Studies in Jungian Thought
JAMES HILLMAN, General Editor

A volume from the *Studies from the C. G. Jung Institute, Zurich*

The Dialogue of a World-Weary Man with His Ba

The Dream of Descartes

Psychological Aspects in Early Hasidic Literature

Timeless Documents
of the Soul

Helmuth Jacobsohn

Marie-Louise von Franz

Siegmund Hurwitz

Northwestern University Press
Evanston 1968

COPYRIGHT © 1968 BY NORTHWESTERN UNIVERSITY PRESS
LIBRARY OF CONGRESS CATALOG CARD NUMBER 68–15329
Composed in Janson and Melior types, printed, and bound by Kingsport Press, Inc., Kingsport, Tennessee

The original German-language edition of TIMELESS DOCUMENTS OF THE SOUL was published in 1952 by Rascher Verlag, Zurich, under the title *Zeitlose Dokumente der Seele*, Studien aus dem C. G. Jung-Institut, Vol. III. Herausgegeben im Auftrag des Curatoriums.

CONTENTS

Preface to the American Edition   ix

- The Dialogue of a World-Weary Man with His Ba   1
  HELMUTH JACOBSOHN
  Translated by A. R. Pope

Foreword		3
Introduction		5
Papyrus lines 1–3	Translation	11
	Notes	11
Papyrus lines 3–30	Translation	12
	Notes	12
	Explanation	17
Papyrus lines 30–33	Translation	21
	Notes	21
	Explanation	22
Papyrus lines 33–55	Translation	22
	Notes	23
	Explanation	25
Papyrus lines 55–68	Translation	26
	Notes	27
	Explanation	28
Papyrus lines 68–80	Translation	29
	Notes	30
	Explanation	30

Papyrus lines 80–85	Translation	32
	Notes	32
	Explanation	33
Papyrus lines 85–103	Translation	34
	Notes	35
	Explanation	37
Papyrus lines 103–30	Translation	38
	Notes	39
	Explanation	40
Papyrus lines 130–47	Translation	41
	Notes	41
	Explanation	43
Papyrus lines 147–54	Translation	44
	Notes	44
	Explanation	47
Papyrus lines 154–55	Translation	49
	Notes	49
Conclusion		49
Bibliography		52

- The Dream of Descartes 55
    MARIE-LOUISE VON FRANZ
    Translated by Andrea Dykes and Elizabeth Welsh
  Introduction 57
  Descartes's Life 59
  The Dream 65
  Interpretation of the First Dream 79
  Interpretation of the Second Dream 116
  Interpretation of the Third Dream 124
  Conclusion 136

- Psychological Aspects in Early Hasidic Literature   149
    SIEGMUND HURWITZ
    Translated by Hildegard Nagel
    Introduction   *151*
    The Great Maggid and Hasidism   *154*
    Consciousness and the Unconscious (*Sekhel* and
       qadmut-ha-sekhel)   *165*
    Sefiroth Symbolism   *179*
    The Symbolism of Numbers and Names   *189*
    Coniunctio Mysticism   *198*
    The Unconscious—Dream—Prophecy   *229*

Indexes   241

PREFACE TO THE AMERICAN EDITION

WITHIN THE COVERS of this small book are three extraordinary documents. Their value lies not only in providing us with important and suggestive source material in fresh translation. They are valuable even more for their contribution to depth psychology.

An aim of this series, "Studies in Jungian Thought," is to stretch the contemporary confines of psychology that have been prejudicially narrowed by its experimental, clinical, and social definitions. We would like to see psychology become, again, a science in an older sense of that term so that it could embrace the psyche in its full peculiarities and reaches. A primary limitation is the present lack of historical dimensions to psychological events—as if the psyche were born a *tabula rasa* anew in each individual, innocent, pristine, without precedent, so that a psychologist might feel justified in approaching it untroubled by his ignorance of psychic history. It is as if everything of value in psychology had happened since William James or, worse, since the publication in a specialists' journal of the latest grant-financed team study. Under the guise of scientific objectivity, myopic subjectivity reigns. These confines are so oppressive that the thrust of the soul's rebellion against being reduced to experimental, clinical, or social descriptions at times unfortunately breaks forth in polemics.

But argument is not the only way to achieve our aim; there is also scholarship. Scholarly research can extend the range of our field. It can bring to light again documents from its past, thereby leading psychology into its own depths. The past of psychology, unlike that of natural science, is not something curiously outmoded. Rather the past is vividly with us because the depths of the human soul and its problems are timeless. As soon as we leave the surface descriptions of the mind and let deeper levels speak, we hear themes common to all men regardless of the conditions imposed by this time or that place. These deeper themes common to all men are archetypal. At this archetypal level, statements from the past have the impact of our own psychological experiences of today. At this level of emotion, dream, and vision we have changed little, if at all.

When we hear, through Professor Jacobsohn's new interpretive translation, a world-weary Egyptian of four thousand years ago speaking with his "soul" and wrestling with the problem of suicide, we can rediscover a connection both to him in that time and to this theme in ourselves today. So, too, when we read the dreams of Descartes or the visionary text of the Hasidic Maggid, we hear examples of man in dialogue with the voice of the unconscious.

Although widely disparate in time and place and content, these three papers stem from the same root. They have one experience in common. They tell of the inroads of the unconscious into consciousness and of the attempts of the conscious personality to come to terms with this other force in the psyche. This experience all of us have in common; the relationship between the conscious personality and its depression or its nightmare or its vision reflects the continuing history of the psyche in its struggle with itself. That this struggle can be a creative relationship these documents show. We know far too little about these crucial psychological events, these moments when an invasion from within demands change in the attitudes of consciousness, not only of one man but in the outlook of a whole period of time. Therefore the study of continuingly valid documents of the soul, especially in unusual individuals, tells us more about how the processes of the psyche work on its objective timeless level.

These documents may also tell us something about the psychological background of history and of historical movements such as Cartesianism and Hasidism. They tell us what was going on in the unconscious of its representatives. The interpretations of the three authors show us a way in which history itself might be approached with the tools of depth psychology. Their method is compatible with that of those historians who examine documents and amplify their contents beyond their immediate context so as to display the fundamental meanings of a period. In order to grasp the quality of consciousness of an age, we need to investigate the archetypal constellation in its representative figures. Dr. von Franz performs this task in her essay on Descartes, thereby shedding light on that particular time as well as on the quality of consciousness of our entire modern period.

A word about the authors: Dr. Helmuth Jacobsohn is Professor of Egyptology at the University of Marburg in Germany. He has been a visiting lecturer at the C. G. Jung Institute every third year since 1948. Dr. Marie-Louise von Franz was trained by C. G. Jung and was his collaborator for more than twenty-five years, working with him especially on his last major opus, *Mysterium Coniunctionis*, of which she wrote the final volume. Other works of hers appear in German in the *Studien aus dem C. G. Jung-Institut Zürich*, and her essay "Evil in Fairy Tales" was published in *Evil*, an earlier volume in this series of "Studies in Jungian Thought." Dr. Siegmund Hurwitz is also a lecturer at the Zurich Institute, specializing in the psychological aspects of Jewish themes. For many years he has been closely associated with the work of the Zurich School. His book *Das Gestalt der sterbenden Messias* was published in the Institute's *Studienreihe*.

The original edition of this book appeared in 1952 as the third volume of the series *Studien aus dem C. G. Jung-Institut Zürich*. It was edited by Dr. C. A. Meier in behalf of the Curatorium of the Institute. The texts in the present edition remain substantially the same as in the original. However, errors have been corrected, some paragraphs have been rewritten, and, where possible, references have been revised. The translations were prepared in close collaboration with the authors so that certain felicities of expression appear in this edition which represent rewriting of the original. Other discrepancies between this and the German edition are the translation into modern idiom (English) of all classical words and passages, and the general index.

The publication of this small volume is the result of thousands of hours of toil and also of cordial cooperation. First acknowledgements must go to the authors for their willingness to take up again work that lay for them in the past and to focus on it in the midst of other research. The translation of Dr. Hurwitz' paper by Miss Hildegard Nagel represents another in a long series of translation contributions that she has made to Jungian scholarship. Despite his other engagements, Dr. A. R. Pope of the Curatorium of the C. G. Jung Institute assumed the responsibility for the translation of Professor Jacobsohn's paper. Dr. von Franz's essay was partially translated by the late Elizabeth Welsh and was then redone by Miss Andrea Dykes. Mr. A. K. Donoghue and Mr. Jay Kugelman helped me with some of the editing. Mrs. Virginia Seidman of Northwestern University Press deserves special mention for her indefatigable, meticulous, and sweet-tempered copyediting of a volume that not only was once in German, and not without errors, but has passages in French, Latin, and Greek as well as transliterations of Hebrew and Egyptian. The index was made by Dr. Nathan Schwartz and Mrs. Maryellen Handel.

JAMES HILLMAN

Zurich
April, 1968

The Dialogue of a World-Weary Man with His Ba

Helmuth Jacobsohn

Translated by A. R. Pope

Foreword

THE NEED for a new interpretation and in part a retranslation of the Berlin hieratic papyrus 3024 is explained in the Introduction, where I also deal briefly with earlier attempts at interpreting this text.

In the Introduction and in more detail in "Notes on the Translation" I have examined critically the views of my predecessors insofar as this was necessary to justify my own divergent point of view. However, for reasons of space, it was not possible to go into, or even to cite, all the different opinions expressed in books, articles, and book reviews.

The papyrus, I feel, deserves more attention than it would if it were just a cultural or historical document. It seems to me as apt and appealing today as it was for its author, who lived in Egypt more than 4000 years ago. I am therefore glad that my interpretation of the papyrus has been included in the series "Studies from the C. G. Jung Institute, Zurich" and thus made available not only to Egyptologists and scholars of ancient history but also to anybody interested primarily in the psyche. Research in depth psychology has shown that there are psychic factors, namely the archetypes, which remain uniform in their structure and which have been alive and effective in all peoples and at all times, though manifesting themselves in varying images.

The Ba of the ancient Egyptians in the papyrus dealt with here reveals itself as a manifestation of such an archetype.

H. JACOBSOHN

Marburg,
July 1951

Introduction

ATTEMPTS at interpreting the Berlin hieratic papyrus 3024, containing "The Dialogue of a World-Weary Man with His Soul" have been going on for some time. About 100 years ago Lepsius published a facsimile of the papyrus (14,* Vol. VI, pls. 111–12) and in 1896 Erman offered a reading of the difficult hieratic text with translation and commentary (3). (Ten facsimile plates, accompanying his work, make the hieratic manuscript more readily and more fully available than do the plates of Lepsius.) Before then the text was considered as good as incomprehensible, but Erman's skill in reading hieratic manuscripts and his self-acquired knowledge of the rules of Egyptian grammar made it accessible and understandable—as far as was possible for an Egyptologist at the turn of the century. Even later, Erman's treatment of the subject remained the basis for anyone working on the papyrus.

Nevertheless, many questions concerning the interpretation of individual passages, as well as the text as a whole, were left unanswered, and since then repeated attempts have been made to deal with the problem. Gardiner (7), Gunn (9), and Sethe (20), in particular, have contributed to the grammatical understanding of difficult passages. Suys (25), Junker (12), Breasted (1), and Spiegel (23) published their views on the text as a whole. In 1937 Scharff worked over the text once again and produced a new translation with detailed commentary (17).

* These numbers refer to the numbers in the Bibliography.

Since then numerous more or less detailed articles on the papyrus or discussions and criticisms of Scharff's work have appeared. Most of them point out that the papyrus is still "one of the most obscure texts in Egyptian literature" (de Buck, 2, p. 20) with regard to the meaning of certain words and sentences as well as "the text as a whole" (de Buck, p. 21). Sainte Fare Garnot (16, p. 18), who follows Scharff's version particularly closely, also feels that we "are scarcely beginning to grasp the whole richness of the text."

All these papers, however, are based on, or criticize, Scharff's translation and commentary and seem to me at essential points to remain stuck in Scharff's errors of translation and interpretation of individual sections, and for this reason they do not carry us much further toward an understanding of the work as a whole.*

This also applies to Raymond Weill's (28) new translation and detailed commentary, with its sociological theories and criticisms of Scharff's interpretation, which space forbids going into here. However, he, too, in defending his own thesis, follows Scharff closely with regard to the interpretation of certain sections of the text.

Scharff himself, in his Introduction (17, pp. 6 ff.), says of this and other texts dating from the same period that "even today, despite advances in grammar and lexicology, all too many questions still remain unresolved. The 'World-Weary Man' is still one of the most difficult Egyptian texts to understand." Scharff describes the aim of his new treatment of the subject as an attempt "to gain an understandable and readable translation of the text by summarizing the results of previous workers and adding numerous new interpretations of my own."

*I cannot agree with Joachim Spiegel's hypothesis about the World-Weary Man in his book *Soziale und weltanschauliche Reformbewegungen im alten Aegypten* (Heidelberg, 1950), pp. 48 ff. (24). The book contains a new interpretation of the World-Weary Man's final speech. Nor do I agree with Günter Lanczkowski's views (15).

7 The Dialogue of a World-Weary Man

Briefly in his Introduction, and in more detail in certain passages of his commentary, Scharff criticizes several of his predecessors, in particular objecting rightly that they let "the soul change its standpoint several times." According to them, "the soul at first favors suicide, then is afraid of it, then is for enjoying life, and finally gives in again." Scharff on the other hand—citing Junker in his support—sees "The Dialogue of a World-Weary Man with his Soul" as representing "the conflict between two philosophies of life (*Weltanschauungen*). One advocates withdrawal from life and longing for death because of the wickedness of the world. The other stands for love of life and enjoyment of all this world has to offer, and contempt for any expectations in the beyond. The author," Scharff continues, "attempts to come to terms once and for all with these starkly contrasting philosophies struggling within himself by having two people voice these conflicting viewpoints. From the outset, however, the author of the text sides with the negation of life; therefore he allocates this viewpoint, which in the end prevails, to man himself. The role of zest for life is attributed to the soul, and finally the soul gives in to the other point of view." Similarly Scharff states in the Epilogue (17, p. 66): "The Egyptian of that day, born and bred as a strict believer in the ancient religious tradition—and we visualize the World-Weary Man as such a one—was sucked into this whirlpool and had to come to terms with new concepts on Death and the Beyond. This takes place in the form of an imaginary dispute with his soul, which confronts him in the role of the new freethinker." Scharff concludes his Introduction by saying (p. 10): "The following translation is therefore intended to show that, without forcing the text grammatically, it is possible to maintain the logical thread of man's and the soul's viewpoints throughout the whole text."

The reviewers of his paper and later workers on the papyrus took Scharff's interpretation as their starting point, either agreeing with it, at least as far as the translation and interpretation of individual passages went, or adding new viewpoints and theories of their own. (See Hermann, 10, in his review of Scharff's paper, and Weill, 28).*

I feel, however, that neither Scharff nor anybody else till now has really done justice to the true significance of the text. Today Sethe's idea of an "exchange of roles" between man and his soul is rightly recognized as false, yet Scharff and later workers still seem to me to have approached the study of the text from false premises. If we read the story of the World-Weary Man once again, unprejudiced and without allowing ourselves to be influenced by what has previously been said on the subject, and if we translate the text as literally as possible, then we obtain an overwhelming impression of a *unique personal experience*. There can be no question that the author consciously intended to demonstrate two conflicting philosophies of life by allocating them to two figures, namely, man and his soul. (Equally untenable is Hermann's and Weill's contention that two philosophic-dogmatic theories about Death are being discussed.)

It seems to me that Scharff, influenced by Junker's comments (12, p. 79), reads his own ideas into the text when he states: "The whole text is a work of poetic invention to account for the problems of the time around 2200 B.C., especially as regards the inner life of the individual . . ." (Epilogue, p. 68). If we let the text itself speak, there can surely be no question of an intentional discussion of "problems of the time," of a conflict between current "trends of thought" (Scharff, p. 68), of a comparison of two different conceptions of life (Scharff, p. 64), or even of a clash of ideas between two different social groups (Weill, pp. 114, 132, and 137 ff.). There is actually no indication of any "exchange of roles" (Sethe [20], *Erl.*, p. 65) or even of an "allocation of roles"

---

* G. Thausing, in her review (26) of Scharff's paper, cautiously points to difficulties and obscurities still existing in the interpretation of the text and rightly stresses that much revision is still required. But she misses the true significance of the text when she speaks of its "abstract philosophical" character.

(Scharff, p. 9). I believe we would do better at first to feel the impact of the meeting with the Ba as a purely human experience, exactly as the World-Weary Man has handed it down to us. Then, perhaps, the experience will indeed tell us something about the historical period in which this work was written.

In contradistinction to the *Ka*, which represents the world-creating power of a god or king and the life force in every human being, the *Ba* stands for an aspect of the soul, connected with the uniqueness of the individual. The Ba is able to separate itself from the world and its polarities.*

In the Pyramid Texts the god-king after his death appears in heaven as Ba or Ba-like, and unites with the other gods to become the Universal Ba, or the Universal God Atum. In the subsequent literature of the dead—the Coffin Texts and the *Book of the Dead*—this quality extends also to the Ba of common man. Since this time—the so-called "Heracleopolitan era," to which, it seems, the original text of the World-Weary Man belongs—the Ba has been an "immanent component of every man" (Eberhard Otto †). The Ba is thus comparable to the Indian concept of Âtman, which is described as "smaller than small and bigger than big" and which also represents both the innermost center of the individual and—as Âtman Purûsha—the all-embracing Deity.

Scharff's reviewers and later workers have all used his translation as their starting point in approaching the papyrus and, apart from minor details, have accepted it as correct.‡ But this is where I think we have to start afresh in order to elucidate the real meaning of the papyrus. I, too, am taking Scharff's work as the starting point for my own translation.

* See "Das Gegensatzproblem im altägyptischen Mythos" (11).

† Eberhard Otto, "Die Anschauung vom B' nach Coffin Texts Spr. 99–104," *Miscellanea Gregoriana* (Vatican City, 1941), pp. 151 ff., and "Die beiden vogelgestaltigen Seelenvorstellungen der Ägypter," *Zeitschr. f. ägypt. Sprache u. Altertumsk.* (1942), pp. 78 ff.

‡ Thausing finds much of the text "unclear and scarcely translatable." As regards de Buck's article, dealing with individual passages and the meaning of the text as a whole, see below, p. 47.

For an account of what Scharff's predecessors—primarily Erman (3), Gardiner (7), Gunn (9), and Sethe (20)—as well as Scharff himself have contributed to a grammatical understanding and translation of individual passages and sections of the text, I refer to Scharff's commentary.

A critical discussion of points of grammar is to be found under the "Notes on the Translation" which follow each section of the text. Some notes also serve toward a better understanding of the text of the translation. The "Explanation of the Contents" following these notes is my own attempt to interpret the section in question. It results from the preceding critical discussion and differs markedly from any comments on the meaning of the text made up till now.

If we look at the text itself without any preconceived ideas concerning the author's intentions, such as contrasting "trends of the time" (Scharff) or sociologically explicable theses (Weill), then we are confronted by a human tragedy of quite unsuspected dimensions.* A man finds himself out of step with his time and for that reason is driven to contemplating suicide. But this is merely the starting point—the exposition of the drama. It is the man who lives far removed from God, who has lost every hold and support, and who now makes a surprising discovery that, as far as we know, no Egyptian had made before him, namely, that the Ba, a man's "soul," is a power to be reckoned with even during this life, a power that man cannot escape by any conscious act of will and cannot entirely grasp by conscious understanding. At first, therefore, man finds himself constantly in rebellion against this power within. It is the tragedy of helplessness, not merely vis-à-vis the outside world but vis-à-vis himself. Such tragedy can never be experienced by a pious and upright man living among unbelievers but only by someone who himself has been gripped by the terror and the despair of godlessness.

* The views of Hermann and Weill preclude all possibility of a human tragedy.

11 *The Dialogue of a World-Weary Man*

What the World-Weary Man in this desperate situation comes to experience at the hands of his Ba is the theme of the following study.

Translation of Lines 1–3

... You [?] will say. ... Incorruptible is their [tongue] ... payment; incorruptible is their tongue. [1]

Notes on the Translation of Lines 1–3

[1] This is where the text as handed down to us begins. Erman (p. 15) considers that probably at least the first 14 lines are missing. The following sentence suggests that these are the last words of a first discourse of the Ba which has not survived (Scharff, p. 13, No. 1). What came before this it is impossible to know. But we may assume that the World-Weary Man began by describing how he came to converse with his own Ba; possibly also that he explains why he came to write down this conversation. Here we can only conjecture.

Scharff rightly emphasizes that there is no evidence that the World-Weary Man tells this story to the dead in the underworld. Such an assumption would indeed be at variance with the text (see Scharff, pp. 65 ff.).

The only thing we can conjecture from these fragmentary lines is that there is already a conflict between the World-Weary Man and his Ba and that the Ba points out the existence of incorruptible arbitrators, to whom one could turn if necessary. It is even questionable whether—as Scharff (p. 11, No. 2) assumes—these incorruptible arbitrators refer to the judges of the dead in the underworld. At any rate, such an assumption does not justify the conclusion that the Ba represents a particular religious standpoint.

Translation of Lines 3–30

Thereupon I opened my mouth to my Ba, that I might answer what he had said: That is too big for me today, that my Ba does not speak in common with me; [1] that is indeed bigger than exaggeration [could describe it]. It is as if he has become indifferent to me. [2] Not go away should [?] my Ba, but stand up for me, if . . . is not [?] . . . he . . . in my body with cord and rope. [3] And he is not free [4] to escape on the day of sadness. [5] Behold, my Ba assails me because I do not listen to him, by lying down for death [6] before I have come to it [by itself]; [7] by laying myself down on the fire [8] in order to burn myself up. . . . May he be near me [9] on the day of sadness; may he stand on that side as the *Nḥp·w* does; [10] he it is who will come out, and to whom he should bring himself. [11] O my Ba, foolish unto despair is a world-weary man. [12] Let me [therefore] drift [13] to death, before I have come to it [by itself]! [14] Make the West pleasant to me! Does it [really] mean sadness? Life is a cycle, even the trees must fall. [15] Disregard the sin, [16] as long as I, O wretched one, still live!

May Thoth, propitiator of the gods, judge me. May Chons, scribe of Maat, defend me. [17] May Ra, who commands the sunbark to rest, try me. [18] May Isdes defend me in the magnificent [?] chamber. . . . My distress [19] weighs [on the brazier?], that she has produced for me [?]. [20] May the gods ward off the innermost secret of my body! [21]

Notes on the Translation of Lines 3–30

[1] The Ba uses a language of his own, he has become independent; see Scharff p. 13, No. 2. Scharff therefore simply translates: "that . . . does not correspond."

[2] *wsf*, "be lazy, be indolent," here used transitively (see Scharff, p. 13, No. 4).

[3] This sentence, although incomplete, contains the idea

13   *The Dialogue of a World-Weary Man*

that the Ba is, or should be, firmly bound in the body of the person, in contrast to "not speaking in common"; see also Scharff, p. 14, No. 8.

[4] According to Sethe, *Erl.*, p. 61 (for *nn* followed by the infinitive see Gardiner, *Grammar*, para. 307). According to Erman-Grapow (6), *WB*, III, 262, bottom, *ḫpr m'* also means "something happens to somebody" (blows of fate, etc.). This would approximate to Sethe's translation. Scharff, with Gunn, takes *nn ḫpr m'* as a nominal clause and translates: "there is not an energetic one who . . ." (Scharff, p. 14, No. 9).

[5] As Scharff surmises, this refers to the day of death.

[6] I agree with Scharff in considering the two infinitive constructions *ḥr št's-j n mt* and *ḥr ḫ"[-j] ḥr ḫt* as further expositions of the negative sentence *n śdm·n-j n-f*. See Gardiner (7), *Grammar*, para. 20: *ḥr* with the infinitive expresses "a concomitant circumstance appended, as an adverbial qualification, to the subject or object of a preceding main clause." According to *WB*, IV, 362 *št[']s* means "lie flat out on the back" (supine position of a patient). If that is what *št's* means here, then we would have to assume its being used transitively. It is not certain how the word should be translated; see Scharff, p. 15, No. 13. (Scharff for other reasons therefore translates: "if I strive after death.")

[7] I.e., without waiting for a natural death.

[8] See *WB*, III, 227. As regards the metaphorical character of this and the corresponding passage, papyrus line 149, see G. Thausing (26).

[9] Erman, pp. 23 ff., surmises that the correct reading here is *tkn-f* (as in papyrus line 71).

[10] I am inclined to take the word *nḥp·w* (the "potter," the "sculptor"), as Scharff and Suys do, as a description of someone taking part in the burial rites.

[11] The meaning remains obscure, since we do not really know the function of the *nḥp·w*. Contrary to what Scharff (p. 16, No. 18) and Weill (p. 117, note d) state, *in-f šw* can only refer to the Ba. This is a nominal clause with the independent demonstrative subject *pw* (a so-called "identity

clause"; see Sethe [21], "Nominalsatz," para. 87) to the predicate of which (*p' iś*) belongs a relative expression *prr* (imperfect participle active) as attribute (see Sethe, "Nominalsatz," para. 92, where the first part of this passage, *p' iś pw prr*, "he it is who will come out," is given as example). This predicate, however, appears to have a second relative expression as attribute, *in-f św r-f* (prospective relative form; see Gardiner, *Grammar*, para. 380, and Gunn [9], *Studies in Egyptian Syntax*, Chap. I, with examples for writing the verb *inj* in this form on p. 12): "to whom he [the Ba] should bring himself" (i.e., apparently on the day of burial).

[12] *wḥ'* is predicate (*śdm-f* form) to the subject *'ḥ ḥr 'nḥ· śdḥ*, "allow to drop" (of the arms, etc.), causative of *dḥ*, "hang down" (see also Weill, p. 116). The man with his hand to his mouth as determinative suggests the meaning: "to allow one's courage to drop, to despair." Scharff's tentative translation, "wanting to convince," is grammatically not possible. When the preposition *r* is used as a conjunction followed by the infinitive, it either expresses the future after verbs of being (Erman, *Grammar*, para. 446, 12) or announces the purpose of a previous action (*ibid.*, para. 411).

Weill overlooks the *r* and translates equally inexactly: "il est insensé de déprimer (davantage encore) un homme lassé de la vie" (Weill, p. 116).

r can only have been used here in its actual sense as a preposition, either as a comparative, "more than," or in the sense "to" (direction toward), or, also, "until" (some condition or other) (see Erman, *Grammar*, para. 446, 3).

[13] Scharff rightly objects to the usual translation of *iḥm r mt*, "to force to death," "to hunt to death." But his own suggestion, "to hold myself back from death," is impossible because *iḥm* is then used as an infinitive; but the absolute pronoun *wj* can never depend as object on an infinitive. *iḥm* is therefore clearly the imperative form. Weill (p. 106), in contrast to Scharff, would like to retain the usual earlier translation of *iḥm*, but he then gives the construction *iḥm wj* in his complete translation equally wrongly (p. 116): "et de me

précipiter à la mort," although, when reviewing Scharff's paper previously, he had recognized the imperative ("conduis-moi à la mort," p. 106). In translating this passage it is essential to retain the imperative.

As regards the meaning of the word *ihm* in this passage and the corresponding passage in papyrus line 50 (see below, p. 23), Scharff (p. 16, No. 22) cites passages from the "Story of the Eloquent Peasant" (B I, 56 / 57, and B II, 104) in which *ihm* is certainly used in the intransitive sense of "to be slow, to go slowly," and another passage of the same text, where *ihm* in the manuscript R, 123, means "delay, put off" (B I, 78), parallel to *swdf*, and thus demonstrates the transitive meaning of "put off, hold back"—literally, "slow down." Concerning the combination of *ihm* with the preposition *r* in the present passage, he refers to the "exact parallel" case *ḥsf r*, "restrain, prevent someone from doing something," in which *r* is used as a conjunction followed by the infinitive. It is therefore not a good parallel for *ihm r mt* in the present passage, since we have to assume that *mt* is used here in its substantival meaning of "death" and that therefore the preposition *r* also has its original significance of "toward something."

For the double use (intransitive and transitive) of *ihm* I should like to suggest the following translations:

1. Intransitive: "to be slow" in the special sense of "drift along." See in particular the passage B I, 57, of the "Story of the Eloquent Peasant" about the ship that should not "drift along," i.e., toward shipwreck.

2. Transitive: "allow to drift." See the corresponding passage of the "Story of the Eloquent Peasant," manuscript R, 123, in which the king tells the official: "If you want to see me healthy (*ihm-k św*), then let him drift along [i.e., the peasant on his stream of words], and do not reply to anything he says, in order that he go on speaking." If we apply this to the present passage, then the imperative really becomes meaningful: *ihm wj r mt*, "let me drift to death!"

[14] I.e., before I would have come to it in a natural way; see above, Note 7.

[15] I follow Erman (p. 25) in the construction of the two short sentences. *phr·t,* "period of revolution of the stars; limited period of time" (*WB*, I, 548), can only refer to the life-span of a man.

[16] *ḫnd ḥr,* "tread on something," also "on something lying on the ground, something hostile, faeces," in the sense of ignoring; in addition it can mean "to pass (lightly) over" (see Erman's examples, p. 27). This can only refer to the intended "sin" of the World-Weary Man and not to a particular sinful philosophy of life of the Ba, as Scharff, p. 18, No. 28, would have it. For the meaning of the passage see below, "Explanation," pp. 20–21.

[17] "Scribe of Maat" is the usual title for the scribe of the Chief Justice; here the moon-god Chons is assistant to the moon-god Thoth.

[18] Ra, who can command the sunbark to stand still and the crew to stop rowing, is particularly suited to "try" the world-weary one, since he also wishes to defy the normal course of nature and make life suddenly stand still. (For the unnatural stopping of the sunbark see the Metternich stele, ll. 217 ff. and 236.*)

[19] *š'r,* "misery, distress" (see Scharff, p. 19, No. 38, and Scharff [18], "Merikarê," p. 15, note 1), "wish" (see *WB*, IV, 18). This "misery" or "distress" is apparently the wish for death which "weighs" him down and cannot be realized.

[20] Scharff relates *f'n-f n-j* questioningly to the Ba, though the Ba is not mentioned before. According to *WB*, I, 573, *f'n* means "to provide somebody with something." If *f'n-f* is the relative form, then the suffix *f* refers to *š'r* as subject of the principal clause, while the missing word in the text would be the object. (For supplying "on the brazier" see papyrus line 149.)

[21] "Ward off" is the literal translation of *ḫsf* with the direct object. At the same time, I agree with Erman and Sethe in taking the horizontal mark below the hieroglyph of the

---

* See Waldemar Golenischeff, *Die Metternichstele* (Leipzig, 1877).

17   *The Dialogue of a World-Weary Man*

god in papyrus line 30 to indicate the plural. Moreover, ḫsf *n* also appears to occur in the meaning of "ward off"; see Papyrus Ebers, 26, 16: ḫsf·w n-f, "he who should be warded off." Scharff, too (p. 20, No. 40), is impressed with Erman's and Sethe's suggestion. But Scharff feels that ḫsf followed by the object, meaning "ward off," does not fit the context and therefore—in line with his premise that a "free death" does not signify anything immoral to the World-Weary Man—proposes ḫsj ḥr in place of ḫsf (or in place of ḫsf n) and translates: "May some god intercede for my most secret wishes" —by which Scharff understands the intended suicide. Hermann (col. 346) and Weill (p. 114) both accept Scharff's conjecture, drawing their own conclusions from it.

On the contrary, I feel that it is just the literal translation of ḫsf, "to ward off," that is the only meaningful one (see below, "Explanation").

Explanation of the Contents of Lines 3–30

From these lines we learn that a man, the author of the text, is "in despair over life," "weary of life"; he wants to "drift toward death" before "he would come to it" in the natural course of events, and he wishes to "lay himself on the fire" in order to "burn himself up." But this is not to be taken literally as death by fire, which would be incompatible with the following sections, where it is made clear that the World-Weary Man is especially concerned about observing the funerary rites with scrupulous care; indeed, observance of the ritual is the only way in which he thinks he can justify his intention. We must therefore assume that "laying oneself on the fire, in order to burn oneself" is a figurative expression for "being consumed with grief." The metaphor reminds us of the oft recurring expression the "hot one," in the sense of the "passionate one," unable to moderate himself, in the Didactic Treatises of the Old Kingdom. At that time "to be hot" could even mean "to be without God," as, e.g., in the following text: "the hot one says: . . . if only I knew where God is, I would assuredly make sacrifice to him!" (Gardiner [8], *Admonitions,* Text, 5, 3). In his grief and despair the World-Weary Man is intent only on dying and says nothing about the way in which he wants to carry it out. At this point he discovers something that for an Egyptian of those times must have been most horrible—more horrible than anything that had previously driven him to despair. His own Ba, the innermost center of his being, his "soul," "does not speak in common with him," "does not agree with him," and offers a certain resistance. The World-Weary Man experiences this opposition as something "bigger than exaggeration" could make it, something for which he can find no words, an enormity that far exceeds his capacity for expressing it.

As I mentioned in the Introduction, the Ba, the "soul," has something to do with the incarnation of a god—his individual form of appearance on earth—or represents an immanent component of a human individual. In general we know that the Ba only attained reality and meaning for the human being after his death. The Egyptian of the third millennium B.C. lived essentially as part of a religious and national group. What we would call "individual" or "personal" remained for him largely unconscious. In his belief, it is only after death, in the Beyond, that certain embarrassing individual impulses play a highly significant role; after having severed his ties with relatives and friends on earth, he appears before the judges of the dead, who examine the life he led on earth. Here he first has to recite the so-called "negative confession," i.e., he enumerates a long list of all conceivable sins, with the assertion that he has *not* committed them. The dead man thus acknowledges the authority of Maat, of "justice"—the prevailing religious and ethical norms—to which every Egyptian had to submit. Indeed, he feels obliged to identify himself with these collective rules (see Joachim Spiegel [23], "Die Idee vom Totengericht in der ägyptischen Religion"). To admit: "I have committed this or that sin" would probably seem like blasphemy to an Egyptian of those days, being

19 The Dialogue of a World-Weary Man

tantamount to admitting that the individual has some degree of free will. The funerary texts describing these judgment scenes are all from the New Kingdom, but, as Spiegel convincingly shows, ideas concerning judgment of the dead originated toward the end of the Old Kingdom and during the following period of unrest, from which the text of the World-Weary Man dates. (These texts were still used in the ritual of burial until a much later period, although the individual's relation to himself and to his own "sin" had in the meantime radically changed.)

But the mere acknowledgment of Maat, an attitude of respect for and identification with the "law," did not suffice; at every statement of the dead man the figure of the divine Maat was weighed in one of the scales against the dead man's heart in the other. The "heart"—for the Egyptian the organ of his innermost thoughts and feelings—could apparently speak a different language from that of the dead man himself. The heart noticed when something in the man's statement acknowledging Maat was not in order, and became "heavy." The scale containing it sank, and the wise and learned moon-god Thoth noted down the result on his slate. Here it becomes clear that the consciousness of an ancient Egyptian did not go beyond the frame of the collective norm. And for this reason he had to identify himself with it and could not make any statement other than what Maat demanded of him. Individual impulses at variance with certain of his statements came from the "heart"—from the unconscious, as we would say today—and were not allowed to reach the threshold of consciousness; he therefore could not express them as his own. They were impulses of a *personal* truth,* still unconscious to the collectively oriented Egyptian of those times.

Significantly enough, there are variants among the representations of the Judgment of the Dead in which the dead man himself sits in the one scale in place of the figure of the

---

* See my paper "Die Bewusstwerdung des Menschen in der aegyptischen Religion," *Vorträge der orientalist. Tagung in Marburg, 1950* (Hildesheim, 1951).

divine Maat, since he is more or less (in his consciousness) identical with her. One variant ("Book of the Dead of Ani," vignette to Chap. 30; see also Spiegel, 23, p. 66) shows the Ba of the dead man sitting, together with the "heart," in one scale; the Ba thus plays the same role as the heart. In the accompanying text the god Thoth says: "I have examined the heart of NN, while his Ba as witness was facing him." The Ba as "witness" is here apparently prepared to testify against the dead man if the latter's statements are not quite right. Here it is the Ba who voices a personal, individual truth.

While life was dominated by the acknowledgment of Maat as the collective moral code, the distressing question of personal truth arose only after death. The funerary inscriptions dating from the end of the third millennium B.C. show that the identification with Maat did not allow doubt as to a man's own integrity. What an overwhelming experience must it therefore have been for the World-Weary Man to become aware of resistance on the part of his Ba toward his own conscious intentions! To learn that even before death the Ba is a real power, with claims of his own, capable of opposing the conscious intentions of a man who had taken it for granted that he was one with his Ba. No wonder it is "too big" for him, "bigger" even than can be expressed "by exaggeration." Nothing but extreme despair, driving him almost to suicide, could provoke such a personal and individual experience.

The Ba obviously exercises a compelling power over the individual which the latter attempts, vainly, to elude. He first begs the Ba to give up its resistance and facilitate the decision for him. A "world-weary man" is, simply, "foolish unto despair," and death is something simple, belonging to the cycle of life. He therefore concludes by telling the Ba: "Disregard the sin" for the short time "that I, O wretched one, still live!" The World-Weary Man is afraid of this "sin," and his fear seems to him to be the voice of the Ba, wanting to prevent him from committing the "sin." In his misery he expresses the wish for four particular gods to "judge," "de-

21 *The Dialogue of a World-Weary Man*

fend," and "try" him. It is not a prayer, but rather a wish expressed in optative form; may the gods take care of him, may they examine whether his intention might not after all be realizable without "sin," whether in his situation he might not be right to wish to depart this life. The way the World-Weary Man voices his wish does not make it sound very convincing, and certainly not as if he actually believed that the wish would be fulfilled. The gods are endowed with magic power; ah, if only they could take away from me my fear of sinning—that is the essence of his wish. It is also literally expressed in the last sentence: "May the gods ward off the innermost secret of my body!" The "innermost secret of my body"—the hidden thoughts—is not his suicidal intention, which he constantly and indeed openly talks of; it is rather the fear of "sin," which he would like the Ba to "disregard," which prevents him from carrying out his intention.

Translation of Lines 30–33

What my Ba said to me [is as follows]: Are not you the man? [1] Are you alive at all? [2] What is your goal, then, that you are concerned about the good [3] as a lord of treasures [is concerned about his treasures]?

Notes on the Translation of Lines 30–33

[1] *ntk* is stressed by means of the enclitic particle *is* (see Erman, pp. 30 ff.). The Ba asks: "Are not you the man, to do it yourself?" See below, "Explanation."

[2] The interrogative particle *tr* seems to be qualified by the sign for the sun; the short, partially destroyed passage is hardly likely to have contained anything else.

[3] Erman (5, p. 124) was certainly right in his translation of this passage; the remnants of the signs of the half-destroyed passage can easily be completed to read *bw nfr* (see

below, p. 38, papyrus line 109: ". . . the good—*bw nfr*—is cast to the ground in all places"). "The good" is certainly meant in a moral sense.

Explanation of the Contents of Lines 30–33

THE BA'S ANSWER to the World-Weary Man's importuning is short and sharp. This answer has thoroughly confounded all commentators and is, to say the least of it, astonishing. It must certainly have been the last thing the World-Weary Man himself expected. The Ba makes no attempt to restrain the World-Weary Man from realizing his intentions and even expresses a certain disdain for the man's indecisiveness: Are you not yourself the man to ward off the fear of "sin" and to "disregard" it? What actually is your goal? A moment ago you were a "hot one," without scruples, and you wanted to be consumed in your own misery and depart this life; now you are concerned about "the good," as a "lord of treasures" is concerned about his possessions, i.e., you want to preserve the good scrupulously and be as innocent as a babe.

The harshness and bluntness of the Ba's short answer (which is also partly a question) shows the Ba to be quite different from what the World-Weary Man had expected (and perhaps what we had expected, too). The Ba does not yet reveal his true nature; he merely hints at what he is *not*. What the World-Weary Man considers to be his "sin" is of little significance to the Ba. Let him cope with his fear himself; this fear is *not* the voice of the Ba. The Ba is not interested in what is conventionally considered good; he obviously wants something else.

Translation of Lines 33–55

I SAID: I have not [yet] gone, [1] for that matter is not yet cleared up. [2] He who removes by force, takes away without considering you. [3] Every robber [4] says: I will carry you off, in that your fate is death [and only] your name remains alive.

The Beyond [however] is the place where one comes to rest, where the heart is led to; home is the West. . . . If [therefore] my Ba listens to me [as one] who is without harm, [5] in that his heart is joined together [6] with me [to a wholeness], then he will be happy. I will [then] let him reach the West as one who lives in his pyramid and at whose burial a relative was present. I will make a . . . over [?] your corpse, so that you will pity another Ba as [the Ba of a] weary man. [7] I will make a . . .—may he not be cold [?]—so that you will pity another Ba who is too hot. I will drink water at the water hole and lift up the . . . , so that you will pity another Ba who is hungry.

If, however, you allow [8] me to drift toward death in this way, [9] then you will find no [place] where you could lie down to rest in the West. Be kind, my Ba, my Brother, till it happens that my heir, who shall sacrifice and stand at my grave on the day of burial, will prepare the bed of the underworld. [10]

Notes on the Translation of Lines 33–55

[1] I.e., to his death. I prefer to retain here the correct translation of the form *n śdm-f* in the perfect tense, as it expresses the meaning of the World-Weary Man's answer more accurately than does Scharff's rendering "I cannot go [from hence], so long as, etc."

[2] *iw r t'*, literally: "since that is to the ground"; see *rdj rf bw nfr r t'*, "what is good is cast to the ground," papyrus line 109.

[3] The Ba is not directly addressed here. The author employs *k*, "you," by way of example, in the sense of "one, anyone."

[4] He feels he does not belong in the same category as a

murderer ("he who removes by force") or a robber ("every robber says . . ."). See "Explanation," below.

Scharff (p. 23, No. 4) sees in "he who removes by force" a description of death as the ravisher and therefore attempts to combine both sentences "[as] any evildoer says" (p. 21). For the consequences which he draws from this see Scharff, p. 24, No. 8. (Weill, p. 119, again follows Scharff's translation: "[tel] un voleur quelconque, disant. . . .") But the word "as" is not in the original, and *nb*, which ordinarily means "every," means "any" in negative clauses only. As is so often the case in Egyptian literature, these are two parallel sentences, each containing slight variations of the same thought.

[5] Scharff suggests completing the partially defective passage to read *iw·t·j bt'* or *iw·t·j bt'-j* (p. 25, No. 12) and points to the use of the expression *iw·tj bt'-f* in the sense of "without guilt." I assume that the oblique sign under the determinative of the striking man (papyrus line 40) as hieroglyph for *f* belongs to it and that we therefore have to read *iw·tj bt'-f*. This *iw·tj bt'* [-f] follows immediately after *b'-j*, but not after the preceding dative suffix *n-j*. It is therefore also in apposition to *b'-j*, "my Ba," and is more fully explained by the following conditional clause *tw[t] ib-f ḥn'-j*. The sign of the seated man following after the relative adjective *iw-tj* cannot therefore be a suffix (*iw-tj* with first-person suffix to my knowledge never occurs) but is apparently a determinative (see also *iw·tj mrḥ·t-f*, "one who has no oil," with the same determinative after *iw·tj*, *Admonitions* [8], 4).

bt' according to *WB*, I, 484, means "crime, etc.," but also "damage" (perhaps therefore best rendered by "fault"). In this passage the World-Weary Man is not pointing out that he is "without guilt" himself but that the Ba, if he listens to him, is "without harm" ("without fault").

[6] The Ba is "without harm" when the individual is "joined together" with his heart to form a whole. There is a close connection between "heart" and Ba (see above, p. 20). The verb *twt* (apart from "be similar to, etc.") means "col-

lect, congregate, bring together" (*WB*, V, 259). It is used in this sense, for instance, for the collecting and putting-together of the parts of Osiris in Ptolemaic texts. This means that the Ba is "without harm" when he is completely united with the individual—when all conflict between them has been resolved.

[7] When the individual and the Ba form a unit, then, after death, the "dead body," the mummy, belongs to the Ba. A "weary man" (see Scharff, p. 26, No. 21) is one who has died without receiving the funeral rites (see below, pp. 26, 28).

[8] See above p. 15, Note 13.

[9] "In this way" refers, not to the manner of death, but to "allow to drift": if you allow me to drift toward death "in this way," i.e., without agreeing with me, then you will not find what you need in "the West."

[10] For *r ḫpr·t* followed by *śḏm-f*, "till it happens that . . . ," see *WB*, III, 263.

Explanation of Lines 33–55

The World-Weary Man has not yet grasped the essential point of the Ba's answer. He is only aware of being reproached with indecision. He therefore picks up the thread where the Ba in his last sentence left off: "You are concerned about what is good . . . ," and he replies: Yes, indeed, that is my concern. (What is "good" means to him the proper funeral rites and an orderly existence in the "Beyond.") He continues: The reason I have not yet gone to the Beyond is that this question remains unclarified. For I am not like a robber or a murderer, who wants to attain his end by force, without concern for the fate of his victim. On the contrary, I ponder well what I do and think everything out most carefully. For—in contradistinction to a robber and a murderer—I want to achieve what is good. My only concern is to find "home" for myself and my Ba in the Beyond. For this very reason my Ba should listen to me and wish what I wish, because only then can he remain unharmed and be united with me to form a whole; only then will he be happy in the Beyond.

The World-Weary Man is perfectly aware that, unless he is reunited with his Ba, "home" will be incomplete and the "Beyond" will be no "home." (This motif of "home" is again taken up by the Ba in his impressive closing remarks; see below, p. 44.)

The World-Weary Man hopes he can himself contribute toward re-establishing the wholeness, the union with the Ba, by impressing upon the Ba how every care will be taken to carry out the religious precepts and funerary rites in the greatest detail. Nothing required by the collective norm will be forgotten. In his opinion, that is the essential thing for the Ba's happiness in the Beyond. He feels justified in begging the Ba once more to be kind to him, until his heir comes and does what is necessary.

Translation of Lines 55–68

THEN MY BA OPENED HIS MOUTH to me that he might answer what I had said to him: If you are thinking of the funeral —that is sentimentality; [1] it is the bringing-forth of tears when a man is made sorrowful, it means [finally] fetching a man away out of the house, in order to cast [2] him on the mound—then [3] you cannot [4] any more rise forth to see the sun. They who have built of granite and have erected as a pyramid something beautiful in beautiful work: [5] while the builders become gods, the tables of sacrifice apportioned to them are empty, [6] like those [of the] "weary ones," who have died on the river bank without an heir; the water has taken its share and likewise the blazing sun its share; [7] the fish speak to them and [?] the river bank.

Hearken now [8] to me! See, it is good, if people listen. Go after the beautiful day and forget the worry!

27 *The Dialogue of a World-Weary Man*

Notes on the Translation of Lines 55–68

[1] When the word ḫ'·t in ḫ'·t-ib, "grief, sorrow," is characterized by a determinative signifying something inferior, something contemptible, then it means a contemptible grief, perhaps best rendered by "sentimentality." I therefore do not agree with Scharff's and Weill's translation of the word as "nonsense." The Ba does not call the funeral itself nonsense; he says that thinking about the funeral is "sentimentality."

[2] Pseudoparticiple of result; literally: "so that he is cast on the mound."

[3] Here the main clause, *nn pr·n-k* etc., follows the conditional clause *ir šḫ'-k krš*. Three short nominal clauses are interposed between the two, with *pw* as subject in each case. This thrice-repeated *pw* refers not to the word *krš*, "funeral," but to the whole subordinate clause *ir šḫ'-k krš*, "if you are thinking of the funeral." (See Gunn's concept of this sentence, 9, p. 127—though he misunderstands the actual character of the three interposed nominal clauses.)

[4] *nn sdm·n-f*-form. See Gardiner, *Grammar*, para. 418 A: "In a few places *nn sdm·n-f* denies with emphasis that something will (or can) occur." "You can" seems to reflect the meaning more precisely than "you will."

[5] My suggested translation of *ḥws·w m mr*. Scharff translates differently, p. 31, No. 11.

[6] *wš*, "empty," also "destroyed, no longer existing."

[7] Those who have died on the river bank lie half in water; the other half withers in the blazing sun (see Scharff, p. 32, No. 18).

[8] *r-k*.

Scharff and Junker have attempted to make these short sentences the key to an understanding of the papyrus and have drawn the conclusion that the Ba once more bluntly rejects the idea of "free death" and advocates uninhibited enjoyment of life. Weill thinks the text represents a conflict between two different concepts of death and that the Ba is inviting the

World-Weary Man to forget his useless concern for the Beyond and make the most of life as it is. Weill (p. 133) also considers the possibility of taking these short sentences as an introduction to the two parables which follow ("apologues," as Weill calls them); but he sees these parables as serving to explain what the Ba recommends. I shall show that the meaning of the two parables is quite different from what Scharff and later workers surmise.

Explanation of the Contents of Lines 55–68

THE BA NOW PLAINLY STATES that merely carrying out formal rites cannot make him happy and that the whole attitude of the World-Weary Man is false. Preoccupation with the funeral gets him on the wrong path; it begins with sentimental thoughts, inevitably leads deeper into misery, and ends finally in death. The Ba is saying: Once there, you cannot come up again any more to see the light of the sun. You cannot emerge from misery, and even less from death itself! You have nothing new to say, and you cannot therefore impress me. And as for graves and tables of sacrifice—which you lay so much stress on—in the long run there is no difference between a Ba who receives the prescribed funerary rites and the Ba of a man who dies on the river bank as a "weary one, without heirs."

The Ba explains in this passage that those who have become "gods," namely, the kings, are no better off than the "weary ones." Offering sacrifices for the dead and having an "heir" care for the Ba is altogether a dubious matter. In this respect the "weary ones" are not worse off than those who have become gods.*

It is true that the words of the Ba express the spirit of the time. But there is nothing superficial or frivolous about them.

---

* See Suys's interpretation of this passage (25, p. 65). Weill (28, pp. 103 ff.) disagrees with Suys's views and presents his own sociological theories.

The Ba does not "ridicule" the funerary rites (Scharff, p. 29) but says that even after death there is something else more important than sticking to the letter of the "law," the collective norm. Whenever people begin to cast doubts on the absolute value of traditional ceremonies, they are not just being frivolous, for new values are emerging. This change begins in the individual, as the text shows.

So far the Ba has explained to the World-Weary Man that his fear of "sin" and his concern about formal rites are worthless. But now he is to "listen" to the Ba, in the sense of "hearkening" to the teachings of wisdom. For he is going to be told something altogether new, and, if he listens carefully, he will learn something that he had not thought of before. To begin with, he should "go after the beautiful day" and forget his futile worries. (The idea that these words are an invitation to an uninhibited enjoyment of life is incompatible with the essential problem the text describes and the role the Ba plays. This will become clearer in the following sections.)

Translation of Lines 68–80

(The First Parable of the Ba)

A MAN TILLS HIS FIELD. He then loads the harvest into the hold of a ship and celebrates the voyage. His festival [1] approaches, after he has seen that a night of storm comes up, and [after he] has kept watch in the ship at the time of the setting of the sun, and [after he] has escaped with his wife, while his child [2] has perished on the waters, which were dangerous [3] in the night because of the crocodiles. Then at the end [of this experience] he sat there and regained his voice and said: [4] I did not weep because of that maiden. [5] She cannot return to earth again [6] from the West. But I grieve [7] for her children, who are broken in the egg [8] and have seen the face of the crocodile-god before ever they have lived.

Notes on the Translation of Lines 68–80

[1] "His festival" is apparently a festival of homecoming and unloading the harvest (see Scharff, p. 35, No. 6). In the construction of the sentence I follow Vogelsang's translation of this passage (27, p. 165).

[2] *mś·w*, literally, also, "descendants"; however, only one daughter is mentioned. Perhaps *mś·w* here stands for "child," just as the singular form *mś* can also stand for "children, descendants" (see *WB*, II, 139).

[3] For *šn* see Vogelsang (27, pp. 164 ff.), to which Scharff also refers. This is apparently the perfect participle passive of the verb *šnj*, "embrace," figuratively, also, "bespeak, enchant" (see Sethe [22], commentary on Pyr. 225 a).

[4] The narrative style of this parable and the next is somewhat abrupt. It is therefore unlikely that a sentence has been lost.

[5] This refers to the "child," the man's daughter, who perished on the waters.

[6] *k·t*, "something different" (see *WB*, V, 112). Hence *r k·t*, "to something different," i.e., "afresh, again." The difficulties inherent in Scharff's translation of this passage are thus avoided. (See also Scharff, p. 37, Nos. 22 and 23. Scharff himself rightly points out that the substantival use of *ḥr t'*, "the one on earth," for "woman," as suggested by him, should correctly read *ḥr·t t'*.)

[7] *mḥ ḥr*, the same expression as above, p. 21: "you are concerned for the good."

[8] A frequent expression for "in the womb."

Explanation of the Contents of Lines 68–80

THE PARABLE has been misunderstood. There is no question here of life on earth representing the "highest value of all" (Scharff) or of its being just "meaninglessly cruel" (Hermann). In this parable the Ba for the first time reveals something of his own nature and something of what he is driving at. If we try to apply the parable to the situation of the World-Weary Man, we arrive at something like the following: The World-Weary Man, having "loaded his harvest," i.e., having settled his account with life, escapes from the "night of storm" of his despair with his Ba, here significantly compared to the man's wife (see also the second parable, below). Their "child," the life they both led together, is thereby destroyed. But that is not the main cause for his grief. Something not yet visible, something still unknown, unborn, that could have developed out of the union of the man with his Ba, has never materialized and has already been destroyed in germ. And this is the real reason for grief and concern. It is particularly subtle that the Ba chooses the symbol of unborn children to express still unrealized possibilities. This symbol further suggests that the Ba is not referring to deeds left undone in the outer world but to something different. It is something potential, lying dormant deep within, a still unconscious inner possibility which, in the "night of storm," would "break in the egg" before it could be born into the world of consciousness.

It is far from the Ba's intention to advocate carefree enjoyment of the good things of this life. Human consciousness was still collectively oriented at that time. Up to the end of the Old Kingdom, claims of the "soul," a man's emotional life, were satisfied by participation in public religious worship and prescribed rites. Neither the colloquial nor the religious language of the time possessed the concepts to express questions arising from personal individual experience. These experiences, emerging for the first time out of man's own depths, were incomprehensible to him and could only be expressed in the form of parables—in symbolic language.

It is the Ba who tells the World-Weary Man the parable. At this point in the text we cannot discern what the Ba means by the treasure, lying dormant in the womb of the future, whose birth is endangered. But the Ba is apparently pointing to a "psychic" possibility that directly concerns himself and his own relation to the World-Weary Man.

Translation of Lines 80–85

(*The Second Parable of the Ba*)

A MAN ASKS HIS WIFE for an evening snack, but his wife says to him: "Only at supper." Thereupon he goes outside, to sulk for a time [?], and then returns home again, being like another, whereas his wife is experienced [1] for him: that he is quite unable to listen [2] to her but has sulked instead, his heart empty for messages.

Notes on the Translation of Lines 80–85

[1] Again a literal translation seems best: *šsʾ* means: "to be experienced" (*WB*, IV, 543). The following *n* stands not for *ḥr* or *m*, but is an ethical dative: his wife is "experienced for him," i.e., just where he is not "experienced"; see below, "Explanation."

[2] Scharff translates here: "he never listens to her" and justifies (p. 41, No. 10) his translation by citing Gardiner, *Grammar*, para. 418, and expressing "this habitual failure to listen, to obey" by the word "never." Weill also translates: "il ne l'écoute pas"; and he agrees with Scharff that the Ba means that the man—who here stands for the World-Weary Man—objects to the given facts but must in the end give in and do what the woman (the Ba) wishes. Gardiner (para. 418 of the *Grammar*) summarizes the function of *n śdm·n-f* as follows: "to deny the occurrence of an action throughout the course of a more or less prolonged period," and he continues in the next section: ". . . and it will often be found that a possible, or even the best, rendering of *n śdm·n-f* is 'he

cannot,' 'could not,' or 'will not be able to hear.' " Gardiner again refers to a tacit implication which we make in English when translating *n sḏm·n-f* and continues: "In such renderings, however, an English standpoint is substituted for the Egyptian; English affirms the impossibility of the act, while Egyptian merely states that over a contemplated period it does not occur." Gardiner once again emphasizes the difference in nuance existing between the two languages in order to justify his proposed translation.

Explanation of the Contents of Lines 80–85

THIS SECOND PARABLE of the Ba, following immediately after the first, brings the story to a dramatic climax: The Ba puts his finger on the real conflict between himself and the World-Weary Man. Again we apply the parable to the situation of the man.

The relation between the World-Weary Man and his Ba is quite clearly shown as the relation between a man and his wife. The man asks his wife for something which she does not immediately grant. The man feels wronged, and his self-esteem as a male is injured. He at once goes "outside" and "sulks" (?), thus making a quarrel out of it. When he returns home again and submits to the inevitable, his wife is "experienced for him"; in other words, she cannot say or do anything more to settle the dispute amicably. "Experienced" as she is, she can merely remain silent; for she knows him better than he does himself. He would be unable to listen to her, he was "sulking" (?), because "his heart was empty for messages." His heart is hardened against her and against anything she could possibly have to say in regard to his wish.

A man's self-assurance and "hardness of heart" apparently caused a woman trouble, even in ancient Egypt. What upsets a woman is not that the man refuses to accord a specific wish of hers or himself wishes something different (this is one reason for rejecting Scharff's translation "he never listens to her" [see above, Note 2]). What depresses her is his lack of understanding of her own nature, his arrogant refusal to "listen" to her. If he did not sulk, his wife could explain her point of view, which might help him to see things in a different light.

The World-Weary Man must have been a fine observer of human nature who understood the deeper significance of the differences occurring in everyday life between man and wife; he was thus one of the earliest Egyptian "poets" to express inner emotional conflicts and what lies behind them. The Ba here uses such observations as a parable in order to show the World-Weary Man something concerning his relation to his Ba: A man's failure to understand the real nature of his wife, his refusal to face facts because of hardness of heart—this is also what separates you and me! I, your Ba, do not demand that you renounce your own wishes. The fear of "sin" and the concern about formal rites which you ascribed to me are really your own; all this leaves me unmoved. I demand neither virtue nor obedience from you. The only thing that matters for both of us is that you recognize and respect my own nature, which is entirely different from what you had believed. Your self-willed arrogance prevented this. You have misunderstood me because you are "hard of heart."

Translation of Lines 85–103

Thereupon I opened my mouth to my Ba, to answer what he had said:

Behold, evil-smelling [1] is [2] my name on account of you, [3] more than the smell of bird dung [?] on summer days, when the heavens burn.

Behold, evil-smelling is my name on account of you, [more than the smell] on receiving fish on the day of fishing and fowling, when the heavens burn.

35 *The Dialogue of a World-Weary Man*

Behold, evil-smelling is my name on account of you, more than the smell of bird dung [?], more than the reed-bank in the swamp where the waterfowl live.

Behold, evil-smelling is my name on account of you, more than the smell of the fishermen, more than the swampy pools they have fished in.

Behold, evil-smelling is my name on account of you, more than the smell of the crocodiles, more than sitting in the company of the river-bank dwellers. [4]

Behold, evil-smelling is my name on account of you, more than that of a woman, about whom rumors are spread because of a man.

Behold, evil-smelling is my name on account of you, more than that of a stubborn [5] child, which it has been decided [6] shall belong to someone it hates. [7]

Behold, evil-smelling is my name on account of you, [more than that of] a dangerous city, [8] contemplating insurrection, and seeing its outside. [9]

NOTES ON THE TRANSLATION OF LINES 85–103

[1] *bʿḥ* is not an adjective but rather the *śdm-f*-form of the verb *bʿḥj* in the intransitive sense of "overflow," here with the particular nuance "spread a bad smell like a flood." (See in this connection Scharff, p. 44, No. 1, who points out the special meaning of *bʿḥj*, "to be flooded" by the stink of corpses flooding a valley, *Urk*;* IV, 84, 8.) I have rendered it by "to be evil-smelling" and would ask the reader to bear this nuance in mind.

[2] Scharff translates: "my name will be rotten (*'anrüchig'*) through you" and states (p. 44, No. 1) that the context demands the use of the future tense. (The World-Weary

* Kurt Sethe, *Urkunden der 18. Dynastie: Historisch-biographische Urkunden*, Section IV, Volume I (2d ed., 1927–30), of G. Steindorff (ed.), *Urkunden des ägypt. Altertums* (4 vols.; Leipzig, 1906–9).

Man assumes that his name "will one day be rotten if he obeys his soul and continues to live.") To my mind the use of the present tense in this important passage supplies the key to an understanding of the whole papyrus (see below, "Explanation"). The present tense is in any case grammatically more probable.

[3] The prepositional expression *m-'-k,* "through you, on account of you," has nothing to do with the similarly written *m-k,* "behold," at the beginning of the sentence. This was correctly recognized by Sethe (*Erl.,* p. 65; see Scharff, p. 44, No. 2). Yet Weill (p. 125) rejects this and each time translates it as "vois" ("see").

According to Weill, the whole reply of the World-Weary Man (from line 85 to line 147) was originally an independent work, lamenting life on earth and extolling death and the Beyond "in the spirit of orthodox religion" (Weill, p. 136). Weill supposes it was inserted later, as a substitute for the man's answer, which was possibly suppressed for political reasons (p. 137). He arrives at this artificial explanation because he feels that the man's last discourse pays no attention to the previous "antireligious thoughts" of the Ba (p. 135). But, as I believe I have shown, both parables, and indeed the whole previous discourse of the Ba, are anything but "antireligious." For the close and logical connection between the World-Weary Man's answer and the Ba's discourse see the following "Explanations."

[4] I.e., the crocodiles.

[5] *kn,* literally: "strong," here in the sense of "defiant, stubborn."

[6] *w*-passive (see Scharff, p. 46, No. 14), here perfect tense.

[7] Literally, "to his hated one."

[8] See above, pp. 29 and 30, Note 3.

[9] The expression "seeing its outside" apparently refers to rebellious inhabitants, who are led away. See the German expression "sich die Tür von draussen besehen" ("look at the door from outside"), in the sense of having been thrown out.

37 *The Dialogue of a World-Weary Man*

Explanation of the Contents of Lines 85–103

Now AT LAST the World-Weary Man's eyes are opened. He has recognized the real cause of the split between himself and his Ba, and, deeply moved, he confesses: my name is evil-smelling, sullied on account of you.

In ancient Egypt a man's name meant more than it does today. The name was intimately connected with the essence of the person and was not merely associated with his reputation. Effacing the name of a god or king from a monument was tantamount to damaging or destroying his very substance. In fact, whoever succeeded in discovering the secret name of a god obtained power over the god himself. When a statement was made about someone's "name," then something was revealed about the intrinsic nature of its bearer.

The name of the World-Weary Man "spreads a bad smell like a flood" (see above, p. 35, Note 1), so that what is rotten and corrupt in the bearer of the name cannot any longer remain hidden. In other words, the World-Weary Man has been unmasked by his Ba. His name is evil-smelling, he himself is defiled, not because of some intended transgression of the law but because of the Ba himself ("on account of you"), against whom he had sinned in pride and hardness of heart. He is so deeply moved by this realization that he has to look for more and more comparisons in his attempt to express it. This self-knowledge is exactly what the Ba had been aiming at, as the World-Weary Man himself was hinting at in the last sentence of his lament over his sin. He compares himself to a "dangerous" rebellious city, whose inhabitants are led away and are thus compelled to view from outside the city in which they had previously lived. In like manner the World-Weary Man has been taken by his Ba out of the narrow standpoint in which he had sought refuge, as in a city, and now sees himself "from the outside," from another standpoint. He has become aware of something that was previously "inside" or unconscious.

Scharff thinks that in the course of the conflict the Ba has become increasingly hostile to the World-Weary Man and that it is senseless for the latter to talk with him. In the following lines he therefore complains that there is nobody else he can turn to. This is hardly compatible with what we have learned so far. On the contrary, although the Ba confronts him as an autonomous power, the World-Weary Man now recognizes that the hostility originated in himself. His hardness of heart blinded him to his own hostility and made him attribute it falsely to the Ba. The shock of this self-knowledge makes him realize that he is responsible to the Ba for his actions and intentions. And this entirely new sense of responsibility is the exact opposite of his earlier anxiety about the failure to observe the prescribed rites. Having confessed and repented his presumptuousness, the World-Weary Man no longer acts like the man in the parable, who went out sulking and then came home again as if nothing had happened. He has gained confidence in the Ba and now explains to him, in detail, why the wish for death has grown so powerful and why he sees no possibility of giving it up. This new feeling of responsibility forces him to account for what is going on in him and makes him able to express adequately his motives.

Translation of Lines 103–30

To whom shall I talk then today? Brothers are bad; friends of today are without love. [1]

To whom shall I talk then today? Covetous are [men's] hearts; everyone steals the property of his neighbor.

To whom shall I talk then today? The gentle one perishes, the impudent one finds entry to all people.

To whom shall I talk then today? Even the one with a contented face is wicked, for the good [2] is cast to the ground in all places.

39 The Dialogue of a World-Weary Man

To whom shall I talk then today? He who makes a man angry because of his wickedness makes [thereby] all [other] people laugh, however bad his offense is.

To whom shall I talk then today? There is plundering [everywhere]; everyone robs his neighbor.

To whom shall I talk then today? The criminal is a confidant; the brother with whom one lives has become one's enemy.

To whom shall I talk then today? One no longer remembers yesterday; no longer does [any]one help him who [once] helped.

To whom shall I talk then today? Brothers are bad; one takes refuge with strangers, in accordance with uprightness.

To whom shall I talk then today? Faces are turned away; [3] everyone lowers his glance before his brothers.

To whom shall I talk then today? [Men's] hearts are covetous; there is not the heart of the man, on whom one can rely. [4]

To whom shall I talk then today? The just [5] no longer exist, the country is left to the offenders.

To whom shall I talk then today? [What is] lacking is a confidant; one takes refuge with a stranger, to complain to him [about one's grief].

To whom shall I talk then today? There is not that one [6] with a quiet heart, with whom one can go; [7] he does not exist.

To whom shall I talk then today? I am burdened with misery and without a confidant.

To whom shall I talk then today? The injustice which strikes the country, it finds no end.

Notes on the Translation of Lines 103–30

[1] Literally, "are not accustomed to loving" or "are not capable of loving." See Gardiner, *Grammar*, para. 418. For *n mr·nj* instead of *n mr·n-śn* see Scharff's reference (p. 50, No. 40) to Gardiner, *Grammar*, para. 486, note 2.

[2] "The good"; see above, p. 21, Note 3.

[3] *ḥtm*, literally, "destroyed, eliminated." Scharff therefore translates "not to be seen."

[4] Spiegel (24, p. 51, note 168) translates in a similar way. Scharff's rendering, "No one on whom one relies has a heart" (similarly Erman), is also possible. Here, however, "the heart of the man on whom one can rely" is apparently contrasted with the "covetous hearts." (See also, below: "There is not that one with a quiet heart, with whom one can go.")

[5] *mꜣ'·t* is at this period still "justice"—ethical norm. The *mꜣ'·tjw* are here contrasted with the *ir·w iśf·t*.

[6] The singular *pf*, "that one," stands, according to Gardiner (*Grammar*, para. 111), nearly always as demonstrative adjective following a noun and therefore here belongs to *ḥrj-ib*, "one with a quiet heart."

[7] *šm* is certainly imperfect participle passive, as Scharff (p. 54, No. 34) explains in detail.

Explanation of the Contents of Lines 103–30

The World-Weary Man suffers from his agonizing loneliness. He feels lost at a time when justice, wisdom, and religious awe no longer mean anything. He suffers most from the lack of a natural relatedness, a rapport between people. A man "with a quiet heart," "a confidant," is nowhere to be found. Nobody wants or is able to "listen" to him—just as he himself was previously unable to "listen" to his Ba. Possibly he was "turned away" (see below, p. 41) when he tried as a "wise man" to bring one of the rulers of his time to his senses. The two parables show how accurate an observer and how fine a thinker the World-Weary Man was. He must have had wider and deeper life-experiences than most; and he suffered the frustration of being able to see further than his fellow men without being able to do anything about it.

Translation of Lines 130–47

Death stands today before my eyes, [as] when a sick man recovers, as when one goes out into the open after being stricken [by illness].

Death stands today before my eyes, like the scent of myrrh, like sitting under the sun-sail on a windy day.

Death stands today before my eyes, like the scent of lotus flowers, like sitting on the bank[s] of the land of drunkenness. [1]

Death stands today before my eyes, like the ending of a storm, [2] as when a man returns home from war.

Death stands today before my eyes, like de-clouding of the sky, as when a man thereby becomes [3] aware of something he did not know [till then].

Death stands today before my eyes, as when somebody longs to see his home again, after he has spent many years held in captivity.

Whoever is there [4] will surely [5] be a living god and ward off the offense of him who wishes [6] to do it.

Whoever is there will surely stand in the sunbark and have the choicest things from it distributed to the temples.

Whoever is there will surely be a wise man, who cannot be turned away, [7] and [may] supplicate Ra, whenever he speaks. [8]

Notes on the Translation of Lines 130–47

[1] This means "on the brink of the coming intoxication." Death appears to the World-Weary Man as a state of blissful drunkenness; it is the theme of liberation and redemption, which he tries to express in various images.

[2] *w'·t*, infinitive of *w'j*, "be distant, withdraw"; see Sethe, *Erl.*, p. 66; Scharff, p. 56, No. 7. For *ḥwj·t*, "storm and rain," see *WB*, III, 49.

[3] This may be a copyist's error (papyrus line 139), similar to the one that occurs in papyrus line 141, where *s*, "man," not only follows *'bb* but had originally followed *m' '* and was subsequently erased by the copyist (see also Erman, p. 70). Perhaps the sign of the seated man follows *sḫt* instead of *s*, "man," and *s*, "man," following *mj* should be expunged. This would give us two infinitive constructions, *kf·t p·t* and *sḫt s:* "like de-clouding of the sky, like making a man aware" (literally, "catching"). At any rate, the meaning is that, when the sky clears, a man becomes aware of something he could not see before.

[4] In the Beyond.

[5] Gardiner (*Grammar*, para. 251) attempts to describe the significance of the enclitic particle *mś* in the following words: "*mś* hints that some thought, statement, or the like has been overlooked by the person addressed, and conveys some tinge of surprise or reproof at this omission." Scharff therefore thinks (p. 58, No. 2) the World-Weary Man is trying to tell his soul something like this: "It's true you don't believe life continues in the Beyond, but I know very definitely it does, and he who is there, etc." But there is not a single passage in the text suggesting that the Ba does not believe in a life in the Beyond; in fact, the end clearly proves the contrary. The particle *mś* (translated here by "surely") rather suggests the thought: "As you surely know yourself," "You, too, must think of that in order to understand me," or the like. The World-Weary Man is now no longer trying to change the Ba's standpoint but feels responsible to the Ba (see "Explanation").

[6] In line with Sethe and Erman, Scharff translates "and visit the sins on him who commits them." According to *WB*, III, 336, *ḫśf n*, "punish someone," is followed by *ḥr*, "on account of" a crime or the like (i.e., not by the direct object). *irr* is imperfect participle active, and, according to Gardiner (*Grammar*, para. 368), often refers to the future. However, I see absolutely no indication of a thirst for vengeance or a play on personal experiences, as Scharff does (p. 60). Even

43 *The Dialogue of a World-Weary Man*

if a "living God" in the Beyond exercises, together with Ra, the divine judgeship in accordance with Maat, then love for one's country is the real motive, as in the following two sentences. This view of the passage, together with detailed reasons for it, provides the main content of Junker's paper "Die Lösung im 'Streit des Lebensmüden mit seiner Seele'" ("The Solution in the 'Conflict of the World-Weary Man with His Soul'"; see Bibliography, No. 13).

[7] For the translation see Gardiner again, *Grammar*, para. 418. *ḫr* here—as in the two previous sentences—introduces the second part of the sentence. (See Spiegel, 24, note 172.)

[8] I.e., the "wise man." (See Erman, p. 73: "every word he speaks is heard by Ra and is a prayer.")

Explanation of the Contents of Lines 130–47

THE WORLD-WEARY MAN continues to account for his conduct to the Ba. His condition is like being stricken by illness, like a storm, or like war; death, then, is like recovery, the way out into the open, returning home, or "de-clouding of the sky," after which everything that is now dark and incomprehensible will become clear. His life in this world is like captivity and overwhelming homesickness. For "there," in the "Beyond," is "home," "his own country." There he will again find everything that has got lost in this world. There justice, wisdom, and religious awe still hold sway. "There" is the longed-for presence of God, whereas life on earth has become captivity remote from God. "He who is there" will himself be a "living god," that is, he will possess the divine power which the World-Weary Man here on earth lacks, namely, the power "to ward off the offense of him who wishes to do it." There without hindrance he will be able to ensure that the temples are provided with the appropriate sacrificial offerings. There he can be the "wise man" he is, which in this life only made him feel different from his fellow men and lonely. And there he will not be "turned away" by some potentate, but whenever he speaks will be allowed to supplicate Ra, the supreme arbiter, in intercession for the oppressed country.

When we reflect upon the World-Weary Man's answer to the Ba's parables, we are struck by the complete change in tone which distinguishes it from everything he had previously said. There is no question here of "summarizing once again" the old standpoint (Scharff, p. 43); on the contrary, the World-Weary Man, now in the grip of a deep, transforming act of self-realization, is for the first time able to express his suffering really adequately. We become witnesses to an inner process of transformation: the pharisaical wrangling and haggling with the Ba that marked the first half of the story have given way to implicit trust, and he now pours out his heart to the Ba without reservation. For the first time the World-Weary Man feels no longer responsible to the traditional collective norm but to his own Ba, his "soul."

Translation of Lines 147–54

That which the Ba said to me: Now let the lamentation be; you, who belong [1] to me, my brother! You may [continue to] weigh [2] upon the brazier, or you may again cling to [3] life, [according] as you will say. [4] Wish [5] me to stay here, if you have renounced the West, or else [6] wish [5] to attain the West and for your body to be given to the earth, and [7] for me to settle [8] here, after you have departed [this life]: in any case [9] we shall share home [10] together.

Notes on the Translation of Lines 147–54

[1] Literally: "O, this one belonging to me," with *pn*, "this," often used vocatively.

45 The Dialogue of a World-Weary Man

[2] I.e., "die of your sorrow." It is just this expression, "weigh upon the brazier," which clearly shows that it is used figuratively; see above, p. 13, Note 8, and p. 17.

[3] This obviously refers to life on earth, since the word *'nḫ* has so far been used only in this sense. *'ḥ ḥr 'nḫ*, "he who is weary of life," is the description the World-Weary Man applies to himself (papyrus line 18). Nowhere does he speak of a "life" after death, but only of "death" or the "Beyond" (*im*, "there"; *imn·t*, "the West," etc.). Moreover, the expression *dmj ḥr*, "cling to, press close to," also suggests that "life" on earth is referred to. Finally, the two sentences *wdn-k ḥr 'ḫ* and *dmj-k ḥr 'nḫ* represent a pair of opposites, just like the two following sentences introduced by *mrj*, "wish," which describe these opposites more fully. (See below, Note 5.)

[4] *mj ḏd-k*, "as you will say," in the sense of "according to that which you will say"; see Gardiner, *Grammar*, para. 170, 5b: *mj* followed by *śḏm-f*: "according as." Gardiner in fact gives this very passage as example, but translates in the present tense: "according as thou sayest."

[5] In the two forms *mr[j]* we have two unmistakable imperatives in hieroglyph of the verb III. inf. *mrj*, "to wish." Scharff's suggestion (p. 62, No. 4), adopted also by Hermann (10, col. 350, note 2) and Weill (p. 130), to consider both imperatives as impersonal forms derived from *mrj*, "to wish," corresponding to the Latin construction *vel-vel*, is not confirmed anywhere else in Egyptian texts. By means of *mrj . . . mrj ḥm . . .* , which follow immediately upon *mj ḏd-k*, "as you will say, according to that which you will say," the opposites just mentioned are dealt with once again, in reverse order, in greater detail, and this time in relation to both the World-Weary Man and the Ba.

[6] It is true that the particle *ḥm* imparts emphasis to an expression, and this certainly means "that the second alternative in the sentence is stressed" (Scharff, p. 62, No. 4); but it does not necessarily mean that it "is the more probable one." The Ba has to emphasize the second alternative in order to stress the point that, even in this case, he and the World-

Weary Man "will share home together." That is just what the Ba wants to reassure the World-Weary Man about in order to reveal to him that he, the Ba, is out for something else (see below, "Explanation").

[7] The parallel nature of the two phrases introduced by *mrj* plainly demands that the words commencing with *ḫnj-j* depend upon the second imperative *mrj*. (See Hermann, 10, col. 351, note 1.) The phrase "wish me to settle here" corresponds to the opposite "wish me to stay here" of the first alternative. The Ba simply leaves the two opposites standing side by side, as of equal value, and this reveals most clearly the Ba's nature and, incidentally, the significance of the papyrus as a whole. The following sentence, introduced by the particle *iḫ*, then shows the consequence to be drawn from the confrontation of both "wishes"; see below, Note 9.

[8] I.e., at the grave or in the Beyond; see Scharff, p. 63, No. 7.

[9] Gardiner, in para. 228 of his *Grammar*, says: "as a particle *iḫ* means 'then' or 'therefore,' often best rendered 'so that.' . . . In its commonest significance *iḫ* expresses a desired future consequence." In the first two examples cited by Gardiner the clauses introduced by the particle *iḫ* follow, as here, on an imperative. "From this meaning," Gardiner continues, "subtle gradations lead to the use in exhortations and even commands. Note, however, that in every shade of meaning the sentence with *iḫ*, 'then,' 'therefore' refers to some still future result of precedent actions." Gardiner then cites the present passage as an example and translates: "then let us make a habitation together." Since, however, the "still future result" can occur following two diametrically opposed "precedent actions" (retaining Gardiner's own words) and will occur in either case, the meaning of *iḫ* is most accurately rendered by "in any case."

[10] *ir-n*, literally: "we make" or "we shall make."

Even in this highly significant final speech of the Ba, Weill (p. 130) again follows Scharff's interpretation, and not quite literal translation, and bases his own thesis upon it. For Weill the final speech of the Ba is merely a compromise, arising out of the author's political sense of caution and designed to "rescue" the work "in order to let the daringly brutal satire appear without causing a scandal" (Weill, p. 137). De Buck, who in his article translates only parts of the work, without a linguistic commentary, is the only one to reproduce the final speech of the Ba in a literal translation (2, p. 30). Though differing from Scharff in the interpretation of certain passages, he also believes that a confrontation is intended between an orthodox and an heretical standpoint; but he points at the end to the "conciliatory" character of the work, which allows the coexistence of the two points of view, thus leading to a typical Egyptian idea of peace and reconciliation.

Explanation of the Contents of Lines 147–54

The Ba now reveals his true nature, and the way in which he does so is surprising: Have done with your complaints: your loneliness and sense of estrangement from the world, your overwhelming longing for "home" and redemption. You belong in any case to me, just as brother belongs to brother. You may continue to be consumed in your grief and finally die of it, or you may gradually "cling to" life again and recover from your grief. Then just voice the wish for me to remain here with you, if you have renounced the longing for death; or express the wish to reach the Beyond and be buried and after your death for me to settle at your grave. Either alternative is possible, but neither of them has anything to do with what had separated us from each other. For the "home" you were looking for—being one with me, joined in human wholeness—this home we shall have in either case. You have already found it here and now.

As I see it, an exact translation, keeping strictly to the wording of the text, permits only the above interpretation.

The final words of the Ba provide the vital clue to the real meaning of the whole papyrus, which goes far beyond any intentional comparison of "trends of the time," "clear-cut philosophical concepts," or any "theses" so far suggested.

We cannot subscribe to the old view that the World-Weary Man and the Ba defend opposite points of view and that now one, now the other, speaks for or against suicide; nor can we agree with Scharff (p. 64) that "the final words of the Soul clearly show that it has abandoned the standpoint it had held so firmly," i.e., that the Ba finally let himself be persuaded into allowing the intended suicide, from which he had till then "shrunk back."

The real aim of the Ba becomes recognizable to the man, and incidentally to ourselves, only at the end. The question which had occupied the World-Weary Man for so long the Ba still leaves open, and in the end this question becomes itself irrelevant. Instead the Ba cautiously leads the World-Weary Man to the real goal: the sense of at-oneness with the Ba, newly gained through self-knowledge—the restoration of the wholeness of the personality, now consciously experienced as the result of the transformation.

The final answer of the Ba shows more clearly than anything that the preceding words of the Ba had ushered in the beginning of an inner transformation. For this final answer of the Ba contains no allusion to hardness of heart nor any reproach of "sentimentality." After having acquired self-knowledge and unequivocal faith in the Ba, he at once obtains an equally unconditional assurance on the part of the Ba, who says: You belong to me; we shall share together the "home" you have been longing for.

We can surmise that those who have so far attempted to interpret the papyrus have not recognized the real nature of the Ba because they failed to recognize the World-Weary Man's own transformation. Scharff sees the relationship between the Ba and the man in exactly the same way as the World-Weary Man must have seen it himself before the second parable of the Ba opened his eyes. The decisive step in

49 The Dialogue of a World-Weary Man

the beginning transformation came when the man renounced his claim to power. The Ba then appears no longer as a hostile power but as "relative" and "brother." That was more than the World-Weary Man himself could, or dared, ever hope for. "Home," the "redemption" for which he had been longing and which he had sought in the Beyond, in death, and with the sun-god Ra, has been vouchsafed to him by his Ba here and now. The possibility hinted at in the Ba's first parable has now become reality. The World-Weary Man has found that pearl of great price which not even death can take away. He is therefore now free to die, if he still wishes to. But the newly achieved wholeness opens up a new possibility for life, and the Ba does not hesitate to point this out. Together with his Ba the man can now quietly watch and see which of the two impulses gains the upper hand: his wish for death or a new will to live.

Translation of Lines 154–55

And thus it has come about from its beginning to its end [1] like that which has been found in writing. [2]

Notes on the Translation of Lines 154–55

[1] This is the usual formula for ending Egyptian books. It confirms the fact that the last words of the Ba really are the end of the whole text.

[2] I.e., the papyrus we possess is the copy of an original (which has not survived). The copy dates from about the middle of the 12th Dynasty (about 1850 B.C.) and was thus made about 300 years after the original.

Conclusion

The World-Weary Man has set down in writing the different phases of his transformation with a fine sense of detail.

We can assume that his ability to give expression to this inner experience was one of the first fruits of the newly achieved wholeness of the personality. Putting it into writing may also have helped him to face life again, to "cling to" life. Whatever his fate may have been, the World-Weary Man revealed to his fellow men and also future generations the possibility of experiences which were at that time unheard of.

For the first time in Egyptian history man was experiencing the terror and horror of separation from God. The omnipotence of the Pharaoh—god and divine son on earth—was broken. The temples and sacred tombs were largely destroyed, and regular participation in religious worship had become impossible. For the first time man was face to face with himself and experienced himself as an individual. This must have been intolerable to an Egyptian accustomed to a collective life; and it must have been to some extent responsible for the high incidence of suicide at that period.

Even where public worship was still in vogue and the sacrificial rites were still carried out, the gods proved entirely inadequate to answer the new "psychic" needs, the needs of the soul, which were reaching the threshold of consciousness for the first time. It was no longer sufficient to "speak" and to "act" in accordance with Maat, the religious "law." The gods who ruled by power were unable to provide an answer to the desperate questions arising from the depths of the individual. The sun-god Ra, heavenly father of the Pharaoh, apparently had real power only in the Beyond. There, at least, it was hoped "the sky would clear," so that what appeared chaotic and insoluble on earth would become clear and harmonious after death. But at first it was the "law" that held the World-Weary Man back from choosing the path of death. The first part of the story makes it clear that he considered suicide as "sin," as an "offense." It was precisely the incompatibility of the "law" with his longing for redemption which drove him to the uttermost limit of despair. In his dire personal need he is suddenly made to feel the real power of the Ba, the center of his individuality, the "soul." And this power appears to man personified, as something coming from outside, which itself carries traits of divinity. In fact, the relation in which the World-Weary Man stands to his Ba resembles very closely the relation between man and God in the New Testament. "Moreover the law entered, that the offense might abound. But where sin abounded, grace did much more abound. . . ." These words were spoken by Paul to the Romans (Romans 5:20), and psychologically they apply equally well to the World-Weary Man.

The newly gained at-oneness with the Ba, the restoration of the wholeness of the individual on a new level, means the realization of what we would nowadays describe as "conscious personality" (see also above, pp. 18 and 31). The realization of his own "personality" was a numinous experience for the World-Weary Man, comparable to the *unio mystica* with a god. Wholeness was not something that he was able to achieve of his own accord or as the result of a pious attitude, but it was granted him by his Ba against all expectation at the moment when he was able to acknowledge: I am defiled "on account of you."

Comparable to "Grace abounding" in Paul's Epistle to the Romans, a divine act has taken place within man.

Bibliography

1. BREASTED, JAMES H. *The Dawn of Conscience.* New York, 1935.
2. DE BUCK, A. "Inhoud en achtergrond van het gesprek van den Lebensmoede me zijn ziel, Kernmomenten der Antieke Beschaving en haar moderne Beleving," *Mededeelingen en Verhandelingen No.* 7 ("Ex Oriente Lux" Series) (Leiden, 1947), pp. 19–32.
3. ERMAN, ADOLF. "Gespräch eines Lebensmüden mit seiner Seele," *Abh. Preuss. Akad. d. Wissensch., Phil.-hist. Kl.*, Pt. II (Berlin, 1896). (Cited as "Erman.")
4. ———. *Aegyptische Grammatik.* 4th ed. Berlin, 1928. (Cited as "Erman, *Grammar.*")
5. ———. *Die Literatur der Aegypter.* Leipzig, 1923.
6. ——— and HERMANN GRAPOW. *Wörterbuch der ägyptischen Sprache.* 5 vols. Leipzig, 1926–31. (Cited as "*WB.*")
7. GARDINER, ALAN H. *Egyptian Grammar.* Oxford, 1927. (Cited as "Gardiner, *Grammar.*")
8. ———. *The Admonitions of an Egyptian Sage from a Hieratic Papyrus in Leiden.* Leipzig, 1909. (Cited as "*Admonitions.*")
9. GUNN, BATTISCOMBE. *Studies in Egyptian Syntax.* Paris, 1924.
10. HERMANN, ALFRED. "Das Gespräch eines Lebensmüden mit seiner Seele," *Orientalistische Literaturzeitung,* XLII (1939), Pt. 6, cols. 345 ff. (Review of SCHARFF's paper; see No. 17, below.)
11. JACOBSOHN, HELMUTH. "Das Gegensatzproblem im altägyptischen Mythos," *Festschrift zum 80. Geburtstag von C. G. Jung,* II, 171–98. Zurich, 1955.

12. JUNKER, HERMANN. "Die Aegypter." Pt. I of Vol. III, *Die Völker des antiken Orients*, in HEINRICH FINKE, HERMANN JUNKER, and GUSTAV SCHNÜRER (eds.), *Geschichte der führenden Völker*. Freiburg i.B., 1933.
13. ———. "Die Lösung im 'Streit des Lebensmüden mit seiner Seele,'" *Anz. d. österr. Akad. d. Wissenschaft, Phil.-hist. Kl.* (1948), No. 17, pp. 219–27.
14. LEPSIUS, RICHARD. *Denkmäler aus Aegypten und Aethiopien*. Berlin, 1849–59.
15. LANCZKOWSKI, GÜNTER. "Zur ägyptischen Religionsgeschichte des Mittleren Reiches. II: Der 'Lebensmüde' als antiosirianische Schrift," *Zeitschrift für Religions- und Geistesgeschichte*, VI (Leiden and Cologne, 1954), Pt. 1.
16. SAINTE FARE GARNOT, J. "La Vie et la mort d'après un texte égyptien de la haute époque," *Revue de l'histoire des religions*, CXXVII (Paris, 1944), 18–29.
17. SCHARFF, ALEXANDER. "Der Bericht über das Streitgespräch eines Lebensmüden mit seiner Seele," *Sitzungsber. d. Bayer. Akad. d. Wissensch., Phil.-hist. Abt.* (1937), Pt. 9. (Cited as "Scharff.")
18. ———. "Der historische Abschnitt der Lehre für König Merikarê," *Sitzungsber. d. Bayer. Akad. d. Wissensch., Phil.-hist. Abt.* (1936), Pt. 8.
19. SETHE, KURT. *Aegyptische Lesestücke*. Leipzig, 1924.
20. ———. *Erläuterungen zu den ägyptischen Lesestücken*. Leipzig, 1927. (Cited as "Sethe, *Erl*.")
21. ———. "Der Nominalsatz im Aegyptischen und Koptischen," *Abh. d. kgl. Sächs. Gesellsch. d. Wissensch.*, XXXIII, No. 3 (Leipzig, 1916). (Cited as "Nominalsatz.")
22. ———. *Uebersetzung und Kommentar zu den altägyptischen Pyramidentexten*. Glückstadt, n.d.
23. SPIEGEL, JOACHIM. "Die Idee vom Totengericht in der ägyptischen Religion," *Leipziger ägyptologische Studien*, Pt. 2. Leipzig, [1935].
24. ———. *Soziale und weltanschauliche Reformbewegungen im alten Aegypten*. Heidelberg, 1950.
25. SUYS, E. "Le dialogue du désespéré avec son âme," *Orientalia*, I (Rome, 1932), 57 ff. (Cited as "Suys.")
26. THAUSING, GERTRUD. "Besprechung," *Archiv f. ägypt.*

Archeologie, I (1938), 162-65. (Review of SCHARFF's paper; see No. 17, above.)
27. VOGELSANG, F. "Ein seltenes Wort nebst einer Textemendation," *Zeitschr. f. ägypt. Sprache und Altertumsk.*, XLVIII (1911), 164 ff.
28. WEILL, RAYMOND. "Le livre du 'Désespéré': Le sens, l'intention et la composition littéraire de l'ouvrage," *Bull. de l'Inst. franç. d'archéol. orientale*, XLIV (Cairo, 1947), 89-154. (Cited as "Weill.")

The Dream
of Descartes

Marie-Louise von Franz

Translated by Andrea Dykes and
Elizabeth Welsh

Introduction

THE SO-CALLED "GREAT DREAM" of young René Descartes has always attracted great interest, for Descartes himself considered it of first importance. He thought it worthy of publication and tried to interpret its symbolism. Indisputably this dream played a decisive role in Descartes's development, but unfortunately we have only an incomplete version of its content, related by the Abbé Adrien Baillet.[1]

The dream has not been investigated much from the standpoint of depth psychology. But Sigmund Freud once said to Maxim Leroy that it was a dream "from above," i.e., from a layer of the psyche very close to consciousness. Therefore, most of its content could have been produced consciously.[2]

---

1. In his *La Vie de M. Descartes* (2 vols., 1691), I, 39 ff., 50–51; reprinted in Ch. Adam and P. Tannery, *Oeuvres de Descartes*, X, 179 ff. (hereafter cited as "*A-T.*") The Adam and Tannery edition of the works of Descartes, published in Paris between 1897 and 1913 in twelve volumes and a supplement, superseded all others.) A German translation of Baillet's account of the dream appears in I. Ježower, *Das Buch der Träume* (Berlin, 1928) (hereafter cited as "Ježower"), and it is Ježower's translation with which I have chiefly worked.

NOTE: In order to simplify the footnotes, titles of many works will be given in full the first time they are mentioned but thereafter will be cited only by author (or abbreviation) and page number. For each work thus cited the reader will also find publication data in the Bibliography on page 144.

2. Jacques Maritain, *Le songe de Descartes* (Paris: Corrêa, 1932), p. 292; English translation by M. L. Andison, *The Dream of Descartes, and Other Essays* (New York, 1944). See also Freud's letter to Maxim

Also, two articles in the *International Journal of Psycho-Analysis* for 1939 and 1947 explain the dream from the Freudian point of view.[3] I shall discuss these articles later, in the course of my own interpretation. An excellent study by J. Rittmeister, "Die mystische Krise des jungen Descartes," written earlier but published later than this paper, interprets the dream in agreement with my own version in many respects. Rittmeister died in Germany in 1943. His paper was posthumously published by A. Storch,[4] who also wrote a short comparison of our interpretations.

Although the articles investigating Descartes's dream have uncovered much information about his personal problems, we believe that the dream, in symbolic form, also throws considerable light on the spiritual situation at the beginning of the seventeenth century, revealing aspects that still interest us today.[5] To use Jung's term, this is an archetypal dream. It

---

Leroy in Freud, *Gesammelte Schriften* (Vienna, 1934), XII, 403 ff.; English translation, "Some Dreams of Descartes: A Letter to Maxim Leroy," in James Strachey *et al.* (eds.), *The Complete Psychological Works of Sigmund Freud* (London, 1927–31), XXI, 203–4. Leroy's book, *Descartes, le philosophe au masque*, was unfortunately not available to me. See also Heinrich Quiring, "Der Traum des Descartes," *Kant-Studien, Philosophische Zeitschrift*, XLVI, No. 2 (1954–55), 135 f. Quiring considers the dream to be merely a consciously formed presentation in cipher of Descartes's theory of cosmogonic vortices. On the other hand, a professional psychologist must object that, throughout, the dream is genuine enough, exhibiting typical motifs that cannot have been invented.

3. I am indebted to E. A. Bennet, M.D., and F. Beyme, M.D., for calling my attention to these articles, which are difficult to find. Dr. Bennet was kind enough to get them for me.

4. *Confinia psychiatrica*, IV (1961), 65–98.

5. Cf. S. Gagnebin, "La réforme cartésienne et son fondement géométrique," *Gesnerus* (a quarterly published by the Schweizer. Gesellschaft für Geschichte der Medizin und der Naturwissenschaften), VII, Fasc. 1/2 (1950), 119: "A la réflexion on en viendrait ... à conclure que ce qui reste vivant du cartésianisme *c'est l'analogie de notre situation actuelle et de celle dans laquelle il s'est formé* ... La chose la plus curieuse c'est que, peut-être, la géométrie sera de nouveau au centre de la nouvelle réforme. C'est une géométrie qui est à la base de la Relativité généralisée." ("Upon reflection one would . . . reach the

contains a suprapersonal message. The dream's basic symbols—the storm, the round fruit, the sparks of fire, and the "magic trickery"—are all *archetypal images* with a collective meaning showing that the events which took place in Descartes's unconscious and pushed their way into the light of his mind were deeply enmeshed in the general religious and scientific problems of his time. Because the personal aspect is also of great importance, we must consider it first.[6]

Descartes's Life

RENÉ DESCARTES was born at La Haye (Touraine) on March 31, 1596, the third living child of Joachim des Cartes,[7] a councilor in the *parlement* of Rennes. His mother, Jeanne Brochard, died a year later in giving birth to a fifth child, who did not survive.[8] His father married a second time. Descartes tells us that he inherited his mother's pale countenance and incessant cough.[9] At the age of eight he was sent to the Royal Jesuit college of La Flèche in Anjou. There Father Etienne Charlet and Father Dinet considerately permitted

---

conclusion that that which remains living of Cartesian philosophy is the analogy of our present situation to that in which it was formed. . . . The most curious aspect is that geometry will, perhaps, once again be at the center of the new reform. It is geometry which is at the basis of generalized relativity.")

6. For the recent literature on Descartes see G. Sebba, *Bibliographia cartesiana: A Critical Guide to the Descartes Literature, 1800–1960* ("Archives Internat. de l'Histoire des Idées," Vol. V) (The Hague: Nijhoff, 1964). See also Wolfgang Röd, *Descartes: Die innere Genesis des cartesianischen Systems* (Munich and Basel: Reinhardt, 1964), and the literature there cited.

7. Originally "de Quartis." Later Descartes's father took the title "gentilhomme de Poitou." His family belonged to the *petite noblesse*. His grandfather and one great-grandfather had been doctors.

8. For further details see Ch. Adam, *Descartes, sa vie et ses oeuvres* (Paris, 1910), p. 9 (hereafter cited as "Adam"; this work is Vol. XII of *A-T*). The eldest son, Pierre, had also died, so that only three children survived (*ibid.*, p. 9).

9. *Ibid.*, p. 15.

him to take good care of his delicate health. Since he had a room to himself, he used to lie in bed meditating—a habit which clung to him throughout his life—and his schoolfellows dubbed him *"le chambriste."* [10] His father had little use for the delicate boy always buried in his books or lost in his thoughts.[11] But Descartes got along well with his sister, later Madame de Crévy, and her son. At sixteen he left La Flèche to live in Paris. Here he associated with his friends, Mydorge and others (possibly Mersenne). With them he devoted himself to mathematics, music, and philosophy—chiefly the writings of skeptics like Montaigne and Charron. He led the life of a typical *gentilhomme*, fencing, riding, playing *jeu de paume*, playing music; women, however, he politely avoided.[12] In Paris, too, he used to spend most of the morning in bed, withdrawing more and more into complete seclusion. He continued these habits when taking part in the Netherlands campaign of Maurice of Nassau (who was Protestant, but allied to France) against the Spaniards.[13]

The protracted siege of Breda was a period of leisure for Descartes, which he employed in indulging his philosophical bent. He also became acquainted with the Dordrecht physicist and doctor, Isaak Beeckmann, with whom he chiefly discussed the application of mathematics to physics, and vice versa.[14]

In 1619 he attended the coronation of Ferdinand II of Austria in Frankfurt and stayed quartered in the neighborhood of Ulm, where he spent the whole winter, spiritually

---

10. *Ibid.*, p. 20.
11. *Ibid.*, p. 7. He once said of his son that "il n'était bon qu'à se faire relier en veau" ("he was good for nothing but to be bound in calf") (*ibid.*, p. 7 n.).
12. He once remarked: "Une belle femme se rencontre trop rarement, aussi rarement qu'un bon livre et un parfait prédicateur." ("A beautiful woman is met with all too seldom, as seldom as a good book or a perfect preacher.") (*Ibid.*, p. 70.)
13. For further details see *ibid.*, p. 41.
14. *A-T*, X, 52. Cf. also Etienne Gilson, "L'innéisme cartésien et la théologie," *Revue de métaphysique et de morale*, XXII (1914), 465.

61 The Dream of Descartes

incubating in a warm room (*"dans un poêle"*) in the house of a German middle-class family. There Descartes experienced his famous "enlightenment," his great mathematical discovery, and the ensuing dream, which we are about to discuss. He was then twenty-three years of age. All we really know further about this important phase of his life is that he was probably already in touch with the Rosicrucian Johannes Faulhaber [15] and was much impressed by the movement.[16] Whether he actually joined the society is uncertain and indeed unlikely.[17] In his *Discours de la méthode* he says he owned to having read the alchemists and magicians enough not to be taken in by them.[18] He was undoubtedly acquainted with Agrippa of Nettesheim's works and Raimundus Lullus' *Ars Magna*,[19] as well as Athanasius Kircher's *De Magnete*[20] and Joannes Baptista's *Magia Naturalis*.

Previously, at La Flèche, he had become acquainted with the works of Galileo, who was only later condemned by the Church. In particular, Lullus and the question of astrology haunted him (*hanté*) for a long time.[21] He had probably read

---

15. See Adam, pp. 47, 49; for further details see *A-T*, X, 252.
16. *A-T*, X, 193: "M. Descartes ... se sentit ébranlé."
17. See, further, Maritain, pp. 13 ff., and *A-T*, X, 193 ff. However, he formed the initials R. C. in his seal, in exactly the same way as the Rosicrucians formed theirs (*A-T*, X, 48).
18. *A-T*, X, 63. In *Discours de la méthode* (*A-T*, VI, 9) he says: "Et enfin pour les mauvaises doctrines je pensois desia connoitre assés ce qu'elles valoient pour n'estre plus suiet a estre trompé, ny par les promesses d'un Alchemiste, ny par les prédictions d'un Astrologue, ny par les impostures d'un Magicien, ny par les artifices ou la vanterie d'aucun de ceux qui font profession de sçavoir plus qu'ils sçavent." ("And as for the false doctrines, I thought I already knew enough of their worth not to be liable to be deceived any more, whether by the promises of an Alchemist, or by the predictions of an Astrologer, or by the impostures of a Magician, or by the artifices or boastings of any of those who profess to know more than they do.") For details see J. Sirven, *Les années d'apprentissage de Descartes (1596–1628)* (Paris, 1925), pp. 50–51, and the literature cited there.
19. Adam, p. 31.
20. *A-T*, X, 6.
21. Sirven, pp. 51, 113, and nn.

the alchemical treatise *Physika kai mystika* of Pseudo-Democritus and had named a work of his own *Democritica*, after it.[22] After countless fruitless wanderings and a relatively passive part in the Battle of the White Mountain near Prague, against the "Winter King," Friedrich von der Pfalz, Descartes returned to Paris. In 1623 he went on a pilgrimage to the Madonna of Loretto near Venice,[23] in fulfillment of a vow which he had made on the occasion of his dream. He then took part in certain Church festivals being celebrated in Rome.

The conflict between the freethinkers (such as Vanini) and the Church made life in France impossible for him; however, when called upon by the Jesuit Cardinal de Berulle to oppose the freethinker Chandoux in a debate, he triumphed over his opponent.[24]

Descartes therefore went to live in Holland, where foreign trade and colonial expansion were at their height; this was the time of Rembrandt and Frans Hals.[25] He changed his lodgings no less than twenty-four times and kept his address as secret as possible. Because he greatly loved nature, he sought places to live in the country. His residence was usually divided into two parts: a *salon de réception* and, behind it, a secret laboratory where he dissected animals (even going so far as to vivisect rabbits),[26] ground and polished telescope lenses, and undertook other kinds of scientific work.[27] During this period he was working on *Le Monde*, a kind of encyclopedia of all the natural sciences. But after Galileo's condemnation he did

---

22. *Ibid.*, p. 69. (*Democritica* has been lost.) Descartes also occupied himself with the meaning of his dream and its "divine character" (*ibid.*, p. 69; see also *A-T*, XI, 468).

23. Concerning his attitude toward the Virgin see Adam, p. 27.

24. Cf. Cay von Brockdorff, *Descartes und die Fortbildung der Kartesischen Lehre* (Munich, 1923), pp. 15 ff., and Adam, pp. 64 ff., 73, and 95.

25. The latter painted his portrait. Cf. Adam, p. 101.

26. Letter to Plempius (*A-T*, I, 527). He believed that animals were automata (cf. Sirven, p. 321).

27. Adam, pp. 161, 193, and 233. He also had an experimental botanical garden (*ibid.*, p. 495).

not dare to publish it,[28] because in it he defended a Galilean theory which was related to some of his own.[29] He distributed its content throughout his other works, with the result that parts of it did not come out until after his death. At this time his first discussions with his orthodox philosophical opponents took place, the latter accusing him of undermining religion. He sought and found support from his old master, Father Dinet of La Flèche, and diplomatic and political protection through the French embassy. Indeed, he was most unwilling to face philosophical battles and avoided them in a peaceable and diplomatic spirit.[30] At this time his *Principia* was published, as well as his correspondence with Elisabeth von der Pfalz on the relation of body and mind. This latter gave rise to his treatise *Les Passions de l'âme*.[31]

At this stage of his life, Descartes entered into a liaison with a Dutch maidservant, Helena Jans, which resulted in the birth of a daughter, Francine. But the little girl died when she was about five years old,[32] and we hear nothing more of the mother. Descartes speaks of this episode as a "dangereux engagement dont Dieu l'a retiré" and emphasizes later "que Dieu par une continuation de Sa même grâce, l'avait préservé jusque-là de la récidive." In a letter he admits to having had in his youth a passing fancy for a girl with a slight squint. The same remarkably cold feeling—or perhaps fear of accepting his feeling—is shown in the expression he uses when speaking

---

28. For details see von Brockdorff, p. 16. Cf. also Gagnebin, p. 109, or Descartes's letter of December, 1640, to Mersenne (*A-T*, III, 263 ff. and 394 ff. Concerning his alleged insincerity and cowardice see Maritain, pp. 50–52.

29. Regarding Descartes's theory of the whirlwind cf. J. O. Fleckenstein, "Cartesische Erkenntnis und mathematische Physik des 17. Jahrhunderts," *Gesnerus*, VII (1950), Nos. 3–4, 120 ff.: "From out of the small spheres of the four basic elements arise vortices that lead to the formation of the world."

30. Von Brockdorff, pp. 24 ff., and Adam, pp. 331, 341, and 366.

31. Von Brockdorff, pp. 19–21.

32. Adam, pp. 230 ff., 287; also p. 575 n.: "La mort de Francine lui causa 'le plus grand regret, qu'il eût jamais senti de sa vie.'" ("Francine's death caused him 'the most regret he had ever felt in his life.'") Cf. also pp. 337 ff.

of the almost simultaneous death of his sister and father, namely, that he experienced a considerable "déplaisir."[33]

In his portraits Descartes appears to us extremely skeptical, with altogether lusterless, mistrustful, and inward-looking eyes. He was small, delicately built, dressed mostly in black, and painfully neat. He wore his hair falling over his forehead like a black curtain reaching almost to his eyes.

In 1649, through his friend Pierre Chanut, French ambassador to Sweden, Descartes was appointed tutor in philosophy to Queen Christina of Sweden,[34] a girl just twenty years old. The poor *chambriste* had to give his lessons in the very early hours of the morning.[35] Moreover, his young pupil, whose Spartan habits and unbounded energy seem to have been the result of a fierce animus-possession, forced on him the reorganization of the academic system in Sweden. However, while devotedly nursing Chanut, who was suffering from inflammation of the lungs, Descartes himself contracted the disease and died on February 11, 1650, in his fifty-fourth year.

The events immediately preceding the dream are vague, but we do know definitely that the young Descartes dreamed it in his *poêle* in Ulm in the first year of the catastrophic Thirty Years' War. This dream made such a deep impression on him that he published it in a special paper, *Olympica*,[36] thus intimating that he felt it had "come from above"—although evidently not from the God of Christianity. Leibniz made fun of the "chimerical" nature of this work.[37] The content of the original work, which was lost, is related in Adrien Baillet's *La Vie de M. Descartes*.[38]

33. Adam, p. 16. Many biographies make much ado about his duel on account of a lady during his student days. But this event strikes me as a purely social affair, with no deeper significance.
34. *Ibid.*, pp. 512 ff.
35. *Ibid.*, p. 549.
36. *Ibid.*, p. 49.
37. For this period of his life see Sirven's standard work (*Les années d'apprentissage*, . . .) and the literature there cited, especially pp. 141 n. and 152.
38. Vol. I, pp. 39 ff. and 50–51. See note 1, above.

The Dream

Descartes begins his account of the dream with the following words: "On the 10th of November, 1619, when I was filled with enthusiasm and discovered the foundations of the marvelous science." [39] In the margin we read: "On November 11th, 1620, I began to understand the fundamentals of the marvelous discovery." [40] It is evidently a case of inspiration or unconscious enlightenment; not until a year had passed did he begin to understand it consciously and to make use of it.[41] At the time of the dream he was in a state of extreme exhaustion, the result of having striven passionately to free his mind from all prejudice so that he could experience his mind in an absolutely pure state (*"intellectus purus"*) and by this means discover the truth—the sole aim of his life.[42] As he tells us in *Discours de la méthode*,[43] he turned his attention entirely within:

> Après que j'eus employé quelques années à étudier ainsi dans le livre du monde et à tâcher d'acquérir quelque expérience, je pris un jour résolution d'étudier *aussi en moi-même* et d'employer toutes les forces de mon esprit à choisir les chemins que je devais suivre; ce qui me réussit beaucoup mieux, ce me semble, que si je ne me fusse jamais éloigné ni de mon pays, ni de mes livres.[44]

---

39. "X Novembris 1619 cum plenus forem Enthousiasmo et mirabilis scientiae fundamenta reperirem, . . ." (*A-T*, X, 179).
40. "XI Novembris 1620 coepi intelligere fundamentum Inventi mirabilis" (*ibid.*).
41. Cf. Sirven, p. 122.
42. He explained "lying long in bed" as *"tristitia,"* and in the *Cogitationes privatae* (*A-T*, X, 215) he says: "Adverto me, si tristis sim, aut in periculo verser, et tristia occupent negotia, altum dormire et comedere avidissime; si vero laetitia distendar, nec edo nec dormio." ("I notice that if I am sad, or thrown in danger, and sad affairs take up my time, I sleep deeply and eat greedily, but if joy fills me, I neither eat nor sleep.")
43. Sirven, p. 114.
44. "After I had spent some years thus studying in the book of the world and in trying to acquire some experience, I one day made the resolution to study *within myself also*, and to use all the powers of my

It is probably no chance event that Descartes's great dream occurred during his German "exile," because, for the French, Germany often represents the "landscape of the soul," upon which they project their unconscious—their shadow and romantic side—as well as their lack of moderation, speculative thinking, and so forth. Descartes describes his new experiment as a wandering in the dark:[45] "Mais comme un homme qui marche seul et dans les ténèbres, je me résolus d'aller si lentement et d'user tant de circonspection en toutes choses, que si je n'avais que fort peu, je me gardais bien, au moins de tomber."[46] Thus he arrived quite close to the threshold of the unconscious and even had a premonition that he would have a meaningful dream that night.[47] He says, in fact, that the same spirit (*"le génie"*) which inspired him with enthusiasm had already predicted the dream when he went to bed and that the human mind had no part in this dream.[48] G. Cohen, who claims Descartes for the Rosicrucians, also calls special attention to the following significant rhythm in his life: on November 10, 1618, the meeting with Isaak Beeckmann, his spiritual awakener, as Descartes calls him; on November 10, 1619, the great dream; and on November 11, 1620, the discovery of the *"scientia mirabilis,"* or the possibilities of its application.[49]

It is impossible to identify with any degree of certainty the

---

mind for the choosing of the paths that I ought to follow; in the which I succeeded far better, so it seems to me, than if I had never left my country or my books."

45. *A-T*, VI, 16–17. Cf. also Sirven, p. 115.

46. "But like a man who walks alone in the dark, I resolved to go so slowly, and to use so much circumspection in all things that, even if I possessed very little, I at least took good care not to fall."

47. In contradistinction to Sirven (p. 116), I consider that Maritain is absolutely correct in comparing this exercise of Descartes's with the *via purgativa* of the mystics, though it is, indeed, actually displaced onto an intellectual plane.

48. *A-T*, X, 189.

49. Cf. Sirven, pp. 121, 298. Unfortunately Gustave Cohen's work, *Ecrivains français en Hollande de la première moitié du XVII⁰ siècle* (Paris, 1920), was not available to me.

67 The Dream of Descartes

"marvelous discovery" which, as he says, he made on the evening preceding the dream.[50] It might consist, first, in his discovery that the four subjects of the quadrivium—mathematics, geometry, arithmetic, and astronomy—can, together with music,[51] all be reduced to one *"mathématique universelle,"* whose basic principles are the seriality of numbers and their proportionate relations;[52] second, that algebra can be expressed by the letters of the alphabet, and the square and cubic numbers, etc., by small superscript numbers instead of by the so-called Cossic signs; and third, that quantities can be expressed by lines and vice versa, whereby geometry, algebra, and mathematics are fused and become *one* scientific discipline: analytical geometry.[53]

G. Milhaud has shown, however, that the "discovery" was in all likelihood first worked out *after* the dream,[54] so I would surmise that at this time Descartes probably perceived these connections only intuitively and then later worked them out in the aforementioned specific formulations.

I should like to illustrate this idea by Poincaré's explanation of the genesis of mathematical discoveries, about which he has written a psychological study of outstanding interest.[55] Poincaré begins with the fact that not all gifted thinkers are mathematically gifted and comes to the conclusion that "A mathematical *proof* is not a simple following-on of syllogisms, but it is a series of syllogisms *that are brought into a specific order,* and the order in which the individual elements

50. For further details see Adam, p. 50, and Sirven, *passim.*
51. Optics and mechanics were subsequently added.
52. *Regulae* (*A-T*, X, 451): ". . . sciendum est omnes habitudines quae inter entia eiusdem generis esse possunt, ad duo capita esse referendas: nempe ad ordinem, vel ad mensuram." (". . . it is necessary to know that all relations that can exist among existents of this kind are drawn up under two headings: namely, hierarchical order and measurable proportion.") Concerning the importance of this experience cf. also Léon Brunschvicg, *Descartes et Pascal: Lecteurs de Montaigne* (Neuchâtel, 1945), pp. 102 ff.
53. Adam, p. 55.
54. G. Milhaud, *Descartes savant* (Paris, 1921), *cit.* Maritain, p. 255.
55. H. Poincaré, "Die mathematische Erfindung," in *Wissenschaft und Methode* (Leipzig and Berlin, 1914), pp. 35 ff.

here appear is far more important than these elements themselves."[56] According to Poincaré, mathematical talent is an intuitive feeling for mathematical order,[57] and mathematical discovery occurs through preconscious selection from the abundance of given possibilities of combinations. Poincaré then relates how he himself made just such a discovery:

> For two weeks I had been exerting myself to prove that there existed no functions of the kind that I have subsequently named Fuchsian functions. At that time I was very inexperienced; every day I sat at my writing-table for one or two hours, experimenting with a great number of combinations without achieving any result. One evening, contrary to my habit, I drank some black coffee and was unable to sleep. A lot of thoughts crowded in. I felt how they collided with one another, until finally two of them clung together and formed a stable combination. By morning I had proved the existence of a class of Fuchsian functions, those very ones that are deducible from the hypergeometric series. I only needed to revise the result, which was accomplished in a few hours.[58]

Poincaré then tells of a further similar discovery that, in the form of a sudden thought, appeared before his eyes with absolute certainty as he was out walking one day. Further on he says:

> The irruption of this sudden enlightenment is very surprising; in it we see a sure sign of prior long-continued unconscious work; the importance of such unconscious work for mathematical discovery is incontestable. . . . When one is working on a difficult problem, it often happens that at the start of the work one makes no progress. One then allows oneself a shorter or longer break for rest and thereafter sits down again at one's desk. During the first half-hour one again finds nothing, and then suddenly the decisive idea presents itself. . . . Probably unconscious work went on during the rest period, and the result of this labor is later revealed to the mathematician. . . . But such a revelation does not only occur during a walk or a journey. It also

56. Quoted *ibid.*, p. 38.
57. *Ibid.*, p. 39.
58. *Ibid.*, pp. 41–42.

asserts itself during a period of conscious work, but in this case it is independent of that work, and the latter acts at most as a catalyst; it is similar to the stimulus that incited the result—gained during the time of rest, but that had remained unconscious—to take on conscious form. . . .[59]

Indeed, the often fruitless exertions concerning the problem bring, as it were, the activities of the unconscious into play, and its results appear in consciousness as inspirations.

The specially privileged unconscious manifestations which are capable of appearing in consciousness are those that, either directly or indirectly, influence our sensibility most profoundly. It will be noticed with amazement that here, on this occasion of mathematical argument which appears to be dependent solely on the intelligence, the feelings have to be brought into consideration. It becomes intelligible, however, if one pictures to oneself the feeling for mathematical beauty. The feeling for the harmony of numbers and forms, for geometrical elegance . . . offers satisfaction to our aesthetic needs and at the same time provides help for our mind, which it sustains and guides. Insofar as it unfolds a well-ordered whole before our eyes, it permits us to anticipate a mathematical law.[60]

I think that these observations of Poincaré's can give us an idea of what happened to Descartes on the eve of his dream. He must have experienced a similar mathematical "enlightenment" or intuitive vision of certain combinations or ordered patterns and may possibly even have drawn the (somewhat premature) conclusion that in this "enlightenment" he had discovered either a kind of universal science or its laws. A passionate war is still being waged today between members of the so-called "formalistic" school of mathematics, who believe that mathematics is based on conscious lemmata (as, for instance, Bertrand Russell and G. Frege, among others), and the intuitives, who concede that mathematical discoveries can originate from an intuitive vision of mathematical order. In

59. *Ibid.*, pp. 44–45.
60. *Ibid.*, pp. 47, 48.

his *The Psychology of Invention in the Mathematical Field*,[61] Jacques Hadamard has shown that mathematical discoveries are in all probability often ruled by preconscious psychic processes. I believe that at this period of his life Descartes had a mathematical intuition, which he later tried to work out through rational thinking.

According to Sirven,[62] Descartes had, even at that time, already intuitively perceived his whole *"méthode,"* i.e., his way of thinking, and the mathematical discoveries were the first of its fruits. Sirven believes, however, that the *"méthode"* was based on the still generally held idea of the unity of all the sciences (*"l'unité des sciences"*). Its first yield is the idea of a *"mathématique universelle."* As E. Gilson emphasizes,[63] for Descartes it is a case of "tout ce qui est susceptible de connaissance vraie ... est par définition susceptible de connaissance mathématique. L'idée de l'unité du corps des sciences [64] ... est donc inséparable, chronologiquement et logiquement, de l'extension de la méthode mathématique à la totalité du domaine de la connaissance." [65] This belief in unity

---

61. Princeton, 1949. Cf. B. L. van der Waerden, *Einfall und Ueberlegung: Drei kleine Beiträge zur Psychologie des mathematischen Denkens* (Basel and Stuttgart: Birkhäuser, 1954).

62. P. 17 and *passim*.

63. In his edition of Descartes's *Discours de la méthode: texte et commentaire* (Paris, 1947), pp. 60, 157, and 214, *cit.* Sirven, pp. 123–24 and 167.

64. My footnote: In *Le songe* . . . Maritain also admits this, but he stresses that Descartes really believed that one man could reform science and that he was that man.

65. ". . . everything that is capable of being truly understood is . . . by definition capable of being known mathematically. The idea of the unity of the body of the sciences . . . is therefore inseparable, chronologically and logically, from the extension of the mathematical method to the totality of the domain of knowledge."

Among other things Descartes also said: "Ces longues chaînes de raisons toutes simples et faciles dont les géomètres ont coutume de se servir ... m'avaient donné occasion de m'imaginer que toutes les choses qui peuvent tomber sous la connaissance des hommes s'entresuivent en même façon." ("These long chains of reasons, all simple and easy, which geometers are in the habit of using . . . caused me to imagine that everything men can learn could be connected in the same way.") Quoted by J. Laporte, *Le rationalisme de Descartes* (Paris, 1945), p. 13.

was easy for Descartes, who considered mathematical knowledge to be "absolute truths." [66]

This conviction has since collapsed, and the reality basis of mathematical thinking has become a matter of passionate discussion. Mathematicians today are aware, as Professor F. Gonseth explains,[67] that mathematical thinking takes place in a "field of consciousness" between two complementary poles of reality: one called "outer" and one called "inner," both of which transcend consciousness.[68] Descartes saw these two realms as coincident in their orderedness and did not concern himself with their consciousness-transcending, "transmathematical" nature.[69] He believed, rather, that he was able to grasp their mystery by mathematics alone. Probably what he

66. For examples see Laporte, p. 7 n. The concepts of dimension, time, and space are for him the constituent concepts of pure knowledge; they are beyond questioning, whether seen waking or in a dream: "Atqui Arithmeticam, Geometricam . . . quae nonnisi de simplicissimis et maxime generalibus rebus tractant, atque utrum eae sint in rerum natura necne parum curant aliquid certi atque indubitati continere. Nam sive vigilem, sive dormiam duo et tria simul iuncta sunt quinque, . . ." ("But arithmetic, geometry . . . deal only with the most simple and general things, and even if they appear in physical nature there is always something free from doubt and certain in them. For awake or asleep, two plus three is five.") (*A-T*, VII, 20, quoted from H. Barth, "Descartes' Begründung der Erkenntnis" [diss., Bern, 1913], p. 33.) Concerning this question cf. also Prof. F. Gonseth, *Les mathématiques et la réalité* (Paris: Alcan, 1936), pp. 55 ff.
67. Gonseth, pp. 58 ff.; cf. also pp. 79 ff., 376 ff.
68. In a letter from Professor Gonseth to the author: "Les mathématiques se situent dans un champ de connaissance placé entre deux pôles complémentaires, l'un étant le monde des réalités dites extérieures, l'autre le monde des réalités dites intérieures. Ces deux mondes sont tous les deux transconscientiels. Ils ne sont ni l'un ni l'autre donnés tels quels, mais seulement par leur traces dans le champ conscientiel. Les mathématiques portent cette double trace." ("Mathematics is placed in a field of knowledge between two complementary poles: one the world of reality called exterior, the other, interior. These two worlds are beyond consciousness. They are not graspable as such, but their imprints appear in the field of consciousness. Mathematics shows this double imprint.")
69. Cf. the criticism of this view of Descartes's, that matter and consciousness are static objective "*entia*," in A. N. Whitehead, *Science and the Modern World* (New York, 1948), pp. 201 ff. Whitehead gives a generally readable sketch of Descartes's ideas and their development.

really had in his mind was the immanent orderedness of the thought processes that had been released [70] by the archetypes (his "numbers" and *"veritates innatae"*) and, with them, *the idea of an "absolute knowledge."* [71] He clearly thought that he could formulate this best through the basic concepts of mathematics or else, more generally, through a universal scientific method and symbolic language.[72] I think this was the reason Raimundus Lullus' *Ars Magna* "pursued" him for so long a period, since it represents a similar effort to "apprehend" an "absolute truth" through the means of mathematical symbolism. Lullus' work was also based on an unconscious inspiration [73] and hence earned him the title of *doctor illuminatus*. It consisted in a correlation of certain ancient mnemotechnical arts whereby the orator hoped to commit his speech to memory without effort. Metrodorus of Skepsis had invented an art by which he associated the parts of any oration he was to deliver with the "magic circle" of the zodiacal houses. This idea, which at first sight seems so absurd, is really not so when we realize that through the present-day depth psychology of Jung it has been discovered that the central ordering of preconscious psychic processes is due to a psychic

---

70. He says of arithmetic and geometry: "Haec enim prima rationis humanae continere et ad veritates ex quovis subiecto eliciendas se extendere debet." ("For this ought to contain the first [things] of human reason and be extended to the truths to be sought from any subject whatsoever.") (*A-T*, X, 374–77, *cit*. Barth, p. 9). On the other hand, he gave up the play of purely numerical symbolism (see Barth).

71. Concerning this idea see C. G. Jung, "Synchronicity: An Acausal Connecting Principle," *The Structure and Dynamics of the Psyche* (*Collected Works*, Vol. VIII, 1960).

NOTE: The *Collected Works of C. G. Jung*, translated by R. F. C. Hull, are published by the Bollingen Foundation (Bollingen Series XX) in the United States of America by Pantheon Books and in England by Routledge & Kegan Paul. The *Collected Works* will hereafter be referred to as "*CW*."

72. Cf. also Sirven's explanation that he had found "les fondements consistant une méthode générale" ("the foundations composing a general method") (Sirven, pp. 126–27).

73. For an over-all view cf. E.-W. Platzeck, *Raimund Lull, sein Leben—seine Werke: Die Grundlagen seines Denkens* (2 vols.; Düsseldorf: Schwann, 1962).

73 The Dream of Descartes

regulatory center which Jung has designated "the Self" and which is wont to manifest itself in mandala form.[74] The horoscope and Lullus' patterns of thought are structures of this kind.[75] In these mnemotechnical mandalas we consequently see a first prescientific idea that the Self can be the ultimate "regulating factor" of our thought processes and memory structures. These mnemotechnical mandalas, which were also meant to serve for the ordering and concentration of the soul, flourished during the Renaissance (Marsilio Ficino and Pico della Mirandola) and were even thought to have a magical regenerating power on the Universe (Giordano Bruno).[76] They were supposed to represent an image of a mysterious all-comprehending order of the Cosmos in the soul of man. As Paolo Rossi has most convincingly demonstrated, these traditions exerted a profound influence on the young Descartes. With this idea—that by constructing a mandala one can find a common structural model of the universe *and* of the human mind—was connected the hope that it would be possible to discover a kind of "ideas-computer"—a generally valid logical system by which all essential knowledge could be collected.[77] It appears extremely probable that Descartes was influenced by ideas such as these and that intuitively he looked to something like a universal order of being (presumably in mandala form) and was emotionally overwhelmed by the thought that he had had a glimpse into the central mystery of all being. It is therefore natural to suppose that his vision was a mandala because the Cartesian system of coordinates that resulted from these intuitions is also a mandala. G. Milhaud considers that he had found "des choses d'en haut, des choses divines ou célestes" and had therefore christened

74. Cf. Jung, *The Archetypes and the Collective Unconscious* (*CW*, IX, Part I, 1959), and *Psychology and Alchemy* (*CW*, XII, 1953), *passim*.
75. Cf. Paolo Rossi, *Clavis Universalis: Arte mnemoniche e logica combinatoria da Lullio a Leibniz* (Milan, 1960), p. 48.
76. Cf. Frances Yates, *Giordano Bruno and the Hermetic Tradition* (London: Routledge & Kegan Paul, 1964).
77. Cf. Rossi, *passim*.

his treatise *Olympica*,[78] just as, in his dream, he had interpreted the storm as the "mind" and the lightning as the "spirit of truth." [79] Milhaud is therefore inclined to think that Descartes had found a *universal language of symbolic interpretation*, something that reaches out even beyond pure mathematics. At all events, it seems probable that Descartes was touched by some archetypal ordered images of the unconscious and sought to comprehend them intellectually. Numbers *are* archetypal representations, which seem to be based on archetypal patterns that actually *do* unite the worlds of psyche and matter in a still unexplained way. Also, the Rosicrucian Johannes Faulhaber, with whom Descartes was probably in communication at the time, had in 1619 brought out a book, *Numerus figuratus sive Arithmetica arte mirabili*[80] *inaudita nova constans*, on the symbolism of numbers.[81] At that time Descartes, too, was planning to write a book entitled "Trésor mathématique de Polybe le Cosmopolite." Perhaps he was seeking to set up universally derived principles of thinking out of the order of natural integers such as, for

78. Milhaud, p. 56, *cit*. Sirven, pp. 55–57.
79. Sirven (p. 151) says: "Ses diverses remarques nous permettent d'expliquer sans peine comment Descartes est passé des 'spiritualia' aux 'Olympica,' des choses de l'esprit aux choses de Dieu. Il est parti du symbolisme mathématique pour former *un symbolisme intellectuel* et s'en est tenu d'abord aux exemples du vent et de la lumière, que lui avait légués la tradition scolaire. Mais la lecture de St. Augustin lui permit de passer aux choses divines et d'exprimer par de nouveaux exemples l'action de Dieu dans le monde." ("These miscellaneous remarks [i.e., Descartes's interpretation of the storm as spirit, etc.] allow us to explain quite easily Descartes's departure from 'spiritual things' to 'Olympica'; from the things of the spirit to the things of God. He left mathematical symbolism to form *an intellectual symbolism* and, at first, stuck to examples bequeathed him by school tradition. But study of St. Augustine allows him to proceed to divine things and to express God's action in the world by means of new examples.")
80. Notice the expression *"arte mirabili."*
81. Cf. Sirven, pp. 279, 298. The title of a publication in my possession runs as follows: *Ansa inauditae et* mirabilis novae Artis *Arcanis aliquot propheticis et Biblicis numeris . . . qua ordo semper a Deo observatus, dum numeris . . . Pyramidalibus observatus est . . .* (Frankfort, 1613). It deals chiefly with speculations concerning numbers mentioned in the Bible.

75 The Dream of Descartes

instance, result from the proportional relations of numbers.[82] He certainly was looking for a mathematical-symbolic universal science and believed that he had had a presentiment of its rudiments [83] and its "language."

Here is Adrien Baillet's rendering of Descartes's account of the dream: [84]

Descartes tells us that when he lay down to sleep on November 10, 1619, he was still filled with enthusiasm and was completely absorbed by the thought of having that day discovered the foundations of a "marvelous science." During the night he had three consecutive dreams, which he thought could only have been inspired by a higher power. Having fallen asleep, he imagined he saw *ghosts* and was terrified by these appearances. He thought he walked through the streets, and he was so horrified by the visions that he had to bend over on his left side [85] in order to reach his objective, for he felt a great weakness in his right side and was unable to hold himself up. Ashamed at having to walk in this fashion, he made a great effort to straighten himself, but *he was struck by a violent wind*. The wind seized him like a *whirlwind* and made him spin round three or four times on his

---

82. Cf. *Cogitationes privatae* (*A-T*, X, 215): "Larvatae nunc scientiae sunt quae, larvis sublatis, pulcherrime apparerent. *Catenam scientiarum pervidenti, non difficilius videbitur, eas animo retinere quam seriem numerorum.*" ("Now the disciplines are masked: these would appear most beautiful if the masks were removed. For anyone contemplating the chain, it seems no more difficult to remember them than the series of integers.") Cf. Sirven, pp. 226–27.

83. Sirven (pp. 123–24) is correct in drawing attention to *"reperirem"* (imperfect), meaning that he was only on the point of finding the *"scientia mirabilis"* and did not, therefore, already possess it. See also *A-T*, X, 360, First rule: "Scientiae omnes nihil aliud sunt quam humana sapientia quae una et eadem manet quantumvis differentibus subiectis applicata." ("All disciplines are nothing but human wisdom, always one and the same thing, applied to as many different subjects as you like.")

84. In general my rendering of Baillet follows I. Ježower's German translation in his *Das Buch der Träume*, pp. 90 ff. I have nevertheless changed a few words ("college" instead of "seminary," "exotic" instead of "strange," and "bend down" in place of "throw down"), in order to remain closer to the French text. I have put certain words in italics which are important in the ensuing interpretation.

85. Ježower translates *se renverser* as "throw down," but in that case Descartes would not have been able to go any farther.

left foot. It was not this, however, which frightened him most. He found it was so difficult to advance that he was afraid of falling at every step, until, perceiving [the gates to] a college standing open on his path, he entered, *to seek refuge* and help in his affliction. He endeavored to reach the *college chapel*, where his first thought was to pray; but, *realizing that he had passed by an acquaintance without greeting him*, he wished, out of politeness, to turn back. [Attempting to do so, however,] *he was thrown back with violence by the wind, which was blowing toward the church*. At the same instant he perceived *another man in the college courtyard*, who called Descartes politely by his name and informed him that, if he were seeking Mr. N., he had something for him. Descartes had the impression *that this [object] must be a melon which had been brought from some exotic land*. Great was his astonishment when he noticed that the people who had gathered around the man, to chat with one another, were able to stand upright and firm on their feet, whereas, on the same spot, he himself had to walk crookedly and unsteadily, even though the wind, which had several times threatened to throw him over, had abated considerably.

At this point he awoke, feeling a definite pain. *He feared it was the effect of evil spirits, bent on leading him astray.* He immediately turned over onto his right side, for it was on his left side that he had fallen asleep and had the dream. He prayed to God to protect him from the evil consequences of his dream and to preserve him from all the misfortunes which might threaten him as a punishment for his sins. He recognized that his sins were grievous enough to call down all the wrath of heaven on his head, although up till then, in the eyes of men, he had led a fairly irreproachable life. *He lay awake about two hours, pondering the problem of good and evil in this world*, and then fell asleep.

Another dream followed immediately. *He thought he heard a shrill and violent report*, which he took to be a thunderclap [*coup de foudre*]. He was so terrified that he awoke at once.

On opening his eyes, he became aware of a multitude of *fiery sparks* scattered throughout the room. This had often happened to him before, and it was not unusual for him to wake up in the middle of the night to find that his sight was clear enough for him to perceive the objects nearest to him. This time, however,

77 The Dream of Descartes

he determined to resort to explanations borrowed from philosophy and, opening and shutting his eyes alternately and observing the nature of the objects which met his sight, he drew favorable conclusions, which appeared convincing to his mind. Thus his fear vanished, and with a quiet mind he again fell asleep.

Soon afterward he had a third dream, which was not so terrible as the previous two.

In this last dream he found a book on his table, not knowing who had laid it there. He opened it and was delighted to see that it was a *dictionary*, hoping that it might be very *useful* to him. The next instant *another book* appeared, just as new to him as the first and its origin equally unknown. He found that it was a collection of poems by different authors, entitled *Corpus Poetarum*, etc. (in the margin: "Divided into five books, printed in Lyon and Geneva, etc.").[86] He was curious to find out what it contained, and on opening the book his eye fell on the line "Quod vitae sectabor iter?" At the same time *he saw a man whom he did not know*, who showed him a poem beginning with the words "Est et non," and extolled its excellence. Descartes told him that he knew the poem, which was among the idylls of Ausonius and was included (*sic!*) in the big collection of poems which lay on his table. He wanted to show it to the man and began turning over the leaves of the book, boasting that he knew the order and arrangement perfectly. As he was looking for the place, the man asked him where he had got the book. Descartes answered that he could not tell him how he had got it but that, a second before, *he had had another book in his hands, which had just disappeared*, without his knowing who had brought it or who had taken it away again. He had hardly finished speaking when the book reappeared at the other end of the table. He discovered, however, that the dictionary was no longer complete,[87] though earlier it had appeared to be so. Meanwhile, he found the poems of Ausonius in the anthology of poets, which he was running through; but, being unable to find the poem beginning "Est et non," he told the man that he knew an even more beautiful poem by the same author, beginning "Quod vitae sectabor iter?" The man begged to let him see it,

---

86. It is fairly certain that he must have read this book at La Flèche. Cf. Adam, p. 21, n. 2.

87. Ježower: "was not so complete."

and Descartes was diligently searching for it when he came upon *a number of small portraits—copperplate engravings*—which made him exclaim at the beauty of the book; but it was not the same edition as the one he knew.

At this point both the man and the books disappeared and faded from his mind's eye, but he did not awaken. The remarkable thing is that, being in doubt as to whether this experience was a dream or a vision, he not only decided, while still sleeping, that it was a dream, but he also interpreted it before waking. He concluded that *the dictionary signified the connection between all the sciences* and that the collection of poets entitled *Corpus Poetarum* pointed particularly and clearly to *the intimate union of philosophy with wisdom*. For he thought that one should not be surprised to discover that the poets, even those whose work seems to be only a foolish pastime, produce much deeper, more sensible, and better expressed thoughts than are to be found in the writings of the philosophers. *He attributed this wonder to the divine quality of enthusiasm and the power of imagination*, which enable the *seed of wisdom (existing in the minds of all men as do sparks of fire in flint)* [88] to sprout with much greater ease and even brilliance than the "reason" of the philosophers. Continuing to interpret the dream in his sleep, Descartes concluded that the poem on "what sort of life one should choose," beginning "Quod vitae sectabor iter," pointed to the sound advice of a wise person or even to Moral Theology. Still uncertain whether he was dreaming or meditating, he awoke peacefully and with open eyes continued to interpret his dream in the same spirit. The poets represented in the collection of poems he interpreted as the revelation and enthusiasm that had been ac-

---

88. The same thought appears in the *Cogitationes privatae* (*A-T*, X, 217): "Mirum videri possit, quare graves sententiae in scriptis poetarum, magis quam philosophorum. Ratio est quod poetae per enthusiasmum et vim imaginationis scripsere: sunt in nobis semina scientiae, ut in silice, quae per rationem a philosophis educuntur per imaginationem a poetis excutiuntur magisque elucent." ("Wonderfully, poets abound more in serious thoughts than philosophers do. Poets write by force of imagination and with enthusiasm; all of us bear the seeds of wisdom within us, like flint, which are brought forth by the philosophers by reason, [but] the poets strike them forth with imagination, and they shine all the more brightly.")

corded him. The poem "Est et non"—which is the "Yes and No" of Pythagoras—he understood as the truth and error of all human knowledge and profane science. When he saw that all these things were so satisfactorily turning out according to his desire, he dared to believe that it was the *spirit of truth* that wished, through this dream, to reveal to him the treasures of all the sciences. There now remained nothing to be explained save the small copperplate portraits that he had found in the second book. These he no longer sought to elucidate after receiving a visit from an Italian painter on the following day.

Interpretation of the First Dream

The exposition of the dream consists in the rather hazy statement that Descartes was frightened by the presence of "a number of ghosts" and thought he was walking through streets toward an (unknown) goal. His fear caused him to bend over on his left side (*"se renverser"*), since he felt a great weakness on the right.

The ghostly apparitions might well be connected with his experience of the previous day,[89] for they are the primordial form of the "spirit," an embodiment, in other words, of the autonomous image-creating activity of the unconscious,[90] which primitive man has always experienced as ghosts or spirits.[91]

While this is the form in which the mind actually confronts primitive man, "with increasing development it enters the realm of human consciousness and becomes a function

---

89. Since the appearance of Milhaud's paper in the *Revue de métaphysique et de morale* (July, 1916), pp. 610–11, it has been customary to look on the "Enthusiasmus" as coinciding with the dream, but I see no reason why Baillet's report should be depreciated; the dream appears to be far more a representation of the "meaning" of the enthusiasm.
90. Cf. C. G. Jung, "The Phenomenology of the Spirit in Fairy Tales," *The Archetypes and the Collective Unconscious*, pp. 212–13.
91. *Ibid.*, pp. 208–9.

under man's control; whereby its original autonomous character is apparently lost."[92] Man, however, should never forget

what he draws into his sphere and with what he fills his consciousness. For he has not created the mind, it is the mind which enables him to create; it gives him the impulse, the sudden flash of insight, endurance, enthusiasm, and inspiration. But it so penetrates the human being that man is sorely tempted to believe that he himself is the creator of the spirit and that he owns it. In reality, however, it is the primordial phenomenon of the mind that takes possession of man, and in exactly the same way as that in which the physical world appears to be the willing tool of his purpose but in reality tears man's freedom to shreds and becomes an obsessing *idée-force*. The mind threatens the naïve man with inflation. . . . The danger becomes greater the more the outer object captivates our interest and the more man forgets that, hand in hand with the differentiation of our connection with nature, there should also go a similar differentiation of our relation to the mind, in order to create the necessary equilibrium.[93]

Without a doubt Descartes was in danger of identifying with his scientific discovery and of overlooking the autonomous nature of his experience. (Just think of his *"Cogito ergo sum"*—*"I think, therefore I am"*![94]) According to his view, all bodily reactions, as well as the feelings and the sense perceptions, can be separated from the ego—as it happens, for instance, in the dream—but thinking cannot be thus abstracted. He says: "Cogitare? Hic invenio: cogitatio: *haec sola a* me divelli nequit." ("To think? Here I discover: Thinking! This alone cannot be taken from me.")[95] Thinking is thus the function of consciousness par excellence, which is completely unified with the ego[96] (and for Descartes the soul

---

92. *Cit.* Jung, *ibid.*, pp. 212–13.
93. *Ibid.*, pp. 212–14. Descartes also hoped that science would make us "the masters and possessors of nature" (Adam, p. 229).
94. *A-T*, VII, 27.
95. Barth, p. 56.
96. The soul is the *"res cogitans"* (Barth, p. 59). See also Barth's comment (p. 53) on the following passage from Descartes's letter to Mersenne (*A-T*, III, 394): "Pour ce qui est de l'Ame, c'est encore une

81   *The Dream of Descartes*

consists only of the thinking ego [97]). In other words, Descartes identifies completely with his thinking function.[98] But for this very reason he is in danger of overlooking the "autonomous" nature of his thinking experience; and therefore the "mind" in its primordial form haunts him most terrifyingly in the night. Also in these phantoms there probably lies hidden all that still surpasses his own comprehension concerning his discovery: [99] the archetypal processes in the background and the dawn of a new spirit of the time, with its dangerous trends, threatening the human order of things. Was not this precisely the time of the outbreak of the Thirty Years' War, whose consequences were destined to destroy all culture in the heart of Europe for a long time to come? [100]

The word "ghosts," moreover, evokes the thought of the dead. Here we may remember that Descartes's mother died

---

chose plus claire. Car n'étant comme j'ai démontré qu'une chose qui pense, il est impossible que nous puissions jamais penser à une chose que nous n'ayons en même temps l'idée de notre âme, comme d'une chose capable de penser à tout ce que nous pensons ... ." ("Concerning the soul, it is something even more intelligible. For being, as I have demonstrated, nothing but a thing that thinks, it is impossible that we should ever think of something without at the same time having the idea of our soul, as of a thing capable of thinking of all that we think about.") It is also indicative of Descartes's type that he relegated feeling to the sphere of the body (see below, p. 87, n. 126).

97. Cf. Jung, *Psychological Types* (*CW*, VI, in preparation), chapter on definitions.

98. His main psychological function was probably introverted thinking. Cf. Fleckenstein's remark (p. 133): "To be sure, the portrayal of all the physical processes thus remains nothing but an image, a model, with which calculations can be undertaken."

99. Cf. Gonseth, p. 378: "Aussitôt qu'elles ont trouvé leur expression *les pensées revêtent une certaine existence autonome.* L'esprit qui les a conçues les reconnaît comme siennes, mais ne les habite plus complètement." ("As soon as they have found their expression, thoughts take on a certain autonomy of existence. The mind that conceived them recognizes them as its own, but no longer inhabits them completely.") The ego is thus only a channel for intellectual contents which announce themselves preconsciously and, after their formulation, autonomously pursue their further development.

100. Quite correctly Maritain speaks, concerning Descartes, of a "mythe de la science." (Cf. Sirven, p. 308 n.)

when he was still an infant. For him the image of the mother remained in the Beyond, and he was doomed to forego the maternal warmth and protection which a child needs to enable him to turn away from the world of images of the collective unconscious and face life. Hence, in his case, undoubtedly a door had remained open into the world of spirits, the land of the dead. No doubt this is why he was never able to project the anima onto a real woman. When the mother dies so early, she often leaves a great secret yearning in her son, so that, as Jung explains, no other woman can attain to the figure—the more powerful for being so distant—of the mother.

The more distant and unreal the personal mother, the more profoundly does the longing for her move the son in the depths of his soul, there to awaken the primordial and eternal image of the mother, for which reason everything that is containing, protective, nourishing, and helpful takes on for us the form of the mother. . . ."[101]

In Descartes's case these mothers were the Mater Ecclesia and Science, the latter of which he often compared with a chaste woman.[102]

To connect these ghosts with the unrealized background of his scientific discovery, on the one hand, and with the image of the mother and the anima, on the other, is not as inconsistent as might appear at first sight: Descartes's simplification of mathematics and the fact that he exalted the latter as the only valid means of representing physical processes contributed,

---

101. Jung says this concerning Paracelsus; see his *Paracelsica* (Zurich, 1942), p. 45. Henri Bergson has also correctly described Descartes's mathematics and *"méthode"* as a *"proles sine matre creata"* ("offspring created without a mother"). (See Sirven [p. 1], who follows H. Bergson, "La philosophie," *Science française* [Paris, 1916]).

102. In the *Cogitationes privatae* (*A-T*, X, 214), he says: "Scientia est velut mulier, quae si pudica apud virum maneat, colitur; si communis fiat, vilescit." ("Science is like a woman, who is cherished if she remains modest with one man, but becomes cheap if she prostitutes herself to many.")

together with the works of Kepler, Galileo, and others,[103] most definitely toward the building-up of a new, purely mechanistic conception of the world, which remained valid up till the end of the nineteenth century. But what was lost at the time, as W. Pauli has shown,[104] was the oneness of the reality which included the observer; also lost was the ancient doctrine of correspondence, in which the psychic factor and the idea of a meaningful teleological order in nature still had a place. Descartes definitely denied the existence of a *causa finalis* in natural events.[105] As Pauli points out further [106]— with reference to Kepler's theories—it was really the image (among other things) of an objectively existing *anima mundi* ("world-soul") and of an objective psychic factor in general which was discarded at that time—which, in other words, became unconscious. The image of the Trinity was

103. Descartes knew the work of "Vitellio" (Witelo) and Kepler's "Paralipomena ad Vitellionem," as well as Galileo's works (see Sirven, p. 283).
104. "Die Einfluss archetypischer Vorstellungen auf die Bildung naturwissenschaftlicher Theorien bei Kepler," in C. G. Jung and W. Pauli, *Naturerklärung und Psyche* (Zurich: Rascher Verlag, 1952); English translation, by Priscilla Silz, "The Influence of Archetypal Ideas on the Scientific Theories of Kepler," in C. G. Jung and W. Pauli, *The Interpretation of Nature and the Psyche* (Bollingen Series LI) (New York and London, 1955).
Professor Pauli had the kindness to send me the following explanations by letter: "There has also been an attempt in principle to take the psychic conditioning factors of the observer into account. Kepler also does this, but with the tendency, ever more apparent, to eliminate them from the 'objective' observation of nature."
105. Cf. *Meditation* IV: "I believe that that whole class of causes that one is in the habit of inferring from their ends should not be used in physics" (*cit.* Carl Felsch, *Der Kausalitätsbegriff bei Descartes* [Langensalza, 1891], p. 11).
106. In his letter, cited above, n. 104, Pauli says: "Concerning the modern 'anima-problem,' [we may remember that] the seventeenth century tried to *eliminate the concept of soul from the physical world*. The tendency was therefore to limit the soul more and more to the individual human being. What was abandoned . . . was the idea of the objective-psychic factor. In the seventeenth century the psyche became purely subjective."

projected into the material world and was sought for there, while the fourth principle was lost once again.[107] With Kepler, the three-dimensional character of space is an image of the Trinity, and the mathematical laws of nature are the laws in the mind of God; with Descartes, the veracity and immutable stability of God guarantee the regularity of the physical laws of movement.[108] In his *Principia* (II, 37) Descartes says that this is first law of nature:

Each thing, insofar as it is simple and undivided, always remains as much as possible in the same state and never changes but by external causes. . . . A second law is that each part of matter, regarded in itself, does not tend ever to continue moving along curved lines. . . . The cause of the latter law is the same as that of the former one, namely, the immutability of God and the simplicity of operation whereby He conserves motion in matter. . . . Through this immutability of His workings God maintains the world in exactly the state in which He first created it.

The knowledge of the simple physical laws of the movement of matter suffice, therefore, fully to explain all natural phenomena.[109] The possibility that God could have a trickster-aspect or could deceive or behave irrationally or acausally is to Descartes unthinkable.[110] God, on the contrary, guarantees that nature obeys laws and also guarantees the clear and distinct ideas in men's minds, which thus constitute an organon for investigating the physical world.[111] He says in *Meditation* I: "Et généralement nous pouvons bien assurer que Dieu peut faire tout ce que nous pouvons comprendre, mais non pas qu'il ne peut faire ce que nous ne pouvons pas com-

---

107. This lack of the conception of the *anima mundi* in Descartes's view of the physical world is consequently also to be connected with his personal problem of not being able to integrate his personal anima.
108. *Meditation* VI and *Principia*, II, 36–37. Cf. Hyman Stock, *The Method of Descartes in the Natural Sciences* (New York, 1931), pp. 11–15.
109. *Principia*, II, 23; cf. also Stock, p. 12.
110. Stock, p. 11.
111. Stock, p. 12, commenting on *Meditation* VI.

prendre." ("Generally we can certainly assert that God can do everything which we are able to comprehend, but not that he cannot do what we cannot understand.") He can, indeed, act differently, but He *will* not do so. As Barth formulates it: "God's acts of will clothe themselves with the laws of the pure conceptions of nature; they coincide with intellectual order." [112]

For Descartes the inner "logic" of physical events is thus completely identical with the inner "logic" of our own thinking.[113] As with Spinoza, the course of our thinking (*ordo et connexio idearum*) is the same as that of physical events (*ordo et connexio rerum sive corporum*).[114] Wolfgang Röd [115] has convincingly worked out this practical (or should one, perhaps, go so far as to call it concretistic?) foundation of Cartesian thinking and has shown how greatly Descartes hoped thereby to arrive at certainty concerning his philosophical and even moral views. For him physical determinism thus almost became a proof of God's existence, for the causal chains of psychic and physical events originate in God as the *causa prima*,[116] and, as Felsch stresses,[117] Descartes also attributed an ordered working to God, i.e., to the metaphysical origins, and only made a few concessions to the freedom of God for reasons of theological prudence. We may therefore conclude that *for him the activity of God is essentially identical with the principle of causality*. He was thus himself aware that the principle of causality belongs to the *notiones communes* or inborn *veritates aeternae*.[118] Felsch lays stress here on the correspondence with Kant, who likewise held that causality belongs to the "categories of pure reason."

Descartes held the view that the working of causality has

112. Barth, p. 87.
113. Cf. Felsch, p. 9.
114. *Ibid.*, pp. 9–10.
115. Röd, *passim*.
116. Felsch, p. 8.
117. *Ibid.*, p. 9.
118. *Principia phil.*, I, 39, 49, 75, *cit.* Felsch, p. 14.

nothing to do with time;[119] for him time itself is a discontinuous series of moments (instants).[120]

It is thus significant that the dreams portray their essential quality by means of ghostly phenomena or parapsychological events. If the unconscious brings up such phenomena in a dream, it wishes to impress the existence of these facts upon the dreamer. Such phenomena are, however, as Jung has shown in his paper on synchronicity,[121] acausal happenings, in which an outer physical event coincides in a meaningful way with a psychically constellated content but cannot be seen as having a causal connection with it. Descartes did not see this principle of synchronicity and in fact rejected its contemporary parallel conception, the doctrine of *correspondentia*. He even excluded it from his thinking.[122] His one-sided and ex-

---

119. Felsch, p. 15.
120. As Fleckenstein (p. 135) stresses: "Descartes was unable to conceive of the mathematical formulation of continuous functions because he tended to eliminate the parameter of time in physics. It was Newton who introduced the time-parameter into physics, and in his private thoughts on metaphysics he even called it a substance of the '*vita divina*'—just as for him space was the '*sensorium Dei*.'" Fleckenstein also remarks (p. 126): "The basis of Cartesian mechanics is the conservation of the impulse or, in its original form, of the quantum of movement which is the product of mass and velocity. Descartes did not yet know of the vectorial aspect of velocity and saw it only as a scalar factor, which led him into contradictions when deriving his laws of impulse. . . . Since Descartes only used the laws of analytical geometry within the framework of Euclidean geometry, he overcame the prejudices of the physics of antiquity in form but not in essence, for his mechanics remain identical with those of antiquity." *Ibid.*, p. 127: "In the world of Descartes there are only rigid collisions which transfer the quantum of movement, but not continually acting forces causing changes of state. He tried to understand cosmic events from the multiplicity of distribution of the movement-quantum instead of understanding it from what remains continuous within the temporal changes. It was Leibniz who later achieved this by his principle of energy, which he had to defend in his dispute with the Cartesians." *Ibid.*, p. 128: "Descartes is unable to grasp a continuous change, especially not in time, for he aims at an elimination of the time-parameter in his 'geometrization' of physics." Cf. also *ibid.*, pp. 123 ff.
121. "Synchronicity: An Acausal Connecting Principle."
122. Naturally Descartes could not recognize the principle of synchronicity in the Jungian sense, but he discarded its earlier manifesta-

clusive acceptance of the laws of causality engendered a lack of clarity in his system concerning the relation of soul and body, which lack one of his pupils, Arnold Geulincx,[123] tried to clarify by introducing the idea that the two factors run parallel to each other, like two watches wound up at the same time.[124]

Descartes surmised that the connection between body and soul was to be sought in the experience of the *"passiones"* (emotions as psychological events);[125] we are reminded that, according to Jung, synchronistic phenomena are especially apt to take place when an archetypal content has been constellated and, with it, a state of emotional tension in the observer. But Descartes was not able to clarify the idea of the mediating *passiones* or to bring it into relation to his views of the physical world.[126] As a consequence he shuts out not only the anima but also the problems of evil and the irrational.

In this illuminating night of terror the unconscious certainly seeks to set precisely this area of facts and problems before Descartes in an impressive fashion, but he does not grasp it. Instead, in the first terrified moment of waking, he thinks of "the influence of evil spirits," though he does not go into this idea more profoundly.

Seen in this connection, it is understandable that Descartes, in the first terrified moment of waking from his dream, should think that evil spirits had been at work; for not only has he excluded the anima from his picture of the world, but he has also shut out the problem of evil as well as the element of the irrational.

---

tions, such as the doctrine of correspondences, the *causa finalis*, and so forth.

123. Concerning whom see von Brockdorff, p. 152.
124. Professor Pauli has drawn attention to these facts.
125. Cf. von Brockdorff, pp. 19 ff.
126. He puzzled over the function of the pineal gland, which he conjectured to be the "connecting place" of body and soul. For details of this particular problem see Geoffrey Jefferson, "René Descartes on the Localisation of the Soul," *Irish Journal of Medical Science*, No. 285 (Sept., 1949), pp. i ff., and the literature cited there. I am indebted to Dr. E. A. Bennet for drawing my attention to this article.

The appearance of the ghosts is the cause for, or coincides with, the fact that Descartes thinks he is walking through streets; he is thrown out of his established introverted life in his room and driven into collective life—a compensation for his fear of entering the life of ordinary human beings.[127] Over and beyond this it is an impulse to strive after collective aims, as yet unknown to him. Furthermore, his fear compels him to bend low down on the left (or throw himself over onto the left side?).[128] This likewise should be understood in the first place as a compensation; the unconscious wants to force him over to the left, onto the *sinister* ("left"), feminine side, which he is far too fond of overlooking and undervaluing.[129]

127. In his paper, "Three Dreams of Descartes," *International Journal of Psycho-Analysis*, XXVIII, Pt. 1 (1947), 11 ff., J. O. Wisdom interprets this motif as Descartes's unconscious fear of impotence (castration complex), though, unless one is inclined to believe in the Freudian theory of the "censor," it is baffling to know why Descartes should suffer from such a fear or why it should be depicted in such a form. No specifically sexual disturbances are perceptible in Descartes's case, but rather an atrophying of the life of feeling. On the other hand, Wisdom (pp. 28 ff.) rightly stresses the conflict in Descartes between his intellect and his urge for life. I wish to thank the author for sending me his article.

128. "*Se renverser*."

129. Cf. J. Rittmeister, "Die mystische Krise des jungen Descartes," *Confinia psychiatrica*, IV (1961), 81, where the "left" is interpreted similarly to the way in which I have sought to work it out. The "left side" corresponds to the dark side of the inferior function, which in intellectual types is usually feeling. For Descartes it becomes the devil, who reverses the previous point of view and (in the case of the dreamer) lames him in the feet. Does it not, says Rittmeister, in fact strike us that the longing for the mother, the home, and so forth applies to all those mythological characters, such as Harpocrates (Horus), Hephaestus, Oedipus, and Philoctetes, who were crippled in their lower limbs? Concerning the left side as feminine and chthonic see Bachofen, *Versuch über die Gräbersymbolik der Alten* (Basel, 1859), pp. 171 ff.: "The left hand of Isis, *aequitatis manus*, is one of the symbols carried around in the procession." Apuleius *Metamorphoses* XI and 1: "The left hand is 'otiosa.'" Macrobius *Sat.* 7. 13: "Boys are begotten from the right testicle, girls from the left one." See also Plutarch *Symp.* 8. 8. and 5. 7. According to Plato (*Laws* 4) the left side and an even number of sacrificial animals were offered to the chthonic gods, while the Olympians received the right side and an uneven number. The left is associated with the North, the right with the South. Sacrifices to or for

89 The Dream of Descartes

It is fear which causes Descartes to bend over to the left. Strangely enough, the ghosts do not appear on the left (where, speaking mythologically, they would seem to belong) but on the right, apparently because on the right there was a weak spot, an open door to the contents of the unconscious. Since the unconscious thrusts him over to the left, it is evident that of himself he has a tendency to diverge too much to the right, which likewise corresponds to a certain *unconsciousness*—for consciousness is a phenomenon of the center, between instinct and spirit. In his "On the Nature of the Psyche," [130] Jung compares conscious psychic life to a ray of light which spreads into a spectrum, one end of which represents the urges and instincts, namely, the psychoid life processes, which gradually go over into the chemical processes of the body, while the other consists of the (equally psychoid) archetypal contents, the element of the spirit.[131] Both poles

---

the dead are performed with the left hand. Cf. Jung, *Psychology and Alchemy*, p. 121, concerning the circumambulation to the left: "The left, the 'sinister' side, is the unconscious side. Therefore a leftward movement is equivalent to a movement in the direction of the unconscious, whereas a movement to the right is 'correct' and aims at consciousness." Cf. also Jung's commentary on dream 22 in the same volume (p. 156), where "The 'left' is to be completely throttled" and where Jung further remarks (pp. 160-61, 163-65): "Just as the 'right' denotes the world of consciousness and its principles, so by 'reflection' the picture of the world is to be turned round to the left, thus producing a corresponding world in reverse. We could equally well say: through reflection the right appears as the reverse of the left. Therefore the left seems to have as much validity as the right; in other words, the unconscious and its—for the most part unintelligible—order becomes the symmetrical counterpart of the conscious mind and its contents, although it is still not clear which of them is reflected and which reflecting. To carry our reasoning a step further, we could regard the center as the point of intersection of two worlds that correspond but are inverted by reflection."

130. In *The Structure and Dynamics of the Psyche*, CW, VIII (1960).

131. In the *Cogitationes privatae* (*A-T*, X, 218), Descartes himself says that the wind is the spirit: "Ventus spiritum designat, motus cum tempore vitam, lumen cognitionem, calor amorem, activitas instantanea creationem." ("Wind designates spirit; movement with time, life; light, cognition; heat, love; instantaneous activity, creation.")

ultimately transcend consciousness. In this sense one might say that Descartes, through his somewhat compulsive meditation, had come too close to the spiritual pole and had thus become too unconscious on this side (in other words, he was in danger of being possessed by archetypal contents). Therefore, he felt "a great weakness" on the right side, and the dream motif endeavors to rectify the situation by taking him over to the left.[132] Moreover, it compels him to bend down low as a balance for his somewhat inflated "enthusiasm" (as Maritain emphasizes, he actually considered himself to be *the* man called upon to reform the entire science of his day).[133]

Ashamed, he nevertheless tries to walk upright, only to feel himself seized by a fierce whirlwind that spins him round on his left foot. The ghosts have now transformed themselves into the πνεῦμα (pneuma or divine spirit), into a storm which threatens him. This spirit whirls him around just at the moment when he endeavors to stand upright: "Take care not to spit *against* the wind!"[134] The man of the Renaissance, who casts off his medieval humility and, raising himself, begins to trust his own thinking—this is the man who is caught by the destructive storm, which had already begun to blow in a threatening way in the "Brothers of the Free Spirit," the "Friends of God on the Rhine," the "Tertiaries," and other Holy Ghost movements.[135] This whirlwind

---

132. Rittmeister (pp. 81–82) thinks that the direction of the storm is a regression into the primordial past and to the Mother of God.

133. See *A-T*, X, 18 ff.

134. Friedrich Nietzsche, *Thus Spoke Zarathustra*, end of Chapter XXVIII, "The Rabble" (New York: Modern Library), p. 111. J. O. Wisdom interprets the wind as the father-image, which appears to be both fertilizing and threatening, when Descartes attempts to consummate the sexual act (Wisdom, pp. 15–16).

135. Maritain (p. 25) stresses the extent to which Descartes felt himself to have been possessed by a kind of "*Sapientia Dei*" or by the Holy Ghost: "C'est ainsi, croyons nous, que Descartes aperçut, ramassée dans une seule intuition, l'idée vitale, le Λόγος σπερματικός ["seminal Word"] de sa réforme philosophique." ("It was thus, so we believe, that Descartes perceived and gathered together into one single intuition the vital idea, the *Logos spermatikos* of his philosophical reform.") He believed (*cit*. Maritain, p. 25) "... à la Science universelle

may have to do with the "storm" of the Reformation and the Counter Reformation, which is beginning to break up the ancient order of things in Germany, where Descartes is now living. The storm tells us that the ghosts in the first dream undoubtedly belonged to the host of the dead, the host of the wild huntsman, Wotan.[136] Descartes is among those who were seized by the new spirit; his discoveries help open the way for the establishment of another *Weltanschauung*, that of a newly dawning age, characteristic of which is the development, on the one hand, of scientific thinking but, on the other, of the growth of a pernicious *hubris* of consciousness for which later generations will have to pay. The left side is again characterized as helpful; only

qui élèvera notre nature à son plus haut degré de perfection" (". . . in the universal science which will elevate our nature to its highest degree of perfection"). Maritain continues (p. 27): "L'enthousiasme solitaire qui l'anime a une origine divine, l'ivresse de la nuit du 10 novembre 1619 est une ivresse sainte, elle est en sa personne comme une pentecôte de la raison." ("The lonely enthusiasm that animates him has a divine origin; the intoxication of the night of November 10th, 1619, is a holy drunkenness; in itself it is like a Pentecost of reason.") (P. 30): "[C'est] la science même de Dieu et des Anges. S'il en est ainsi, c'est sans doute par un effet de l'idéalisme et si j'ose dire de l'angélisme qui caractérise en général la philosophie cartésienne." ("It is the very science of God and the angels. If it be thus, it is without doubt as a consequence of the idealism, or, if I may say, the angelic quality, which in general characterizes Cartesian philosophy.") Maritain (p. 31) understands very clearly the *hubris* of the new scientific thinking and for that reason believes that "c'est le songe d'une nuit d'automne *excité par un malin génie* dans un cerveau de philosophe ..." (". . . it is the dream of an autumn night, *instigated in the brain of a philosopher by a malicious spirit* . . .").

136. Concerning the idea that behind this outbreak of the German spirit stands the image of Wotan cf. Jung, "Wotan" (*CW*, X, 1964), esp. pp. 16 ff. Wotan (Odin) is a wind- or storm-god, the leader of the *wüetis heer*, i.e., the host of the dead, the great magician who, as Jung says (*ibid.*), embodies ". . . the impulsive emotional, as well as the intuitive and inspirational side of the unconscious." For the mythological phenomenology see Martin Ninck, *Wodan und germanischer Schicksalsglaube* (Jena, 1935), and E. Mogk, *Germanische Religionsgeschichte und Mythologie* (Berlin and Leipzig: Gruyter, 1927), pp. 64 ff. Wotan also behaves like a ghost-figure (*ibid.*, p. 65). He is the first engenderer of enthusiasm (*ibid.*, p. 67); he is also a deluder of women (*ibid.*, p. 74) and a magician.

on his left foot is Descartes still able to maintain his standpoint on earth, but even so the wind whirls him round three or four times (!) in a circle.

This whirling causes him to turn on his own axis, so that he has to look in all the directions of the compass in turn—a compensation for his one-sided point of view. The unconscious is aiming at a widening of his horizon and a shifting of the center of rotation from the outer world into his own sphere. This image of the whirlwind also appears to be projected into Descartes's cosmogonic theory, according to which the world proceeds from a continuously expanding equal diffusion of extended matter in which the small spheres of the four primal elements fall into a spiral movement and begin to rotate around themselves and around certain outer central points, which are now the stars.[137] As Fleckenstein remarks, these bizarre Cartesian vortices constitute "the first effort in the direction of a continuum physics."[138] In themselves creation myths are representations from the unconscious of the emergence of consciousness, so that from Descartes's own theory one might conclude that these spiral movements in the dream could mean the inception of an awakening new consciousness.

There is a noteworthy detail in the fact that Descartes is whirled around *three or four* times. The problematical relation of three to four is precisely *the* psychologically significant matter, which is already expressed in the alchemistic axiom of Maria Prophetissa, "One becomes two, two becomes three, and out of the third comes the one as the fourth."[139] "This uncertainty," comments Jung,

has a duplex character—in other words, the central ideas are ternary as well as quaternary. The psychologist cannot but mention the fact that a similar puzzle exists in the psychology of the unconscious: the least differentiated or 'inferior' function[140] is so

---

137. According to Fleckenstein, pp. 122–24.
138. *Ibid.*
139. Cf. Jung, *Psychology and Alchemy*, p. 23.
140. The present writer's note: Cf. the chapter on "Definitions" in Jung's *Psychological Types*.

93 The Dream of Descartes

much contaminated by the collective unconscious that, on becoming conscious, it brings up the archetype of the Self as well —τὸ ἓν τέταρτον, as Maria Prophetissa says. Four signifies the feminine, motherly, physical; three the masculine, fatherly, spiritual. Thus the uncertainty as to three or four amounts to a wavering between the spiritual and the physical. . . .

As already mentioned, that is precisely *the* problem for Descartes, who tore the physical and the psychic apart with his causal thinking and its corresponding mechanistic view of the world and who was unable to integrate the fourth—the feminine and maternal—into his personal life. It might be possible to object here that too many motifs are pulled into the detailed interpretation of the dream, but, after all, the dream *does* exactly state—and this is typical for such "big dreams"—that Descartes is whirled around three or four times, neither more nor less.[141] It might be further mentioned that the name "Descartes" was originally "de Quartis"!

While he is being whisked around to such an extent, Descartes is tormented by a constant fear of falling, of touching the earth, i.e., reality, the maternal / feminine. He then notices a college, which stands open, and resolves to seek help and protection by offering up a prayer in its chapel. As Maritain stresses, this place might well be connected with the Jesuit college of La Flèche, in which Descartes grew up,[142] and would therefore represent the spiritual training and the whole framework of orthodox conceptions in himself, by means of which—like so many others at the time of the Counter Reformation—he sought to save himself from being possessed by the new spirit (at the time of the dream he was serving in the army of Maximilian of Bavaria). The storm is blowing in the direction of the church, so it cannot be the wind that once filled the early Church. It is rather a storm which has its

---

141. Cf. *Psychology and Alchemy*, pp. 101–4, 119–20, and esp. 144, 148, and 153.

142. Thus does Maritain conclude his paper "Le songe . . ." (pp. 5–7). Unfortnuately he considers that to Catholics "le commerce avec les génies excitateurs des songes" ("traffic with spirits instigating dreams") can only seem suspect.

origin not *in* the Church but *outside* it. It "bloweth where it listeth," and the Church is no longer its vessel but, according to circumstances, either an obstacle on its path or a refuge for those who fear the wind. The situation at that time could hardly be more aptly represented symbolically! Descartes himself was puzzled by this paradox: he interpreted the wind as "le mauvais génie qui tâchait le jeter par force dans un lieu où son dessein étoit d'aller volontairement" ("the evil spirit which tried to push him forcibly to a place where he wanted to go voluntarily").[143] A marginal note adds:

A malo Spiritu ad Templum propellebar: C'est pourquoi Dieu ne permit pas qu'il avançât plus loin et qu'il se laissât emporter, même en un lieu saint, par un Esprit qu'il n'avait pas envoyé: quoy qu'il fût très-persuadé, que c'eût été l'Esprit de Dieu qui luy avoit fait faire les premières démarches vers cette Église.[144]

(I was pushed by an evil spirit toward the church: This is why God did not allow him [Descartes] to go further and be carried away—even into a holy place—by a spirit which He had not sent, though he [Descartes] was completely convinced that it had first been the spirit of God who made him take the first steps toward that church.)

Descartes is quite naturally in doubt as to whether this wind is the spirit of God or the spirit of Satan, which was also thought to be a *ventus urens*, coming out of the North.[145] Descartes's uncertainty concerning the moral significance of the storm may be compared with the doubt experienced by Ignatius of Loyola when, in a profoundly beneficial vision, he saw a snake "which was full of luminous eyes, although they were really not eyes." [146] Later, however, he concluded that it

---

143. *A-T*, X, 185.
144. *Ibid.*
145. Cf. the following articles in *Patr. Lat.* (ed. Migne): "Rhabanus Maurus," Vol. CX, col. 860; "Adam Scotus," Vol. CXCVIII, col. 760; "St. Eucharist.," Vol. L, col. 739; "St. Victor Garnerius," Vol. CXCIII, col. 59; "Gregor Magnus," Vol. LXXVI, cols. 1019, 1026, and 1054; etc. Further details in Jung, *Aion* (*CW*, IX, Part II, 1959).
146. See Philipp Funk, *Ignatius von Loyola* (Berlin, 1913), pp. 57, 66. Cf., further, Jung's exposition in "The Process of Individuation"

95 The Dream of Descartes

must be a diabolical apparition.[147] Niklaus von der Flüe also had subsequently to tone down his terrifying vision of God, for the personal experience of it almost disrupted him.[148] This, too, is a somewhat similar case; in itself the storm is a morally unbiased image, emerging spontaneously from the unconscious and symbolizing a primordial experience of the spirit whose effects could be various: he who allowed himself to be carried away by it stormed against the Church, whereas he who fled was bound to dig himself into the Church, with windows and doors tight shut, and could not leave it and go about freely again without danger. Few indeed had sufficient humility to bend low down toward the earth—certainly not Descartes, and therefore he decided subsequently to explain the storm as the work of the evil spirit.

In his haste, however, he notices that he has passed an acquaintance without greeting him, but when he endeavors to go back and make good this omission, the wind stops him. Unfortunately, we lack any associations or statements which might tell us who this Mr. N. might be and are therefore unable to discover what role he played in Descartes's psyche;[149] but he was evidently a man for whom Descartes must have had a positive feeling or a certain respect, since he regretted not having greeted him. We can only say, therefore, that the "acquaintance" represents a part of Descartes's personality which, in his state of enthusiasm, he is in danger of overlooking. The unusual gift which this young man of only twenty-three possessed in the realm of thinking—amounting indeed to creative genius—obviously suggests that he developed in a very one-sided way and in a measure far

---

(Eidgenössische Technische Hochschule Lectures, Zurich, June, 1939—March, 1940; privately printed); by kind permission of Professor Jung.

147. Jung, "The Process of Individuation," p. 24.

148. Cf. Jung, "Brother Klaus," *Psychology and Religion* (*CW*, XI, 1958).

149. Freud has already rightly expressed regret that Descartes's associations, needful for a *certain* interpretation, are lacking—which is particularly the case with these human figures.

outran his own nature, leaving parts of his personality undeveloped behind him. Moreover, his natural inclination to escape life and his fear of love involvements, as well as his skepticism, encouraged still further this one-sided development of his introverted thinking.

We know that, at the time of the dream, Descartes was making a particular effort to become conscious of his own thinking; so we may assume that the aspect of the personality which he negligently passes by is connected with his emotions and his feeling side and, in a wider sense, is bound up with his undifferentiated fourth function. It may therefore not be misleading to surmise a shadow-figure of Descartes in Mr. N., which nonetheless has a rather positive meaning for him and which he had only overlooked, not rejected. It would be interesting to know what Descartes said in his lost treatise "De genio Socratis"; for in Socrates' case, too, there was a really split personality, connected with the pronounced Cabiric traits exhibited by his daimonion. Descartes was probably interested in Socrates because he projected his own problem onto him. He also speaks of the fact that *"le génie"* gave him notice in advance of the great dream.[150] It is not clear exactly what he meant by his *"génie";* he probably conceived of it, as Sirven surmises, as a kind of *spiritus familiaris* or *"cousin de l'ange gardien."* [151]

In the dream Descartes does, certainly, try to make up for his fault; but then he comes up against the wind. The attempt to compensate would have been a step toward the attainment of inner wholeness; but precisely at such a moment the whole resistance of collective trends makes itself felt. This confrontation with the *Zeitgeist*, demanding an effort to come to

---

150. *A-T*, X, 186: "Il ajoute que le Génie qui excitait en luy l'enthousiasme dont il se sentait le cerveau échauffé depuis quelques jours, luy avoit prédit ce songe avant que de se mettre au lit et que l'esprit humain n'y avoit aucune part." ("He adds that the spirit which had excited in him the enthusiasm by which he had felt for several days that his brain was being heated, had predicted the dream to him before he went to bed, and that the human mind had no part in it.")

151. Cf. Sirven, pp. 131–32.

97 The Dream of Descartes

terms with it and an individual self-assertion in face of it, is a step which, as his biography shows, Descartes never uncompromisingly attempted. Did he himself not say, speaking of his appearance in the world, *"Larvatus prodeo"* (["Only] with a mask do I appear in public!").[152] But it is not only outwardly that he avoided any risk of disclosing himself; inwardly, as well, he remained curiously undecided in regard to the most critical religious questions of his time and in the personal conduct of his life. The lack of a mother deprived him of the vitality and rooted contact with the earth which would have enabled him to maintain himself against the storm.

Even so, his attempt to reach Mr. N., who has been left behind, brings about a positive change in the dream: in the college quadrangle another man calls to him, saying that, if he is going in quest of Mr. N., he would like to give him something for him, and Descartes thinks the object is a melon, which has been brought from an exotic land.

The Church as a spiritual shelter has somehow disappeared from Descartes's field of vision in the dream, but in its stead the college quadrangle still serves him as a maternal, sheltering "temenos."[153] The college quadrangle represents the rigid spiritual training which Descartes had received at the hands of the Jesuit fathers and which never ceased to color his entire philosophy.[154] The people within this frame are all able

152. Adam, p. 305, and *A-T*, X, 213 (*Cogitationes privatae*): "Ut comoedi, moniti ne in fronte appareat pudor, personam induunt, sic ego, hoc mundi theatrum conscensurus, in quo hactenus spectator exstiti larvatus *prodeo*." ("Just as comedians, warned that shame may appear on the face, put on a mask, so I go forth masked when I am to go into the theater of the world, in which until now I was only a spectator.")
153. J. O. Wisdom interprets the school as "mother" in the typical Freudian personalistic sense, although the church, as well as the school, probably held a maternal significance in the wider meaning of the word for Descartes.
154. Cf. Adam, p. 22. For details of the school curriculum and Descartes's teachers see Sirven (pp. 27 ff., 31 ff.), who notes that Aristotle and Thomas Aquinas, in particular, were studied extensively. Sirven stresses (pp. 31 ff.): "Nous saisissons ainsi sur le vif l'interaction

to stand quietly upright; he alone continues to be hampered by the wind.

He is one "possessed," one who has been touched by the *Zeitgeist*. Here the dream emphasizes his individual situation. The unknown man whom Descartes meets in the college quadrangle might well represent the side of himself which has still remained completely within the framework of the spirit of the Church—a figure who stands for the traditional spirit or for the Catholic in him. It has often been pointed out, and with justice, that somewhere within himself Descartes cherished a kind of rigid, static belief, something quite separate from his living intellectual spiritual search—a "fides *non* quaerens intellectum" ("a faith which does *not* seek understanding"), as Maritain so trenchantly puts it.[155] Very likely it is this aspect of Descartes that is embodied by the man in the quadrangle. This man gives him an interesting mission: He must take something to Mr. N.—and Descartes thinks in the dream that it is a melon.

Hence between Mr. N., who has been passed by in the street, and the man in the college quadrangle there is evidently a connection, a sort of system of barter or trading in presents, in which Descartes is called upon to play an instrumental role. Evidently this inner side in Descartes, which has "remained behind," is still to a great extent maintained by the traditional spirit of the college. Mr. N., as already mentioned, stands for an unconscious part of the personality but one

---

des diverses influences qui se sont exercées sur son [Descartes's] esprit et que nous sommes obligés de séparer pour rendre notre exposé plus précis. Mais *l'idée primitive qui l'a orienté dans ce sens* [of an intellectual discipline of thought] *lui est venue de la logique de l'Ecole dont il a simplifié peut-être à l'excès les directions générales*" (my italics). ("Thus we grasp the essence of the interaction of the diverse influences that were exercised over his [Descartes's] mind and that we are obliged to separate in order to add precision to our *exposé*. But the first primitive idea that oriented him in this direction [of an intellectual mental discipline] came to him from Scholastic logic, the general instructions of which he simplified, perhaps to excess.")

155. P. 86. Cf. also the additional literature there cited concerning this problem.

which—and this is significant—does not coincide with the Catholic in him, for in the dream he appears outside the "framework" of the Church, in the street, in the collective, profane sphere. So he might possibly represent an un-Christian shadow-figure. Since Descartes never troubled about this unconscious part of his personality, it must have got its nourishment elsewhere, presumably from the college. This may perhaps be connected with the fact that, whenever attacked, Descartes always sought the help of his old schoolmasters, Père Charlet and Père Dinet. Since, as a personality, he was never inwardly united and never had his shadow with him, he lacked the strength to face the spiritual battle of his time.

The object which Descartes has to take Mr. N. is really rather unexpected: a melon, which, he presumes, must have been brought from an exotic land.

In the East, as in Africa and southern Europe, the melon has an important symbolic meaning. It was already known in the West and in the Mediterranean regions in antiquity and had probably spread from Egypt in all directions.[156] As early as the time of Moses, melons were among the fruits for the sake of which the children of Israel hankered after the land of Egypt:

And the mixed multitude that was among them fell a-lusting: and the children of Israel also wept again, and said, Who shall give us flesh to eat? We remember the fish, which we did eat in Egypt freely; the cucumbers, and the melons, and the leeks, and the onions, and the garlic: But now our soul is dried away: there is nothing at all, besides this manna, before our eyes.[157]

This passage is important insofar as in the patristic literature the departure of the Jews from Egypt is understood as a breaking-away from polytheistic pagan unconsciousness.[158] Melons are consequently the much-loved food of the *pagan*

---

156. Cf. Celsius, *Hierobotan.* I. 356 and II. 47.
157. Numbers 11:5–6.
158. For the material see M.-L. von Franz, "The 'Passio Perpetuae,'" *Spring* (New York: Analytical Psychology Club of New York, Inc., 1949).

shadow of the Jews, or else of the Christians. This is significant, because we have speculated that Mr. N. might have represented a non-Christian shadow of Descartes. This passage from the Bible would, moreover, have been known to Descartes.

In the Greek sphere of culture the melon is called πέπων ("ripe, completely cooked"; also a pet name for children). In a scholium it is called *spermatias*,[159] probably on account of its abundance of seeds. To distinguish it from the watermelon, the round edible melon was specially known as μηλοπέπων ("quince-apple")[160] on account of its apple-like shape (*mēlon* = apple). This is the origin of the Latin word *melo, melonis* and of our word "melon." It was already a matter of wonder to the ancients why this fruit in particular should be called "ripe," as all fruit presumably deserves that name.[161] It was prized for the amount of water it contained and for its refreshing and aperient effect.[162] In medieval popular medicine its seeds, cooked in milk, were used as a remedy for phthisis.[163] This is worth mentioning, inasmuch as Descartes suffered from weak lungs and died of inflammation of the lungs (contracted in Sweden's cold, stormy, northern winter).

In the Chinese imagery of the *I Ching*,[164] the oracular *Book of Changes*, the melon is symbolized by the sign Ch'ien, "heaven," because Ch'ien is round. But it is emphasized that the melon spoils easily and therefore belongs to the feminine principle of darkness, Yin. The image of "a melon covered

---

159. Pollux on Athen. VI. 46C.
160. Pliny *Nat. hist.* XIX. 67.
161. See Pauly-Wissowa, *Realencycl. des Altertums*, s.v. "Melone."
162. Pliny *Nat. Hist.* XXI. 6: "caro peponis mirifice refrigerat" ("flesh of melon is wonderfully [refreshing] cooling"). It is considered to be particularly ὑγρός ("damp").
163. See O. von Hovorka and A. Kronfeld, *Vergleichende Volksmedizin* (Stuttgart, 1909), II, 34.
164. *The I Ching, or Book of Changes,* translated into English by Cary F. Baynes from Richard Wilhelm's German edition (London: Routledge & Kegan Paul, 1951), Vol. I, No. 44, "Coming to Meet." In regard to "nine in the fifth place" see Vol. II, p. 260.

with willow leaves" is therefore interpreted as "hidden lines"—then it drops down to one from heaven."[165] "Hidden lines" means in China a pattern of the Tao which man does not yet know and which, when it becomes suddenly conscious to him after a ripening process in the unconscious, is compared with the falling of a ripe fruit from above. So the oracle evidently means that *the melon represents a latent conscious order within the darkness, which suddenly and unexpectedly becomes manifest.*

The main theme of this whole section of the *I Ching* depicts the unexpected meeting of a bold and shameless girl who associates with five men, for which reason, we are told, one should not marry her.[166] The Commentary continues:

> However, things that must be avoided in human society have meaning in the processes of nature. Here the meeting of earthly and heavenly forces is of great significance, because at the moment when the earthly force enters and the heavenly force is at its height—in the fifth month—all things unfold to the high point of their material manifestation, and the dark forces cannot injure the light force.

According to the Commentary this dark Yin principle is, however, *symbolized by the melon*. The melon thus connects here with the image of a dark hetaeristic anima, who still displays a piece of unadulterated and unassimilable nature, which is dangerous for the conventional human order. (Descartes's liaison with Helena Jans comes to mind.) This connection of the symbol of the melon with the image of the anima is due to the fact that it is a very watery fruit, and water is a widespread symbol for the living essence of the psyche.[167] The old alchemists never tired of devising new and expressive synonyms for this water. They called it *aqua nos-*

---

165. A Spanish proverb also says of the melon: "Por la mañana oro / a mediodía plata / por la noche mata" ("In the morning gold, at midday silver, but at night death"). Another one says: "If you eat melon at night, even the neighbor feels sick."
166. *I Ching*, II, 257.
167. Cf. Jung, *Psychology and Alchemy*, pp. 71 ff.

tra, mercurius vivus, argentum vivum, vinum ardens, aqua vitae, succus lunariae, and so on, by which they meant a living being not devoid of substance, as opposed to the rigid immateriality of mind in the abstract.[168] The expression *succus lunariae* ("sap of the moon plant") points exactly enough to the nocturnal origin of the water, and *aqua nostra*, like *mercurius vivus*, to its earthliness. *Acetum fontis* is a powerful corrosive water that dissolves all created things and at the same time leads to the most durable of all products, the mysterious *lapis* ("stone").[169] These alchemistic amplifications will prove not to be so far-fetched as they might at first appear; this watery element in the melon undoubtedly hints at the anima and the problem of evil, as can be shown even more clearly in a Japanese fairy tale, "Princess Melon," [170] which runs as follows:

An old childless couple lived alone in the mountains. While the woman was washing in the river, she saw a huge melon floating toward her from the upper reaches of the stream and took it home. When the old people cut it open, they found inside it a wonderfully beautiful tiny girl, whom they called "Princess Melon." She grew up to be a sagacious and beautiful maiden. One day when the old couple went off to a village festivity and she was minding the house on her own, the evil demon Amanojaku came and dragged her away and bound her to a plum tree in the garden. He then took on her form and sat himself in her place. But she succeeded in calling out to her homecoming parents, telling them what had happened, so that they were able to kill the demon.

According to another version, the demon devours the princess but is then convicted of the murder and executed; and it is the blood he sheds that dyes the millet flowers so red.

In connection with the foregoing associations to the dream

---

168. It is possible to compare this with the ghostly phenomena in Descartes's third dream, where this "subtle-body" quality of the psychic is also indicated.
169. Quoted from Jung, *Psychology and Alchemy*, pp. 71–72.
170. In *Japanische Volksmärchen*, ed. E. Diederichs (Jena, 1938), pp. 185 ff. ("Die Märchen der Weltliteratur" series, ed. F. v. d. Leyen).

it is important that this melon-spirit originated in the water ("washed up by the stream of life and of happenings") and that she secretly drew to herself an evil demon because she possessed a similar dark background. This melon-princess recalls one of the central motifs of a group of European fairy tales of the type of "The Three Lemons" (or oranges): [171] A prince seeks a beautiful wife and with the help of a little old woman finds a lemon tree by a spring. Three times he cuts a fruit off; each time a beautiful woman immediately appears and says: "Give me something to drink." Only at the third attempt does he succeed in giving it to her quickly enough so that she does not die, as did the first two women, but stands before him in her naked beauty. He allows her to hide herself in a tree while he fetches her clothes. But during his absence she is discovered by an evil Moorish woman (cook, witch, etc.) who kills her and puts herself in the victim's place. The dead woman reappears as a dove, is killed once again, and from her blood grows a lemon tree. When the prince once again opens one of its fruits, she steps forth redeemed, and the Moorish woman is punished. Here, too, the anima [172] is concealed in the round yellow fruit; and like the melon-princess, she, too, attracts a correspondingly dark, chthonic figure that, for men, constellates the problem of the confrontation with evil.

This problem of evil leads over to a further meaning of the melon. As the ritual food of those known as the *electi*,[173] this

---

171. Cf. J. Bolte and G. Polivka, *Anmerkungen zu den Kinder- und Hausmärchen der Brüder Grimm* (Leipzig, 1912-32), IV (1930), 257, and the versions there given. Further variations may be found in Vol. II (1915), p. 125.

172. Cf. A. Fischer, "Die Quitte als Vorzeichen bei Persern und Arabern und das Traumbuch des 'Abd-al-Ranī an-Nabulūsī," *Zeitschrift der deutschen morgenländischen Gesellschaft*, LXVIII (Leipzig, 1914), 301, according to which quinces, lemons, pears, oranges, and "small melons" are frequently used poetic similes for women's breasts. Among the Persians the quince was a "*symbolum boni*" (p. 275) because it smells like musk, is gold-colored, and is shaped like a full moon (p. 300).

173. *Electi* = "high initiates."

fruit plays a symbolically significant role in Manichaeism. The whole meaning and purpose of the Manichaean way of life is to save the "germs of light" imprisoned in darkness and convey them back to the original realm of light. Plants and trees are particularly rich in these germs of light; in them lives the *anima passibilis* of the Savior (that aspect of the soul of the Savior which was capable of suffering), "who is crucified in every tree." [174] Plants and human bodies contain the greatest number of these germs of light because they have their origin in the seeds of the Archons, the planetary gods who compose Yaldabaoth's following. The *electi*, the higher adepts among the Manichaeans, were therefore strictly vegetarian; they ate only plants containing a large quantity of these germs of light, among which cucumbers and melons are especially mentioned. The aim was to store up the element of light contained in such fruit in the body—which lived a chaste life—and thus withdraw it from the process of procreation. In a small way the *electi* were, like the water wheel of the cosmos,[175] a sort of machine for saving the element of light; through their digestion they set free the particles of light, and at their death these returned to the realm of light.[176]

The pleasant taste and smell of the melon, as well as its beautiful color, are doubtless the reason why (according to St. Augustine) it belonged to the "golden treasures of God." [177] As a light-containing fruit it recalls the role of the

---

174. See H. Ch. Puech, "Der Begriff der Erlösung im Manichäismus," *Eranos-Jahrbuch 1936* (Zurich, 1937), esp. pp. 258–59.

175. See *Acta Archelai*, ed. C. Beeson (Leipzig 1906), pp. 12–13, and Jung, *Psychology and Alchemy*, pp. 364–65.

176. See Puech, p. 259, and Ferd. Chr. Baur, *Das manichäische Religionssystem* (Tübingen, 1831), esp. p. 287. St. Augustine *Contra Faustum* V. 10: "Si melioris meriti sunt (auditores) in melones et cucumeres vel in alios aliquos cibos veniunt, quos vos manducaturi estis, ut vestris ructatibus cito purgentur." ("If they [the hearers] are worthy of something better, they come to cucumbers, melons, and other foods which you will eat that *they* be quickly purged of your eructations.") Cf. also Baur, p. 250.

177. Cf. Baur, p. 250, *viz.*, Augustine *De moribus Manichaeorum*, chap. 16 (Migne, *Patr. Lat.*, Vol. XXXII, col. 1362): "Cur de thesauris

105 The Dream of Descartes

apple of Paradise, the partaking of which mediated to humanity the knowledge of good and evil that had until then belonged only to God. The apple really contains in embryo the possibility of becoming conscious, the γνῶσις θεοῦ ("cognitive experience of God"), through the understanding of the opposites of good and evil contained within Him. Descartes would fairly certainly have known of the Manichaean significance of the melon, since he was acquainted with Augustine's work *De Genesi contra Manichaeos* [178] and therefore would probably also have read his further treatises against the Manichaeans, which were usually printed with it. It might therefore be assumed that for him the melon, like the apple of Paradise, could have signified an attempt to ponder more deeply over the problem of good and evil and, in contradistinction to the ecclesiastical conception of evil as a *privatio boni* ("privation of good"),[179] to participate in the Manichaean recognition of the divine reality of evil. At that time

---

Dei melonem putatis aureum esse et pernae adipem rancidem? . . . [col. 1363:] An bona tria, ubi simul fuerint, i.e., color bonus et odor et sapor, ibi esse maiorem boni partem putatis?" ("Why do you consider, from the treasures of God, the melon gold, and the rancid fat of ham? . . . Do you think if these are good together, i.e., . . . good color, flavor, smell, that there is the better part of good?") See, further, A. von le Coq, "Die buddhistische Spätantike in Mittelasien: Die manichäischen Miniaturen, II Teil," *Ergebnisse der kgl. preuss. Turfan-Expedition* (Berlin: Reimer, 1923), where, on Plate 816, melons are depicted. As von le Coq realizes (p. 52), it concerns a representation of the so-called βῆμα festival in honor of the martyrdom of Mani in A.D. 273. This ceremony was solemnized in the presence of the empty tribune (βῆμα), the master's chair. The five steps that led up to it signified the five elements or grades—the Magistri, Episcopi, Presbyteres, Diaconi, and Electi. To the right and left were the sun and moon, for Mani is "medius Solis et Lunae" ("between the Sun and Moon"). In front of the tribune stood a bowl with three layers of fruit: at the bottom, yellow melons; in the middle, grapes; and on top, green melons. On the table lay wheat loaves in the shape of the sun's disk, with the sickle of the moon laid round it. I thank Professor Jung for the reference to this material.

178. Cf. Sirven, pp. 145 ff. and esp. pp. 147–48. Descartes's definition of God as *"purus intellectus"* plainly stems from the treatise *De Genesi contra Manichaeos* (Sirven, p. 147).

179. For further details see below, p. 127.

he felt himself oppressed by a *"mauvais génie,"* but he did not subsequently face up to the problem more deeply on the philosophical level. It is certainly no accident that he dreamt of this Manichaean symbol and, on first waking, as he himself records, "for two hours had many thoughts about the good and evil of this world." The image of the melon actually suggests the idea of an achievement of consciousness based on an experience of life—through the acceptance of the anima and of the conflict of good and evil. This image is at the same time the feminine, which mediated between Descartes's ecclesiastical element and his nonecclesiastical inner side.

The Manichaean idea of the liberation of the germs of light is also to be found in various Gnostic systems. The Sethians, for instance, advocated the following doctrine.[180] The All consists of Three Principles (ἀρχαί): the Light above, the Darkness below, and, in between, a pure, sweet-scented Pneuma. The Light shone forth in the Darkness, which was a "terrible water," which thereafter strove to hold onto the germs of light by means of the scent of the Pneuma. But the powers of these three primordial principles (δυνάμεις) were infinite, "each one rational and capable of thought" (φρόνιμοι καὶ νοεραί). They collided, and their collision was "like the impression of a seal";[181] and since there were endless numbers of these powers, endless collisions took place, and countless impressions (εἰκόνες) of endless seals resulted.[182] Thus the Cosmos in its multiplicity came into being. Each

---

180. Hippolytus *Elenchos* V. 19-22 (ed. P. Wendland; Leipzig, 1916); cf. also H. Leisegang, *Die Gnosis* (2d ed.; Leipzig, 1924), pp. 151 ff.

181. . . . γίνεται γὰρ τῶν δυνάμεων συνδρομὴ οἱονεί τις τύπος σφραγῖδος (". . . for there is born from the powers a tumultuous concourse like some impression of a seal").

182. Αὗται οὖν εἰσιν αἱ εἰκόνες αἱ τῶν διαφόρων ζῴων ἰδέαι. ("These are the pictures, the 'ideal forms' of various living things.") The first collision makes the ἰδέα σφραγῖδος ("impress of seal") of heaven and earth and so forth. Expressed in modern language, these "seals" are the archetypes which engender the "images."

part of the Cosmos is, however, a monad which recapitulates the whole Cosmos in miniature. The perfume of the Pneuma, which floated up together with the light, now sown in this infinity (as σπινθὴρ φωτός, "spark of light"), and *a mighty generating wind,*[183] *which gave rise to all things,* rose up out of the primal waters and whipped up its waves, which became pregnant and caught hold of the light that, together with the Pneuma, had been scattered down. This is only a small (trifling) spark,[184] "like a piece separated from a ray of light, that is brought down into the multifariously combined, mixed, physical world and 'calls out from many waters' (Ps. 29:3)." The thinking and aspirations of the upper Light proceed toward the redemption, once again, of this spirit,[185] and for this reason Man, too, must exert himself in the same direction.

Another (Ophitic) sect describes the creation of the world in the following manner:[186] the Father and Primal Man is a Light that lives holy and ageless in the power of the βυθός ("abyss"). From him proceeds the Ennoia ("Thought, Reflection") as the Son and second man; beneath him lies the Pneuma; and still farther below are Darkness, Chaos, Water, and the Abyss, above which hovers the spirit, the first woman. From this woman the Father engendered the third man, Christ. The woman, however, cannot endure the greatness of her light and rushes and flies over to the left, down to the earthly world. This light streaming toward the left possesses a dew of light in which the Prunikos (i.e., the "left one") is enveloped and is flung down, and it strives to raise itself up again with the help of this dew of light. The consummation will take place when the complete dew of light

---

183. ἄνεμος σφοδρὸς καὶ λάβρος καὶ πάσης γενέσεως αἴτιος ("a keen, boisterous wind and the cause of all beginnings"). This may be compared with the storm in Descartes's dream.

184. σπινθὴρ ἐλάχιστος ("the least spark").

185. In that he drinks the "drink of living water" and lays aside the "form of the servant."

186. Irenaeus *Haer.* ch. 30; cf. also Leisegang, pp. 174 ff.

is gathered up and changed into the everlasting Aion.[187] The idea of the light lost in matter also appears here.

The "Barbelo" Gnostics taught the following.[188] From the primal Father proceeds Barbelo (possibly, "Out of the Four comes God"). But her son Yaldabaoth (or Sabaoth, the Lord of the Seventh Heaven) becomes arrogant and declares himself to be the only God. Barbelo weeps over his trespass "and now appears before the Archons (gods of the planets, who formed Yaldabaoth's following) in a ravishing form and robs them of their seed through their ejaculation in order by this means to bring their powers, which were scattered in many creatures, back to herself."[189] This is the reason why man must also withdraw his procreative power or his semen from the earthly process of becoming and guide it, once more, to the divine. Leisegang remarks:

> From this we can understand the passage from the "Gospel of Eve," quoted by Epiphanius:[190] "I stood on a high mountain and saw a vast man and another shrunken figure, God the Father with Barbelo, who is shriveled up because her power has been taken from her; and I heard something like a voice of thunder, and I came closer in order to hear, and it spoke to me and said: 'I am thee and thou art me, and where thou art, there am I, and I am sown in all things. And when thou wilt, gather me up; when, however, thou gatherest me, thou gatherest thyself.' "[191]

This gathering of the power was then symbolically expressed through their spermatic union, which they also conceived of as a "fruitfulness" of the body. For them redemption consisted in uniting their seed with the procreative substance of the universe, i.e., withdrawing it from its earthly destiny and leading it back to the divine original source of all seed.[192]

Closely allied spiritually with the Manichaean ideas is the doctrine of the Gnostic Basilides. According to him the "non-

---

187. Leisegang, p. 183.
188. Epiphanius *Panar.* 25–26; cf. also Leisegang, pp. 186 ff.
189. Leisegang, pp. 189–90.
190. *Panar.* 26. 3. 1.
191. Leisegang, p. 195.
192. *Ibid.*, pp. 196 ff.

109 The Dream of Descartes

being" (potential) God first creates a seed of the Cosmos;[193] "just as the seed of mustard contains, at the same time, everything comprised in the smallest space . . . ," so this unmanifest seed comprises the seed-entirety of the Cosmos. In this sperm sojourns the "thrice-divided sonship," of which the finest element straightway hastens back to the Father above and the second element also hurries aloft again, borne on the wings of the Pneuma. Only the third part, "in need of cleansing," remains below, caught in the mass of the cosmic entirety of seeds, and "does good and allows good to be done to it."[194] This third sonship has still to be redeemed through the process known as $\phi\nu\lambda o\kappa\rho\iota\nu\eta\sigma\iota s$, the separation of the natures.[195] Here, too, man must cooperate in bringing this power of God, that is ensnared in matter, back to its realm up above.

The Manichaean idea of the salvation of the germs of light is made clearer by the help of these Gnostic parallels. According to the Manichaean conception these germs are contained especially in cucumbers, melons, and similar fruit, whose mass of seeds probably suggested the idea of a *thesaurus* or totality of seeds.[196] A transverse section of both these fruits yields the design of a mandala,[197] which certainly also explains the Manichaean meaning of the melon as a "golden treasure" of God: it is a symbol of the Self. It is not by chance that its Greek name also emphasizes its round (apple-like) form, which resembles the images of psychic totality, of the Self.[198]

The symbol of the melon could be compared with the "round body of light" of the alchemists, which they also describe as "yolk of egg" or "the red point of the sun in the

---

193. *Ibid.*, pp. 215 ff.
194. *Ibid.*, pp. 218 ff.
195. Cf. Jung, *Aion*, p. 80.
196. *Thesaurus* also means "treasure house, treasure chest."
197. For this term see Jung, *Psychology and Alchemy*, p. 42, and more especially "Concerning Mandala Symbolism," *The Archetypes and the Collective Unconscious*, p. 355 and *passim*.
198. Cf. *Psychology and Alchemy*, pp. 41–42.

middle."[199] It is an image similar to the one which the alchemist Gerhardus Dorneus describes as the "infallible center of the middle." Commenting on this idea, Jung says:

> The point in the center is the fire. Upon it is based the simplest and completest form, which is what the roundness is. The point comes closest to the nature of the light, and the light is a *simulacrum Dei*. The firmament was created in the midst of the waters, so to speak . . . ; in man too there is a *lucidum corpus*, namely, the *humidum radicale*, which stems from the sphere of the waters above the firmament. This corpus is the sidereal balsam which maintains the body heat. . . . The *corpus lucens* is the *corpus astrale*, the firmament or star in man.[200]

These amplifications from Paracelsus' range of thought seem to me to be enlightening about the melon as well.

The green network on a melon looks like the lines of meridian on a globe of the world, so it is obvious to look upon the melon as a sort of microcosmos. It is an image of the inner "firmament," of the psychic totality, that is here brought forth by the unconscious as a counterbalance to the phenomena of the macrocosm, which had so greatly fascinated Descartes.[201]

In this instance the *"rotundum"* is manifestly a fruit, whereby the Self is described as something that has grown naturally, the result of a quiet process of ripening. It is a symbol of a light and an order which, however, ripens in the darkness of natural creation. As Jung demonstrates in his article "The Philosophical Tree,"[202] tree and plant motifs have an important meaning, which is greatly clarified by amplifications from the realm of alchemy. In the "Visio Arislei,"[203] for instance, a precious tree is mentioned whose fruit satisfies the hunger of mankind forever, like the *panis vitae* ("bread of life") of John 6:35. The sun- and moon-trees

---

199. Jung, *Paracelsica*, pp. 116–18.
200. *Ibid.*, pp. 116 ff.
201. Remember that he wanted to write a book called "Le Monde," in which he wished to draw up a complete picture of the macrocosmos.
202. *CW*, XIII (in preparation).
203. An old alchemical text quoted *ibid*.

111   *The Dream of Descartes*

of the "Legend of Alexander" are also often quoted, and Benedictus Figulus equated them with the apple trees in the Garden of the Hesperides and their rejuvenating fruit.[204] The tree symbolizes the entire alchemical opus; [205] at the same time it is also "a metamorphic form of man, so to speak, since it proceeds from the primal man and becomes man."[206] Jung concludes his interpretation of the tree in the following manner:

> Insofar as the tree, both morally and physically (*tam ethice quam physice*), symbolizes the opus and the process of transformation, it is also clear that it indicates the life process in general.[207] Its identity with Mercurius, the *spiritus vegetativus*, confirms this idea. Since the opus represented by the tree is a mystery of life, death, and rebirth, this interpretation also applies to the *arbor philosophica*, as does also the attribute of wisdom; which offers a valuable hint to psychology. Since times long past the tree has served as a symbol of Gnosis and wisdom. Thus Irenaeus says that, for the Barbelites, the tree is born out of man (i.e., the Ἄνθρωπος) and the Gnosis, and these, too, they called Gnosis. In the Gnosis of Justinus the angel of the revelation, Baruch, is designated as τὸ ξύλον τῆς ζωῆς, which reminds us of the future-discerning sun- and moon-trees of the "Legend of Alexander." [208]

But, as Jung explains in another passage, Gnosis means "a perception that wells up from the inner experience, a type of perception that is at the same time a vital experience." [209] Descartes lacked this type of perception because he put too much emphasis on conscious thought and not enough on unconscious inspiration. This is why the unconscious set it before him as a goal.

204. *Ibid.*, p. 416, with further examples.
205. *Ibid.*, pp. 418–20.
206. Quoted *ibid.*, p. 421, with further examples.
207. My note: Cf. also the cabalistic Tree of Life, which grows from above downwards and which, as S. Hurwitz has informed me, is identified with *adam qadmon*.
208. *Ibid.*, p. 422.
209. "Seminar über die psychologische Interpretation von Kinderträumen 1931–40," pp. 18–19. Quoted from the privately printed edition with the kind permission of C. G. Jung.

Melons grow in the shade of the leaves of a ground-growing runner, close-pressed against the earth. (Consider Descartes's compulsion to bend down.) This motif of "growing out of and on the earth" thus strongly emphasizes that for which his shadow was longing: to become caught in earthly reality.

In the dream Descartes thinks that this melon comes from an exotic land. It comes from far away; it is something "strange," of a different nature, unfamiliar. As Jung says, in the beginning the Self often appears as something strange, as the "wholly other," because to the ego it will seem to be completely remote as long as the latter remains caught up in its own fictions.[210] A consciousness like Descartes's, whose interests were so definitely directed toward the outer object, would more particularly have to meet this aspect of the Self, since

The Self, regarded as the opposite pole of the world, its "absolutely other," is the *sine qua non* of all empirical knowledge and consciousness of subject and object. Only because of this psychic "otherness" is consciousness possible at all. Identity does not make consciousness possible; it is only separation, detachment, and agonizing confrontation that produce consciousness and understanding. . . . Even today Western man finds it hard to see the psychological necessity for a transcendental subject of cognition as the opposite pole to the empirical universe, although the postulate of a world-confronting Self, at least as a "point of reflection," is a logical necessity.[211]

Descartes did, indeed, perceive this necessity logically but did not fully recognize its psychic reality, for which reason the melon appeared in the dream as something strange. Later, he used to wander with delight around the Dutch docks, looking at the curious new imports from overseas, which he also liked to investigate in his secret dissecting room. By this means he

---

210. Cf. the example in *Psychology and Alchemy*, pp. 176–77.
211. Quoted from C. G. Jung and C. Kerényi, *Introduction to a Science of Mythology* (London: Routledge & Kegan Paul, 1951), p. 125.

sought to discover the manifestations of the *lumen naturale* ("natural light"), in the existence of which he believed, as he also believed in the existence of the revealed light. This natural light is, according to him, the reasonableness of our clear and distinct ideas and of the mechanical laws of nature, which have been created by God and whose regularity is assured.[212] Descartes often, moreover, made use of the image of the seed and the fruit when speaking of the inner process of thought. For instance, in his *Regulae ad directionem Ingenii* (*Rules for the Direction of the Mind*) he says:

. . . the human mind contains something divine in which the seeds of profitable thoughts are so well sown that they often, even when neglected and stifled through false application, bear spontaneous fruit. This we experience the most easily in arithmetic and geometry. Their discoveries were "spontaneous fruits" which were engendered through the inherent principles of the method . . . ; if they are tended conscientiously, they can achieve full maturity.[213]

Descartes himself interpreted the melon as a symbol "*des charmes de la solitude*," [214] an interpretation which was evidently suggested by the meaning of πέπων, "secret ripening." [215] This inner ripening of the personality is the compensation for the fact of being overwhelmed and swept along by the storm and torn away from his own nature. In later life Descartes actually strove in this direction, but one thing remained an impossibility for him in this endeavor: to take root in the earth.

212. Cf., among others, von Brockdorff, pp. 48–49, and S. Gagnebin, p. 117.
213. *A-T*, X, 33. In this same passage he also says: "Habet enim humana mens nescio quid divini, in quo cogitationum utilium semina iacta sunt." ("For the human mind possesses something divine in which the seeds of useful thoughts are sown.") He also speaks of "*quaedam veritatum semina*" ("certain seeds of truth") (*A-T*, X, 376) and, in the *Cogitationes privatae* (*A-T*, X, 217), of "*semina scientiae*" ("seeds of science"). Cf. also Laporte, pp. 116–17, and Gagnebin, p. 118.
214. *A-T*, X, 185 and n.
215. Or, as Wisdom (p. 16) very pertinently says, "a serene relation to mother-earth."

In the dream Descartes has to take the melon to Mr. N., whom he had passed by—the part in himself with which the symbol should unite him.[216] One cannot help wondering why this shadow is not able to live simply by the ecclesiastical symbol of Christ and the means of grace which the Church affords. Presumably it is because these symbols of the Self no longer exercise a sufficiently immediate and natural effect to appeal directly to the unconscious parts of the personality. Therefore, although these unconscious parts are still nourished within the framework of the Church, they need "light" in the form of a "natural food," [217] which, according to the dream, the Church actually does give incidentally but which it looks upon as profane. The symbols of the Self within the framework of ecclesiastical conception are all, for their part, of a "pneuma-like nature," in particular, they are *sine umbra peccati* ("without the shadow of original sin"). The image of Christ or of the Host, for example, incorporates only the light, redemptive aspect of the Self.[218] With these means of grace Descartes's shadow would only be able to raise itself up spiritually, away from the earth, but they cannot help him to root himself. He does not in this way find himself implicated in the physical reality which the Mr. N. within him requires and which would create the correct compensation for his intellectual attitude toward life. This explains the design of the unconscious that Descartes should be instrumental in the proceedings, that *he* should bring the melon to Mr. N. In other words, he should be consciously concerned with the needs of his shadow and bring the latter its food, as a Manichaean *auditor* to the *electus*. In this way he would even be serving the Church in a certain sense, for at that time the Church, blinded by its desire to stem the Reformation, was

---

216. Concerning the "uniting" function of the symbol see Jung, *Psychological Types, passim.*

217. Cf. the "*Aniada*" in Paracelsus, which he calls "fruits and powers of Paradise and of the heavens, and also the Sacraments of the Christians" (Jung, *Paracelsica*, pp. 122–24).

218. For further details see Jung, *Aion, passim,* esp. p. 80.

anxious, as the dream says, to "give away" the natural, individual experience of the Self, presumably as a thing of no use and "exotic," in other words, as strange, foreign, and not belonging, since the Self, as already mentioned, is experienced as being different—as the "wholly other."

Even so, in the first instance the melon is in the possession of the Church, very probably because the unconscious feminine principle is projected onto it. It also, however, represents that natural symbol tradition, taken over from paganism, which still survives within the framework of the Church—in the outer court, as the dream so pertinently says—and to which the Manichaean problem also belonged.[219] The man in the quadrangle and Mr. N. are both unconscious parts of Descartes, and it is interesting to see how they wish to be connected through him or by means of his intercession. He must find a place for them in consciousness so that they can unite; at the same time, the melon, which depicts the feminine, acts as the mediating principle or as the "uniting symbol." It might be possible to go so far as to say that, inasmuch as it represents not only the Self but the anima as well, the mediating function of the melon in the dream is not unconnected with the fact that, on awakening, Descartes vowed to go on a pilgrimage to the Madonna of Loretto. Here an attempt at a solution of the tension in the Christian way of life is hinted at which has only now found official expression in the "Declaratio Solemnis" of the "Assumptio Mariae."

In the same moment that Descartes is given the commission of handing over the melon, he notices that he is the only one of the group in the college quadrangle who is unable to stand upright against the wind, although the wind has abated. As has already been suggested, he is one chosen, moved by the

---

219. Compare with this Descartes's "provisional" moral doctrine, which, according to him, consisted in the commandment "d'obéir aux lois et aux coutumes de son pays, retenant constamment le religion en laquelle il avait été instruit dès son enfance" ("to obey the laws and customs of his country, holding fast to the religion in which he had been brought up from infancy") (*cit.* Gagnebin, p. 108).

Zeitgeist, and therefore he must hand on the "round thing," he must turn to the inner ripening of his personality, even if he is alone in doing this.

When Descartes wakes up after the dream, he is greatly oppressed by the thought of his sins and feels himself endangered by the evil spirit. Although—as he says—"in the eyes of men" he had led a spotless life, he knows that he has sinned sufficiently to call all the wrath of heaven down on his head in punishment. It is significant that, like most people who try to interpret their own dreams, he should connect the meaning with his personal life and, as a good Catholic, should at once resort to a sort of self-examination. In so doing, however, he overlooks the deeper meaning of the dream—the problem of the reality of evil—and diverts it into the channel of his conscious thinking. Also, even if he did not altogether understand the dream, it mitigated his inflationary enthusiasm and permitted him somehow to feel the evil in the new intellectual attitude; the dream also stemmed the impetuous outward flow of his thoughts and brought them back to dwell on himself and his own life.

Interpretation of the Second Dream

The next so-called "dream" is no real dream; Descartes hears a sharp explosion like a thunderclap and sees—when already awake—fiery sparks glowing in the room. In most pagan religions a peal of thunder has a numinous significance.[220] In Germanic mythology it occurs when Thor rides across the heavens with his team of goats; the thunderbolt of the Greeks and Romans belongs to the supreme deity, Zeus or Jupiter, who uses it to frighten his enemies, the Titans, and human beings possessed by *hubris*. In late antiquity there existed the so-called "Brontologia," a science which dealt with the interpretation of thunder. Jupiter can also cause thunder to resound out of a clear sky as a sign of his approval

220. Vergil *Aeneid* II. 690–95.

117   The Dream of Descartes

and assent.[221] In common parlance, "lightning" and "thunder" stand for violent outbursts of affect. These frequently accompany the constellation of archetypal contents, which would also fit in with Descartes's experience. Although he did not really understand the first dream, it evidently "struck home" and touched him in his innermost being.

Descartes himself interpreted the *"coup de foudre"* as the descent of the *"esprit de la vérité."* [222] Lightning, as Jung explains,[223] indicates a sudden enlightenment and change of attitude (*mentis sive animi lapsus in alterum mundum* ["rapture of the mind or soul into another world"], as Rulandus' alchemistic lexicon defines it [224]). Jakob Boehme describes the Messiah and also the "Source-Spirit" Mercurius as thunder.[225] "Of the innermost birth of the soul," Boehme again says that the bestial body attains "only a glimpse, just as if it lightened." [226] Caught in the four spirits, the lightning then stands "in the midst, as a heart." [227] Or: "For when you strike upon the sharp part of the stone [cf. Descartes's comparison of the sparks in the flint], the bitter sting of nature sharpens itself and is stirred in the highest degree. For Nature is dissipated or *broken asunder* in the sharpness, so that the *Liberty shines forth as a flash."* [228] The lightning is the "birth of the Light." In his *Vita longa* Paracelsus recommends a

221. *Ibid.*
222. Cf. Sirven, p. 129. For this reason I think it correct, in contrast to Sirven, to call it a "mystical crisis" and a genuine religious experience. Maritain speaks of a "Pentecost of reason." But Sirven objects: "Then, again, since this mysticism ought to be a secular mysticism, *clearly related to the subconscious,* its source is in the inspiration of the poets. . . ." Psychologically, the dream should be analyzed as a phenomenon of the unconscious only, without going into the problem of whether God is, in the final analysis, behind it, which cannot be established scientifically!
223. Jung, "A Study in the Process of Individuation," *The Archetypes and the Collective Unconscious,* pp. 295 ff.
224. *Cit., ibid.,* p. 295, n. 7. Cf. also Jung, *Paracelsica,* pp. 118-19.
225. Jung, "A Study in the Process of Individuation," p. 296.
226. *Ibid.*
227. *Ibid.*
228. *Ibid.,* p. 295.

constantly repeated Distillation of the Center, or, as Jung explains, an awakening and development of the Self.[229] At the end of the process a "physical flash" appears, and the flash of Saturn and that of the Sun are separated from each other, and in this flash appears that which appertains "to long life." [230] Descartes does not pay attention to the thunder, which he only later mentions and interprets, but only to the lightning, the emotional shock. The flash of lightning, on the other hand, he sees as a multitude of sparks.

These fiery sparks recall the alchemistic idea of the *scintillae* or *oculi piscium* ("fishes' eyes"), which Jung has explained in the sixth chapter of his paper "On the Nature of the Psyche." [231] At the primitive level, he says, consciousness is as yet not a unity; in other words, it is not yet centered on a firmly structured ego-complex but flares up here and there, wherever outer or inner experiences, instincts, and affects call it up.[232] The developed ego-complex should also be thought of as surrounded by many small luminosities, which can be demonstrated out of the dreams of modern people as well as in alchemistic symbolism. The alchemists often maintained that the transformative substance (the unconscious) contained many "small white sparks." [233] Heinrich Khunrath explains these as rays or sparks of "the Anima Catholica," the universal soul which is identical with the Spirit of God.[234]

229. *Paracelsica*, p. 118.
230. *Ibid.*, pp. 118–19.
231. "The Unconscious as a Multiple Consciousness," section 6 of "On the Nature of the Psyche," pp. 190 ff.
232. *Ibid.*, p. 189.
233. *Aurora Consurgens. II: Artis Auriferae* . . . (1593), I, 208 (quotation from Morienus, *cit.* Jung, *ibid.*, p. 190, n. 54).
234. H. Khunrath, *Amphitheatrum* (1604), pp. 195, 198: "Variae eius radii atque Scintillae, per totius ingentem materiei primae massae molem hinc inde dispersae ac dissipatae; inque mundi partibus disiunctis etiam et loco et corporis mole, necnon circumscriptione, postea separatis . . . unius Animae universalis scintillae nunc etiam habitantes." ("The various rays and sparks in the huge mass of all matter in the first lump are [now] dispersed and scattered into the disjunct parts of the world which were later separated by mass and boundaries . . . which

(The human mind is also one of these sparks.[235]) They are seeds of light in the Chaos,[236] "sparks of the fire of the soul of the world as pure *Formae rerum essentiales*" ("essential ideal forms of things").[237] The idea of the *lumen naturale* in Paracelsus is based on a similar conception,[238] which originates in the inner *astrum* or "firmament" in man and is a light that is bestowed on the "inward man."[239] The light of nature is "kindled by the Holy Ghost"[240] and is an "invisible light," an invisible wisdom which is "learned," among other ways, through dreams.[241] Paracelsus' student Gerhardus Dorneus also held to the doctrine of the *scintillae* which are perceived by the spiritual eyes, shining resplendently.[242] According to Paracelsus the natural light is also innate in animals,[243] for which idea he is indebted to Agrippa von Nettesheim, who speaks of a *"luminositas sensus naturae"* (the light or consciousness immanent in instinctual nature).[244] This is specially

---

even today constitute the sparks of *one* universal world soul.") (*Cit.* Jung, *ibid.*, n. 55.)

235. *Amphitheatrum*, p. 63 (*cit.* Jung, *ibid.*, p. 191, n. 57): "Mens humani animi scintilla altior et lucidior." ("The mind of the human spirit is a higher and more lucid spark.")

236. *Amphitheatrum*, p. 197 (*cit.* Jung, *ibid.*).

237. *Von hylealischen Chaos* (1597), p. 216 (*cit.* Jung, *ibid.*).

238. Paracelsus, *Philosophia sagax* (cf. Jung, *ibid.*, p. 191).

239. *Paracelsus . . . Sämtliche Werke* (ed. Karl Sudhoff and Wilhelm Matthiessen) (Munich: Otto W. Barth, 1922-32), XII, 23 (*cit.* Jung, *ibid.*, p. 193).

240. *Cit.* Jung, *ibid.*, p. 194, from *Paracelsus . . . Sämtliche Werke*, XIII, 325.

241. *Cit.* Jung, *ibid.*, p. 195, from *Paracelsus . . . Sämtliche Werke*, XII, p. 53.

242. "Thus little by little he will come to see with his mental eyes a number of sparks shining day by day and more and more and growing into such a great light . . ." ("De speculativa philosophia," *Theatr. Chem.* [1602], I, 275; *cit.* Jung, *ibid.*, p. 192).

243. See Jung, *ibid.*, p. 195.

244. *De occulta philosophia* (Cologne, 1533), p. 48. (*Cit.* Jung, *ibid.*, p. 195. Cf. also, *ibid.*, Jung's further researches concerning the history of this conception of the *"sensus naturae"*; see also his *Paracelsica* for the early alchemical history of the idea.)

worth mentioning, since Descartes had evidently read Agrippa. As Jung explains, these alchemical *scintillae* are descriptions of the archetypes of the collective unconscious, which must accordingly possess a certain inherent luminosity or autonomous latent element of consciousness.[245]

Among the many sparks, the seedlike luminosities of the contents that shine forth out of the darkness of the unconscious, the alchemistic authors often emphasized *one light* as being central and of peculiar importance.[246] In Khunrath this is designated as Monas or Sun,[247] in Gerhardus Dorneus as *sol invisibilis* ("invisible sun").[248] Many more examples of this conception, to which I should like to refer, are quoted by Jung from numerous other alchemistic and Gnostic sources.[249] In conclusion he says:

Since consciousness is characterized from of old by expressions taken from the manifestations of light, the hypothesis that the multiple luminosities correspond to small phenomena of consciousness is not, in my view, too far-fetched. If the luminosity should appear as monadic, as a single star for instance, or as an eye, then it easily takes on mandala formation and is then to be interpreted as the Self.[250]

I have gone into these analogous ideas at such length because I believe that Descartes's conception of the *lumen naturale* can be connected with these contemporary notions and is, in any case, based on a similar inner original experience. As Stephen Schönenberger points out in his article "A Dream of Descartes': Reflections on the Unconscious Determinants of the Sciences," [251] alchemistic ideas often played a definite role

---

245. Jung, "The Unconscious as a Multiple Consciousness," pp. 191, 192, 195.
246. *Ibid.*, p. 192.
247. *Ibid.*
248 *Ibid.*, p. 193.
249. *Ibid.*, pp. 196 ff.
250. *Ibid.*, p. 199.
251. In *The International Journal of Psycho-Analysis*, XX (1939), 43 ff. Schönenberger's article is not given further consideration here

121 *The Dream of Descartes*

in Descartes's thought,[252] although, for the most part, he misunderstood alchemical symbolism, taking it in a concretistic sense [253] and therefore rejecting it. As, in Paracelsus, the "natural light" also signifies human reason, so, according to Descartes, *"la raison"* consists of multiple *"semina scientiae"* ("seeds of science") or *"naturae simplices"* ("simple natures or beings") or *"veritates innatae"* ("inborn truths"). He also termed the ideas "notions primitives" or "originaux, sur le patron desquels nous formons toutes nos autres connoissances," but he reduced them to the conception of space, number, time, and one or two other elements.[254]

The image of the central sun was not lacking, either, in

because the author bases practically all his interpretations on quotations from Descartes's writings rather than on the dream motifs.

252. Especially in the *Discours* (*A-T*, VI, 44–45), where he speaks of the transformation of ashes into glass.

253. See Schönenberger and *A-T*, VI, 26.

254. In a letter to Elizabeth von der Pfalz, May 21, 1643 (*A-T*, III, 665), Descartes says: "... je considère qu'il y a en nous certaines notions primitives qui sont comme des originaux sur le patron desquels nous formons toutes nos autres connoissances. Et il n'y a que fort peu de telles notions; car après les plus générales de l'estre, du nombre, de la durée etc. qui conviennent à tout ce que nous pouvons concevoir; nous n'avons pour le corps en particulier que la notion de l'extension, de laquelle suivera celle de la figure et du mouvement, et pour l'âme nous n'avons que celle de la pensée, en laquelle sont comprises les perceptions de l'entendement et les inclinations de la volonté, enfin, pour l'âme et le corps ensemble nous n'avons que celle de leur union, de laquelle dépend celle de la force de l'âme de mouvoir le corps, et le corps d'agir sur l'âme en causant ses sentiments et ses passions. ..." (". . . I consider that there are certain primitive ideas in us, which are like the patterns upon which we form all our other knowledge. And there are but very few of these ideas, for after the most general ones of being, number, duration, etc., which agree with everything of which we can conceive, for the body in particular, we have nothing but the idea of extension, from which will follow that of form and of movement, while for the soul we have only that of thought, in which are included the perceptions of understanding and the inclinations of the will; and finally, for the soul and body together we have only that of their union, on which depends the idea of the power of the soul to move the body, and of the body to act upon the soul by causing its feelings and its passions. . . .") It is indicative for Descartes's type to equate feelings with bodily reactions and to look on them as secondary.

Descartes; in the *Regulae*[255] he says: "In their totality the sciences are nothing but human knowledge (*humana sapientia*), which ever remains one and the same, no matter how many objects are applied to it, just as the light of the sun is single among all the multiplicity of objects upon which it shines."[256] However, while these formulations shape the *intellectual working-out* of the original experience, it is the fiery sparks of the dream—as it were, its primal form or immediate, psychic manifestation—which, in their autonomy and reality beyond the scope of consciousness, terrify Descartes most profoundly.[257] These sparks are connected with the motif of

255. Quoted from the translation of E. Cassirer, Descartes's *Kritik der mathematischen und naturwissenschaftlichen Erkenntnis* (Marburg, 1899), p. 3.
256. Cf. also Barth, p. 12. Cf., further, the important part played by the image of the sun in Kepler's view of the world. See also W. Pauli, *op. cit.*
257. The Stoic doctrine of the *igniculi* or σπινθῆρες as the simplest elements of human reactions was known to him from Justus-Lipius, *Manuductio ad philos. stoic.* Part I, Book II, diss. II (1st ed., p. 72); cited in Gilson, p. 481, n. 2: "Igniculi isti non aliud quam inclinationes, judicia, et ex iis notiones sunt, a recta in nobis Ratione. Scito enim Stoicis placere partem in nobis divini spiritus esse mersam, id est illam ipsam Rationem, quae si in suo loco et luce luceat, tota pura sincera, recta divina sit; nunc corpore velut carcere clausa, coercetur et opinionibus agitatur aut abducitur, et tamen retinet originis suae *flammulas* et Verum Honestumque per se et sua indole videt. Istae flammulae, sive igniculos mavis dicere Graeci σπινθῆρας, ζώπυρα, ἐναύσματα appellant exserunt se et ostendunt in sensibus aut judiciis, quae omni hominum generi fere, et optimae cuique naturae eximie sunt insita aut innata. Id Graeci Ἐννοίας sive Notiones vocant item προλήψεις *Anticipationes* et quia passivae atque insitae κοινὰς καὶ ἐμφύτας communes et ingeneratas agnominarunt." ("These sparks are nothing but inclinations, judgments. From them come notions, by right reasoning within us. Because the Stoics liked to call that part lodged in us the spirit of the divine, i.e., that very reason which, when placed and shining in its own place, is pure, sincere, whole, and justly divine; now in the body as if shut in a prison, it is coerced, led astray, and agitated by opinions, and yet it retains the little flames of its origins and sees the true and honest by itself and its inborn quality. These little flames—or you may prefer to call them little fires [the Greeks call them 'sparks; life-giving sparks']—poke out and show feelings and judgments. These are innate in almost every sort of human and are excellently placed in the best natures. These the Greeks call 'reflections, conceptions, or notions.' Likewise they

The Dream of Descartes

the melon in the first part of the dream; for, as we have seen, the melon was considered by the Manichaeans to be a sort of "light-germ receptacle." This has now burst open, so to speak, and the luminosities appear directly before Descartes's eyes.[258] In a certain sense the sparks occurring in the second dream correspond to the ghosts and the tempest in the first one, and, like the latter, they symbolize emotionally charged archetypal contents of the unconscious which were not contained in the framework of the Church nor yet in Descartes's intellectual conception of the world.

Descartes shuts and opens his eyes until his fear and the phenomenon both vanish. He evidently tries to rationalize them away, just as he was altogether convinced that all so-called "miraculous" phenomena of nature could be rationally explained away.[259] This had a quieting effect, which is likewise evident in the atmosphere of the third dream, which is far less dramatic.

---

call them 'preconceptions, anticipations.' And because they are passive and placed there, they call them 'common and inborn.'") As Gilson emphasizes (*ibid.*, n. 3), Descartes's phrase "*bona mens*" can probably also be traced back to the same work (*Manuductio*, pp. 70–71), where it says: "Ecce Natura bonae Mentis nobis ingenuit *fomites et scintillas*, quae in aliis magis minusque elucent." Cf. also P. Gibieuf, *De libertate Dei et creaturae* (Paris, 1630), I, 1: "Primae et universalissimae rerum qualitatumque notiones non concinnantur hominum arte et industria, nec ad arbitrium etiam philosophorum effinguntur, sed in mentibus nostris reperiuntur a natura consignatae. Qui autem animo ad tranquillitatem composito naturam audiunt, vel si paulo dignius loqui mavis, qui veritatem intus presidentem et responsa dantem consiliunt [must mean: 'consulunt'] illas tamquam in alto puteo delitescentes percipiunt." ("First and most universal notions of things and qualities are not constituted by the art and industry of men. They are not fashioned by the arbitrary judgment of philosophers but are set in our minds by nature—they are discovered there. Moreover, whoever listens to nature with a mind kept tranquil—or to put it in a little less dignified way, whoever proceeds to the truth that presides within and gives answers—will catch sight of them as if they were hidden in a deep well.")

258. Because (*vide* Descartes's associations) the sparks originate in the collision of two stones, Schönenberger interprets them as coitus—to my mind an incomprehensible violation of the dream symbol.

259. For further details see *A-T*, X, Pt. I, 183, n. Cf. Stock, pp. 60 ff.

Interpretation of the Third Dream

IN THE THIRD DREAM Descartes sees a book on the table but does not know who has placed it there; it is a dictionary, and he thinks that it will be very useful. But suddenly he finds that, instead of the dictionary, he is holding another book, without knowing where it has come from; it is a collection of poems, "*Corpus omnium veterum poetarum latinorum, etc.,* Lugduni, 1603," [260] a book he had probably used at La Flèche.

The unmistakably magical way in which, throughout the third dream, books appear on the table or disappear suggests the influence of ghosts and thus takes up the theme of the first dream; [261] but this time the ghosts play about with books but do not themselves appear. It seems to be the purpose of the unconscious to make clear to Descartes that, just as the creations of art are not "made" by consciousness, neither are the contents of all rational human knowledge (the dictionary undoubtedly stands for this); both *owe their existence to incalculable unconscious influences* and to their creative activities. In a certain sense, this is what Descartes tried to formulate in his *Cogito ergo sum,* in that for him the lucid awareness of one's own act of thinking, the immediate fact of oneself as a thinking being, in short, this consciousness of oneself, is that which guarantees not only the existence of one's own being but also that of God, inasmuch as God is the primal cause and source of all truth and of reality.[262] From this source come all those judgments which are irrefutably convincing to everybody, the sum total of which constitutes the *lumen naturale* [263] which originates in the *naturae purae et*

---

260. For further details concerning this publication see *A-T*, X, 183, n.
261. Also worth noting is the connection with Wotan, who is related to storm, the spirits of the dead, and to *magic*.
262. For details cf. Stock, p. 11. God *cannot* deceive, neither can the thinking substance in us; at most it is our understanding that cheats.
263. Or a "*Sapientia generalis.*" Cf. Regulae (*A-T*, X, 360-61).

125 The Dream of Descartes

simplices ("pure and simple natures")—the inborn ideas.[264] These latter he also compares with the *"tableaux ou images"* in the individual soul.[265] They are stored away *"in mentis thesauro"* ("in the treasury of the mind"),[266] from whence they must be lifted up. The "natural light" is the *res cogitans* in us;[267] it stems from God.[268] I consider it most probable that these fundamental premises of the Cartesian philosophy were born of the experience of the night of November 10 / 11, 1619—*that they represent, so to speak, the form in which Descartes endeavored to master, with his thinking, this incursion of the unconscious. But he only partially succeeded in doing justice to the contents of the unconscious* because he tried to grasp them with his thinking only (his superior function) and possibly with his intuition, and he did not consider

---

264. Cf. *A-T*, X, 383: "Notandum 2. paucas esse duntaxat *naturas puras et simplices,* quas primo et per se, non dependenter ab aliis ullis, sed vel in ipsis experimentis *vel lumine quodam in nobis insito* licet intueri; . . ." ("Second to be noted: [Such] pure and simple natures are not really very many. Firstly they are to be seen only through themselves, or in experiences, or by a certain light placed in us.") And, *ibid.,* p. 419: "Pure intellectuales illae *(scil.* res) sunt, quae per lumen quoddam ingenitum et absque ullius imaginis corporeae adiumento ab intellectu cognoscuntur. . . ." ("Those things are purely intellectual which are learned by the intellect through a certain inborn light without the aid of any corporeal form.")

265. Meditation III *(A-T,* IX, 33). For this reason Leibniz *(Philosophische Schriften,* ed. G. L. Gehrhardt [Hildesheim: Olms, 1960], IV, 328, 371), criticizes: "veritatis criterium nihil aliud esse quam visionem" ("the criterion of truth being nothing but a vision"). Cf. Laporte, p. 21, n. 1.

266. Meditation V. Cf. Laporte, pp. 116, 117.

267. "Recherche de la vérité par la lumière naturelle" *(A-T,* X, 527; cf. also p. 495).

268. Cf. Laporte, p. 319: "L'ensemble des idées distinctes dont se compose notre raison est littéralement non pas une 'vision en Dieu' (Descartes ne dit rien de tel mais une *révélation naturelle que Dieu nous fait)."* ("The harmony of the separate ideas of which our reason is composed is quite literally not a 'vision in God' [Descartes says nothing of the kind, but a natural revelation that God grants to us].") Cf. Karl Löwith, "Das Verhältnis von Gott, Mensch und Welt in der Metaphysik von Descartes und Kant," *Sitzungsberichte der Heidelberger Akad. der Wiss., Phil.-hist. Klasse* (1964), Transaction 3.

the feeling and sensation side of his experience.[269] Besides, the irrational way in which the books are conjured up and then disappear—which cannot be explained causally [270]—contradicts his contention that the original substance of our thinking can only be clear and lucid and can only operate according to reason. Descartes was undoubtedly seriously concerned with the question of the illusion of reality, as experienced in dreams, and with the possibility that a cunning evil spirit lays "traps" for our thoughts, leading us astray into illusions and wrong conclusions; [271] but certain truths, above all the realization of oneself as a thinking subject, are somehow left out. The act of reflection—in its literal sense, the thought which bends back on itself—is for him the ultimate basis of reality of human existence and leads to the discovery of our consciousness of God,[272] which is set above man's existence and encompasses it. *But what the source of the illusions is, Descartes never investigated more closely;* no doubt in his opinion it is the *passiones animae* ("emotions") [273] and the sense perceptions which mislead

269. Goethe revolted with feeling against this one-sidedness: "He [Descartes] makes use of the crudest sensory similes in order to explain the impalpable, indeed the inconceivable. His various material examples, his vortices, his screws, hooks, and pointed curves, thus drag the spirit down. When ideas of this sort are accepted with approval, then it shows that just the rawest, clumsiest views harmonize with the general outlook." Quoted from Fleckenstein, p. 124.

270. Wisdom (p. 14) says that Descartes laid these realizations aside and then took them up again. But in the dream it is *not* Descartes who does this. "It" conjures the books from here and there.

271. For material see Stock, p. 10.

272. God is *"intelligentia pura"* ("pure intelligence"); see *Cogitationes privatae* (*A-T*, X, 218).

273. See von Brockdorff, p. 36, and *Regulae* (*A-T*, X, 368): "Per intuitum intelligo non *fluctuantem sensuum fidem* vel male componentis imaginationis iudicium fallax; sed mentis purae et attentae tam facilem distinctumque conceptum, ut de eo, quod intelligimus nulla prorsus dubitatio relinquatur." ("By intuition I mean not our wavering trust in our senses nor the fallible judgment of a disorderly imagination, but the easy and clear distinctions of a purified and attentive mind so that no further doubt remains about what we understand.") Concerning his doctrine of sensory perception through *"phantasmata"* see Gilson, pp. 470 ff.

people into wrong conclusions, but who or what engenders them he does not inquire. It is therefore significant, as Felsch notes,[274] that his application of the principle of causality is, especially in all psychological connections, dark and illogical. He projects the mystery of the connection between psyche and body onto the pineal gland,[275] which ostensibly rules the "spirits of life" in the ventricles of the brain. A continuous something must somehow exist between the *"res extensa"* and the *"res cogitans,"* but Descartes is unable to define it more closely.[276] The same lack of clarity prevails in regard to both his definition of imagination—which to him is a psychophysical event [277]—and the "passions of the soul" (*passiones*), which are allegedly brought about, now by the "spirits of life," now by the *"actio animae"* ("activity of the soul"), and then again by the impressions affecting the brain (*"impressiones quae casu occurrunt in cerebro"* ["impressions occurring in the brain by chance"]), or else by sensory objects.[278]

The unconscious inhibition that hindered Descartes from investigating this complex of problems more deeply must, in the final analysis, have been his adherence to the Christian definition of evil as a mere *privatio boni*,[279] a question that I would, in principle, refer to Jung's exposition in *Aion*.[280] In his *Cogitationes privatae* [281] Descartes says that God is *"intelligentia pura"* ("pure intelligence") and that, when He separated the light from the darkness, He separated the good from the evil angels. Since the *"privatio"* could not be separated from the *"habitus"* ("habitual behavior"), the darkness and the evil angels are only a *privatio* and its form of existence. As Sirven points out,[282] he is here quoting word for

---

274. Felsch, p. 19, and esp. pp. 44 ff., 49.
275. *Ibid.*, p. 49.
276. *Ibid.*, p. 50.
277. *Ibid.*, pp. 50–51.
278. *Ibid.*, p. 53.
279. That this was the case, see Sirven, pp. 146 ff.
280. *CW*, IX, Part II.
281. See *A-T*, X, 218.
282. See *ibid.*, p. 146.

word from Augustine's *De Genesi ad litteram liber imperfectus* [283] and *De Genesi contra Manichaeos*.[284] Just at the time of his dream, Descartes was himself considering the idea of writing a commentary on Genesis and had been reading these works of Augustine's.[285] We may assume that he took the *privatio boni* over from Augustine [286] and half-unconsciously, as it were, blended it with his declaration that God is *"intelligentia pura"* and is thus absolutely veracious and unable to deceive.[287] With this view Descartes remains ensnared in a Christian prejudice; it is as if the Trinitarian system should be applied to matter and cosmic reality but, again, without asking the question about the Fourth, the Totality. Maritain is therefore correct in saying that Descartes's philosophy appears with an "air d'héroisme géomètre et chrétien"—measuring the earth and straightway finding God in the soul.[288] He further emphasizes (see Gilson for supporting evidence) that Cartesian philosophy "breaks into two contrasting bits, which it asserts as separate existents never again capable of being reunited into those higher conciliations Scholasticism had made between the great antinomies of reality." [289] I believe this breaking-in-two of the Scholastic view of the world may be looked upon as a *doubling* of

283. Migne, *Patr. Lat.*, XXXIV, col. 229.
284. *Ibid.*, col. 176, and XLI, cols. 332–33.
285. Sirven, pp. 147–48.
286. Cf. *ibid.*, p. 149.
287. Cf. Laporte, p. 171, where he shows that Descartes deduces the veracity of God from the fact that God cannot introduce any nonbeing into his being: "Mais le mot 'tromper' n'a pas de sens où il signifie le substitution du faux au vrai. En faisant de la tromperie un bien Dieu introduirait en soi du non-être: ce qui reviendrait à s'ôter un peu de son être ... ." ("But the word 'to deceive' has no sense where it means the substitution of the false for the true. By committing deceit, a good 'God' would introduce into himself some nonbeing: which would amount to removing a little of himself. . . ."
288. Maritain, p. 41: "mesurant la terre et trouvant tout droit Dieu dans l'âme."
289. *Ibid.*, p. 55: "brise ... en deux morceaux contrastant, qu'elle affirme chacun à part sans pouvoir désormais les réunir, les conciliations supérieures, en lesquelle la scolastique resolvait les grandes antinomies de réel ... ."

129 *The Dream of Descartes*

the same, in other words, as an unconscious realization of its "lower" correspondence. As Jung has explained,[290] the divine Trinity has its counterpart in a lower, chthonic triad [291] which "represents a principle which, by reason of its symbolism, betrays affinities with evil, though it is by no means certain that it expresses nothing but evil." This lower element has the relation of *correspondentia* ("correspondence") with the higher, but, in contradistinction to quaternary symbols, the triadic ones are not symbolic of wholeness. Jung continues: "If one imagines the quaternity as a square divided into two halves by a diagonal, one gets two triangles whose apices point in opposite directions. One could therefore say metaphorically that as the whole symbolized by the quaternity is divided into equal halves, it produces two opposing triads." The lower triangle represents a "dark spirit," which is indeed the cause of the present-day collective catastrophes but which, when rightly understood, can also become the *causa instrumentalis* of the process of individuation.[292] *This* spirit which seized Descartes is from the point of view of the Church a *malin génie* ("evil spirit"); but it is also a *spiritus familiaris* ("familiar spirit") that incites toward the achievement of wholeness. As Pauli explains in his article on Kepler, the latter's three-dimensional scheme of space is dependent on the Christian idea of the Trinity; and, similarly, Descartes's mechanistic, purely causal comprehension of nature, on the basis of the simple laws of movement, is founded on the Christian image of God. Thus it becomes evident that materialism, so-called, among whose founders Descartes must be numbered, really has its roots, as Brunschvicg remarks,[293] in

290. "The Phenomenology of the Spirit in Fairy Tales," *The Archetypes and the Collective Unconscious*, pp. 234–35.
291. The three-headed Satan, and so forth. In folklore a similar triad also often appears, for Satan is given a "grandmother" and a beautiful daughter with "human" feelings.
292. *Ibid.*, pp. 251–52.
293. Brunschvicg, pp. 117–18: "Une physique où le mécanisme est pratiqué avec autant de rigueur et dans une semblable extension ne risque-t-elle pas de frayer la voie à la renaissance du matérialisme

an extreme form of spirituality. Thus, basically, Descartes completely "dematerialized" matter, in comparison with the way in which it is described in the newer physics, for, according to definition, he only concedes it a geometrically comprehensible dimension of space in three parameters, but not density, mass, or qualities of energy.[294] This connects up with the fact that he denied any movement of light taking place in time. He believed in an absolutely instantaneous spreading-out of light, a point against which Beeckmann, his contemporary, was already raising objections.[295] The uncritical acceptance of the definition of evil as a *privatio boni* and the identification of God's workings with logical, rational, causally explainable events made it impossible for him, in the sphere of his researches into natural science, to give further thought to an acausal description of occurrences. For this reason the unconscious emphasizes the reality of such phenomena in a compensatory manner and displays an autonomous ghostly effect.

Descartes's own association to the dictionary is that it represents the sum total of all the sciences (whose basic principle he believed he had just discovered mathematically); the collection of poems, on the other hand, stands for wisdom,

---

épicurien? ... mais tout au contraire, parce que la manière dont il introduit et justifie la vérité du mécanisme intégral, immanent en quelque sorte à lui-même, *plonge ses racines dans une métaphysique dont on ne doit pas dire seulement, qu'elle est radicalement spiritualiste, mais qui renouvelle, en la portant à un degré de pureté jusqu'alors insoupçonné, la notion de spiritualité.*" ("Does not a physics where the mechanism is practiced with as much rigor and to such an extent risk opening up the road to a rebirth of Epicurean materialism . . . ? But quite the contrary! Because the manner in which it introduces and justifies the truth of the integral mechanism, immanent in some way in itself, *plunges its roots into a metaphysics of which one not only ought to say that it is radically spiritual but that it even renews, by bringing to it a degree of purity unsuspected up to now, the notion of spirituality.*") This "abstraction" is grounded in the geometric nature of Descartes's physics. Cf. Gagnebin, p. 117.

294. Cf. Stock, pp. 75 ff. Descartes hypostasizes space as absolutely existent; cf. Gagnebin, p. 116: "la géométrie de Descartes est déjà une physique" ("Descartes's geometry is already a physics").

295. Cf. Stock, p. 49, and Gagnebin, p. 116.

131 The Dream of Descartes

enthusiasm, divine inspiration, and the seed of wisdom (which is to be found in the soul of man, as sparks in flint). However satisfying this thought may be at first sight, one cannot help being surprised that two poems by the Gallic poet Ausonius (fourth century A.D.) should represent this world of wisdom and inspiration; for the poems of this skeptical "poet," who wrote in a purely rhetorical style and merely went over to Christianity conventionally (!), contain, from our point of view, very little poetic inspiration. On the other hand, the two idylls which appear in the dream are both confessions of a possibly ingenious but purely skeptical *Weltanschauung*,[296] that of a man who is weary of life and even opposed to it. At first Descartes's eye falls on Idyll XV ("Ex Graeco Pythagoricum de ambiguitate eligendae vitae"), which begins with the words: "Quod vitae sectabor iter? Si *plena tumultu / sunt fora;* si curis domus anxia: si *peregrinos /* Cura domus sesequitur, . . ."[297] These first lines fit Descartes's own situation in an amazing way—namely, that of the *peregrinus* ("stranger in the land, wanderer") in the very heart of Germany, then endangered by war. The poem then proceeds to state that neither work nor marriage nor riches, neither youth nor age, not even eternal life or mortality, can bring man happiness, and it ends with the words: "Optima Graiorum sententia: Quippe homini aiunt / non nasci esse bonum, natum aut cito morte potiri."

In a certain sense, the question in the introductory sentence of the poem is on the same lines as the symbolism of the first dream, which showed that, "gripped" by the raging storm, Descartes was in danger of overlooking the rounding-out and maturing of his own personality. Here, also, the question calls his attention back, as it were, to the moral and

---

296. Concerning Descartes's "sceptique chrétienne" see Adam, p. 57. It might perhaps be still more important to stress that Descartes really only thought about an intellectual solution to the moral problem and did not look on morality as a concern of the feeling-function.

297. The full text and translation of each of these poems—Idyll XV, which begins "Quod vitae sectabor iter?" and Idyll XII, which begins "Est et Non"—will be found on pp. 138–41.

personal problem [298] of his feeling, to the choice or decision in favor of the personal life. But here again another man appears, this time an unknown man, who draws his attention to yet another idyll. *This unknown person might be the figure of the "trickster,"* [299] *now become visible*, who spirited the books about in such an uncanny way. In any case, he represents an unknown, unconscious part of Descartes's personality, which might perhaps be a parallel to Mr. N. of the first dream, although Mr. N. was merely overlooked by Descartes, whereas this new arrival is completely unknown to him. The stranger recommends to him an idyll by Ausonius beginning "Est et Non" ("Yes and No").[300] Idyll XII = Ναὶ καὶ οὐ Πυθαγορικόν ("The Yes and No of the Pythagoreans"). The theme of the poem is that these two little words, "yes" and "no," govern all human life, set men at variance, and that everything can be affirmed and denied, so that many would prefer to remain completely silent.

If the poem "Quod vitae sectabor iter" tried to awaken doubt and insecurity where the values of life are concerned, this last poem kindles doubt as to the reliability of all human statements; the "yes" and "no" are entirely relative. *The unknown man appears to be bent on undermining Descartes's belief in the possibility of absolutely valid proofs* and on convincing him of the paradoxical character of every really psychologically true statement—presumably with the intention of thus detaching him, as previously by means of the first poem, from his thinking function, which was growing more and more absolute, and of leading him toward the problem of his own self. At the same time the two poems *mirror Des-*

---

298. Descartes himself calls it "Le bon conseil d'une personne sage ou même la Théologie Morale" ("the good counsel of a wise person or even of Moral Theology").

299. In the history of religion this is the name specially given to the divine savior-figures in many American Indian tribes, because they are particularly noted for their queer, elfish tricks. The alchemistic Spirit Mercurius is likewise fond of appearing as a "trickster."

300. For the text and translation of this poem, see below, pp. 140 f.

133 The Dream of Descartes

cartes's *unconscious feeling attitude:* [301] he has no faith at all in life and none in himself or in any other person. In his portraits one cannot help being struck by his hopelessly skeptical, timid, lifeless expression. It is without doubt the fact of his mother's early death which robbed him of any zest for life, of any faith in life and in his own feeling, so that he shut himself off in the sole activity of his mind. Also, it seems to me that his apparent lack of character is better explained as a certain deficiency of this sort of vital substance than as a flaw in his nature.

In the dream Descartes takes up the stranger's suggestion, appears to be quite *"au fait"* and wants to show the stranger the poem in his book but is unable to find it. The trickster's game starts anew; the stranger inquires where he got the book. He evidently wants to make it clear to Descartes—as we have already hinted—that all his sudden ideas and inspirations, his thinking and feeling, which he firmly believes to be under his control, being convinced that *he* is doing it all ("Je *pense donc* je *suis*"), are in reality entirely dependent on the good grace of the unconscious—on whether it chooses to supply them or not. This is why the dictionary appears again. But it is no longer complete: parts of it have crumbled away, since the problem of feeling has come up. Descartes then finds the idylls of Ausonius in the anthology, but not the poem "Est et Non," and he wants to recommend the other one ("Quod vitae sectabor") to the stranger instead. He tries to turn away from the problem of the doubtful nature of all thinking statements and, at the same time, to accept consciously his skeptical feeling side, which is inimical to life. But once again the unexpected happens: he finds small colored portraits, copperplate engravings, which do not figure in the actual edition. The fact of touching the problem of feeling, the fourth function, has the effect of bringing up the idea of

---

301. Wisdom (p. 14) also stresses this point: ". . . the anthology meant the knowledge of what is real in the life of the living."

the individual personality [302] and of interest in the individual value and actual reality of each unique human being. This was just the period of the great Italian and Dutch portraitists, and this interest in individual personality corresponded to the tendency of the age. There is a multiplicity of portraits, which suggests an initial state of the as yet dissociated fragments of Descartes's personality. Like the many seeds of the melon, these are, as it were, the components inherited from the ancestors, out of which the "united personality" is gradually brought together.

In the first dream the symbol of the Self consists of a round object—the Monas. Emphasis is laid on unity. In the two following dreams, on the other hand, the new content of the Self is pictured as a plurality of sparks or portraits. It appears in multiple form, so to speak. This points to the fact that through the first meeting with the center, the Self (which is not the same as the ego), a duplication of the personality takes place. The unity of consciousness (and Descartes himself certainly saw the *âme pensante*, the thinking ego, as the only psychic reality) is cracked open. The dream shows that inwardly man is in reality manifold and inextricably bound up with the many. The ideal, connected with Christian monotheism, of the unity of consciousness and will, which was especially striven after by the Jesuits, is here called into question. For the Self, as Jung says, comprises not only the single man but also many others. "It is paradoxically the quintessence of the individual and at the same time a collectivity." [303]

Whereas Descartes's own dream interpretation is, on the

---

302. In the "Recherche de la vérité" (*A-T*, X, 507) Descartes speaks of the deceptions of the senses as being inferior pictures, painted by apprentice artists, to which the master (Reason) puts finishing touches. But according to Descartes, the master would do better to start from the beginning again.

303. Jung, *Paracelsica*, p. 116. Concerning the *Multiplicatio* cf. Jung, "The Psychology of the Transference," *The Practice of Psychotherapy* (*CW*, XVI, 1954), pp. 304 ff., and for the Self as the condition of relatedness see *ibid.*, pp. 233 ff.

whole, somewhat feeble and optimistic, in the final motif of the portraits it misses the mark altogether: he takes it to be a forecast of the visit of an Italian painter, who did in fact come to see him on the following day.[304] At least he sees that there might be a *"valeur prophétique"* in his dream and feels himself confirmed in seeing the operation of God in it. Therefore he says that "l'esprit humain n'y avoit aucune part." Although the incident was calculated to stress the importance of the portraits, Descartes does not appear to have grasped that they could be connected with his feeling side. The later development of his thought actually put more and more distance between himself and the "pictures." In his earlier writings and studies of the phenomenon of memory he granted a far higher value to the symbol of the pictures and to imagination, as "shadows" or images of a higher truth, as it were; but later he dissociated himself from these conceptions.[305] Perhaps this was the reason why the dream refers with such emotional intensity to just this particular aspect of the spirit. In this connection the visit of the painter on the following day should be looked upon as a synchronistic event, which intensified the significance of the dream. It is amazing how the statement about the *"valeur prophétique"* of the dream appeared to be a satisfactory "explanation" for Descartes, who normally dismissed the thought of an acausal connection of events. The implications of his remark seem to have eluded him. Subsequently, however, he did instinctively do something for his feeling side, which, in his case, was doubtless bound up with his dead mother: he vowed to go on a pilgrimage to the Madonna of Loretto, to pray for inner guidance in his *"recherche de la vérité,"* for after the dream he felt deep contrition as a sinner. His feeling of contrition (of being overwhelmed with regret) was caused in all probability by an illegitimate shifting of his feeling of inferiority onto certain

304. *A-T*, X, 185; Sirven, p. 129.
305. Cf. J. H. Gouhier: "Le refus du symbolisme dans l'humanisme cartésien," *Umanismo e simbolismo: Atti del VI convegno internat. di studi umanistici* (Padua, 1958), p. 67, and Rossi, pp. 154 ff.

sins of the past;[306] his real feeling of inferiority was doubtless based on the fact that the dream had touched the split-off problem of his feeling and the religious problem of evil.

What makes these dreams so impressive to me—quite apart from all they tell us about Descartes—is the fact that they already sketch, in a nutshell, the actual problem of the man of our time, the heir to that epoch of eighteenth-century rationalism, at the dawn of which Descartes stands, and, through the symbols of the melon and the individual portraits they point to the process of individuation as a possible lysis. Even though it is evident, not only from the conclusions which Descartes himself drew from the dreams but from the later trend of his life, that in some respects he failed to follow the way indicated by the unconscious, it is yet his merit to have worked with such passionate devotion for the "purification" of his mind and for the *"recherche de la vérité."* [307] This is undoubtedly the reason he was granted this important manifestation from the unconscious.

Conclusion

My interpretation of the dreams may seem rather critical and be felt to disparage Descartes's personality, but this is by

306. This is a typical phenomenon, i.e., that people suffering from feelings of inferiority do not connect them with their actually inferior side but shift them to a side where they have no need to feel so inferior.

307. Cf. *A-T*, X, 180, where A. Baillet remarks, concerning his condition before the dream: "Avec toutes ces dispositions il n'eut pas moins à souffrir que s'il eût été question de se dépouiller de soy-même. Il crût pourtant en être venu à bout. Et à dire vrai, c'étoit assez que son imagination *lui representât son esprit tout nud*, pour lui faire croire qu'il l'avoit mis effectivement en cet état. Il ne lui restoit que l'amour de la vérité dont la poursuite devoit faire dorénavant l'occupation de sa vie." ("With all those preparations, he suffered no less than if it had been a matter of stripping himself of himself. He thought, however, that he had reached the end. And truth to tell, it was enough that his imagination should show him his mind entirely naked, to make him believe that he had in fact reduced it to that condition. Nothing remained for him but the love of truth, the pursuit of which was to be the occupation of his life from that time on.")

no means my intention. My criticism is directed against Cartesian rationalism, which still influences man today. In other words, I have sought to demonstrate the inadequacy of a purely rational view of the world, which was a historically conditioned reaction against certain uncritical trends in medieval thought. From the opposing standpoint, Rittmeister has given more prominence to Descartes's merit in having established an ego-strength and an ego-freedom in his work, through which the development of modern science first became possible.[308] This is undoubtedly very much to the point. Today, however, the rationalism of science has become so rigidly established that it discards and even threatens to destroy feeling and with it our whole soul. It seems interesting, therefore, that already in Descartes's dream (which stood at the beginning of this recent development) this danger was symbolically indicated. The dream itself shows that the unconscious does not criticize the dreamer; he commits no offense in it, apart from failing to greet Mr. N. However, the unconscious does underline Descartes's relative lostness in an uncanny suprapersonal situation which occurred as a result of his intense preoccupation with the problems of spiritual truth. He was certainly deeply touched and stirred by the dream-images, although his reasonable thinking extracted from them only a partial insight. But, looking at the symbolism with hindsight and from our modern standpoint, we can see how, through him, the archetype of the Self was seeking to become integrated, not only in his new thinking but in his human being as a whole, a task which still awaits the scientist of today.

308. *Confinia psychiatrica*, IV (1961), *passim*.

Idyll XV

QUOD VITAE SECTABOR ITER? Si plena tumultu
sunt fora; si curis domus anxia: si peregrinos
Cura domus sesequitur, mercantem si nova semper
damna manent, cessare vetat si turpis egestas:
Si vexat labor agricolam, mare naufragus horror
infamat, *poenaeque graves in coelibe vita:*
Est gravior cautis custodia vana maritis
sanguinem si Martis opus, si turpia lucra
Foenoris et velox inopes usura trucidat.
Omne aevum curae cunctis sua displicet aetas
sensus abest parvis lactentibus et puerorum
dura rudimenta et juvenum temeraria pubes
afflictat fortuna viros per bella per aequor
irasque insidiasque catenatosque labores
mutandos semper gravioribus. Ipsa senectus
Exspectata diu votisque optata malignis
obiicit innumeris corpus lacerabile morbis
spernimus in commune omnes praesentia quosdam
Constat nolle Deus fieri. Iuturna reclamat
quo vitam dedit aeternam? Cur mortis ademta'est
conditio? Sic Caucasea sub rupe Prometheus
testatur Saturnigenam nec nomine cessat
Incusare Iovem, data sit quod vita perennis
Respice et ad cultus animi. Sic nempe pudicum
Perdidit Hippolytum non felix cura pudoris
At contra illecebris maculosam ducere vitam
Quem iuvat, aspiciat poenas et crimina regum.
Tereos incesti vel mollis Sardanapali
Perfidiae vitare monent tria Punica bella
Sed prohibet servare fidem deleta Saguntos
Vive et amicitias semper cole, crimen ob istud
Pythagoreorum periit schola docta sophorum
Hoc metuens igitur nullas cole. Crimen ob istud
Timon Palladiis olim lapidatus Athenis
Dissidet ambiguis semper mens obvia votis
Nec voluisse homini satis est. Optata recusat
Esse in honore placet. Mox poenitet. Et dominari
Ut possit, servire volet, Idem auctus honore

139 The Dream of Descartes

> Pernox est cura disertis
> Sed rudis ornatu vitae caret, esto patronus
> Et defende reos sed gratia rara clientis.
> Esto cliens, gravis imperii persona patroni
> Exercent hunc vota Patrum. Mox aspera curis
> Sollicitudo obit. Contemnitur orba senectus
> Et captatoris praeda'st haeredis egenus.
> Vitam parcus agas, avidi lacerabere fama
> Et largitionem gravius censura notabit
> cuncta sibi adversis contraria casibus. Ergo
> Optima Graiorum sententia: Quippe homini aiunt
> non nasci esse bonum, natum aut cito morte potiri.

WHAT WAY OF LIFE shall I choose? When the streets are filled with tumult, and cares oppress the home with anxiety? When the traveler is dogged by domestic cares, when fresh reverses constantly await the merchant and yet ignominious poverty forbids any wavering. When labor harasses the peasant, when the sea depicts the terrifying horrors of shipwreck, and heavy penalties weigh on the bachelor's life. And yet no careful guarding of his spouse will avail the cautious husband when the work of Mars claims his blood and when all petty gains are swallowed up by the rent, and the poor are crushed by the usurer. Every generation is dissatisfied with its own age on account of its difficulties; the little sucklings lack consciousness; hard indeed is the first training and the petulant age of youth; fate afflicts men with wars and the dangers of seafaring, strife, ambush, and a network of troubles which constantly increase. Even old age, yearned for and desired with insidious vows, exposes the decaying body to countless illnesses. We all join in scorning the present; in the case of some it is evident that God did not wish them to live. Iuturna claims back eternal life from him to whom she gave it. Why have I been robbed of the state of death? Thus cries Prometheus on the rock of Caucasus to the daughter of Saturn and ceases not to blame Jupiter for having endowed him with eternal life. Glance also at the spiritual values: chaste Hippolytus, namely, was destroyed by his infelicitous chastity. Yet, he who finds pleasure in wasting a life sullied by lust, let him glance at the punishments and judgments of kings. The three Punic wars warn us against the incest of Tereus and the faithlessness of effeminate Sardanapalus, yet Saguntum in ruins forbids us to remain faithful. Very well, then live and forever cultivate friendship—yet it is owing to this sin that the learned school of the Pythagoreans was destroyed. Fearing this, on no account cultivate friendship—for this fault Timon was once stoned in Athens. An inner meaning forever contradicts ambiguous vows, and it does not suffice a man to have desired something—he afterwards rejects the very object of his longing. We like to be esteemed. We soon learn to regret it. And to be capable of ruling, one must be willing to serve. He who is held in honor is constantly plagued by glib talkers, yet the uncultured man foregoes the enrichments of life. Be a patron and defend the accused, your client's thanks are rare indeed. Be a client, the patron's yoke is heavy, he is plagued by the senators' wishes. Soon comes anxiety laden with cares. We despise old age, and, when in need of help ourselves, we are the prey of the legacy-hunter. Live frugally, you will be dubbed avaricious, and prodigality will be even more severely censured. Everything has its opposite side. Therefore the Greeks' saying is the best: they hold that it is fortunate for a man not to be born, and, if he is, then to die quickly. (Translated from the author's German rendering of the Latin.)

Idyll XII

EST ET NON, cuncti monosyllaba nota frequentant
His demptis nihil est hominum quod sermo volutet
Omnia in his et ab his sunt omnia sive negoti
sive oti quicquam'st seu turbae sive quietis
Alterutro pariter nonnumquam saepe seorsis
obsistunt studiis ut mores ingeniumque
Vel faciles vel difficiles contentio nacta'st.
Si consentitur mora nulla intervenit Est, Est.
Si controversum dissensio subiiciet Non.
Hinc fora dissultant clamoribus, hinc furiosi
iurgia sunt Circi, cuneati hinc laeta theatri.
Seditio et tales agitat quoque Curia lites
Hinc etiam placitis schola consona disciplinis
Dogmaticas agitat placito certamina lites

The Dream of Descartes

Hinc omnis certat dialectica turba Sophorum
Est lux estne dies ergo, Non convenit istuc
Nam facibus multis aut fulgoribus quotiens lux
Est nocturna homini non est lux ista diei
Est et non igitur quotiens lucem esse fatendum'st
Sed non esse diem. Mille hinc certamina surgunt
Hinc pauci, multi quoque talia commeditantes
Murmure concluso rabiosa silentia rodunt
Qualis vita hominum, duo quam monosyllaba versant!

YES AND NO: everyone uses these well-known words of one syllable. When they are lacking, human conversation is incapable of expressing anything. Everything is contained in these, and everything proceeds from these—be it connected with work or with leisure, in the crowd or in repose. With both equally people often oppose each other with contrary opinions, according to their nature and their attitude, whether they are pliable or difficult in a discussion. When we are in agreement, it is: Yes, Yes! forthwith. When, on the contrary, a difference of opinion flares up, it is: No, No! Therefore the forum resounds with clamor; hence the fierce fights in the circus; therefore the shouts from the tiers of seats in the theater; thus are disputes discussed in the Senate; therefore the school of philosophers, of one mind in its dogmas, discusses axiomatic conflicts with differing opinions, hence the whole voluble band of sophists' quarrels. It is light—is it then day? This is not accepted, for how often does light proceed from a number of torches, or from lightning, that is man's nocturnal light, not daylight. Yes and No. We must therefore admit that whenever there is light, it is not necessarily day. Thus a thousand discussions arise. A few, therefore—yea, indeed many—who ponder over such things bite their lips in angry silence. How sad in reality is this life of man, forever swayed by these two words of one syllable. (Translated from the author's German rendering of the Latin.)

Bibliography

ADAM, CHARLES. *Descartes, sa vie et ses oeuvres.* Paris, 1937. (Vol. XII of C. ADAM and P. TANNERY, *Oeuvres de Descartes.*)

ADAM, C., and TANNERY, P. *Oeuvres de Descartes.* 12 vols. Paris, 1897–1913.

BACHOFEN, J. J. *Versuch über die Gräbersymbolik der Alten.* Basel, 1859.

BARTH, HEINRICH. "Descartes' Begründung der Erkenntnis." Dissertation. Bern, 1913.

BAUR, FERD. CHR. *Das manichäische Religionssystem.* Tübingen, 1831.

BEESON, C. (ed.). *Acta Archelai.* Leipzig, 1906.

BERGSON, HENRI. "La philosophie," *Science Française.* Paris, 1916.

BOLTE, J., and POLIVKA, G. *Anmerkungen zu den Kinder- und Hausmärchen der Brüder Grimm.* Leipzig, 1912–32.

BROCKDORFF, CAY VON. *Descartes und die Fortbildung der Kartesischen Lehre.* Munich, 1923.

BRUNSCHVICG, LÉON. *Descartes et Pascal: Lecteurs de Montaigne.* Neuchâtel, 1945.

CASSIRER, E. *Descartes' Kritik der mathematischen und naturwissenschaftlichen Erkenntnis.* Marburg, 1899.

COHEN, G. *Ecrivains français en Hollande de la première moitié du XVIIe siècle.* Paris, 1920.

FELSCH, CARL. *Der Kausalitätsbegriff bei Descartes.* Langensalza, 1891.

FISCHER, A. "Die Quitte als Vorzeichen bei Persern und Arabern und das Traumbuch des 'Abd-al-Ranī an-Nabulūsī," *Zeitschrift der deutschen morgenländischen Gesellschaft*, Vol. LXVIII. Leipzig, 1914.

FLECKENSTEIN, J. O. "Cartesische Erkenntnis und mathematische Physik des 17. Jahrhunderts," *Gesnerus* (a quarterly published by the Schweizer. Gesellschaft für Geschichte der Medizin und der Naturwissenschaften), Vol. VII. 1950.

FRANZ, M.-L. VON. "The 'Passio Perpetuae,'" *Spring*. New York: Analytical Psychology Club of New York, Inc., 1949.

FUNK, PHILIPP. *Ignatius von Loyola*. Berlin, 1913.

GAGNEBIN, S. "La réforme cartésienne et son fondement géometrique," *Gesnerus* (a quarterly published by the Schweizer. Gesellschaft für Geschichte der Medizin und der Naturwissenschaften), Vol. VII. 1950.

GIBIEUF, P. *De libertate Dei et creaturae*. Paris, 1630.

GILSON, E. "L'innéisme cartésien et la théologie," *Revue de métaphysique et de morale*, Vol. XXII. 1914.

———. (ed.) [Descartes's] *Discours de la Méthode, texte et commentaire*. Paris, 1947.

GONSETH, F. *Les mathématiques et la réalité*. Paris, 1936.

GOUHIER, H. "Le refus du symbolisme dans l'humanisme cartésien," *Umanismo e simbolismo: Atti del VI convegno internat. di studi umanistici*. Padua, 1958.

HADAMARD, JACQUES. *The Psychology of Invention in the Mathematical Field*. Princeton, 1949.

HOVORKA, O. VON, and KRONFELD, A. *Vergleichende Volksmedizin*. Stuttgart, 1909.

The I Ching, or Book of Changes. Translated by CARY F. BAYNES from RICHARD WILHELM's translation into German from the Chinese. New York, 1950; London, 1951.

Japanische Volksmärchen. Edited by E. DIEDERICHS. "Die Märchen der Weltliteratur" series, edited by F. v. d. LEYEN. Jena, 1938.

JEFFERSON, GEOFFREY. "René Descartes on the Localisation of the Soul," *Irish Journal of Medical Studies*, No. 285. 1949.

JEŽOWER, I. *Das Buch der Träume*. Berlin, 1928.

Jung, Carl Gustav. *Aion. Collected Works,** Vol. IX, Part II. 1959.

———. *The Archetypes and the Collective Unconscious. Collected Works,* Vol. IX, Part I. 1959.

———. "Brother Klaus," *Psychology and Religion. Collected Works,* Vol. XI. 1958.

———. "Concerning Mandala Symbolism," *The Archetypes and the Collective Unconscious. Collected Works,* Vol. IX, Part I. 1959.

———. "On the Nature of the Psyche," *The Structure and Dynamics of the Psyche. Collected Works,* Vol. VIII. 1960.

———. *Paracelsica.* Zurich, 1942. *Collected Works,* Vol. XIII (in preparation).

———. "Paracelsus as a Spiritual Phenomenon," *Alchemical Studies. Collected Works,* Vol. XIII (in preparation).

———. "The Phenomenology of Spirit in Fairy Tales," *The Archetypes and the Collective Unconscious. Collected Works,* Vol. IX, Part I. 1959.

———. "The Process of Individuation." Lectures given at the Eidgenössische Technische Hochschule, Zurich, June, 1939—March, 1940.

———. *Psychology and Alchemy. Collected Works,* Vol. XII. 1953.

———. "The Psychology of the Child Archetype," *The Archetypes and the Collective Unconscious. Collected Works,* Vol. IX, Part I. 1959. Also published, in collaboration with Carl Kerényi, in *Essays on a Science of Mythology* (American title), New York, 1949, and *Introduction to a Science of Mythology* (British title), London, 1950.

———. "The Psychology of Transference," *The Practice of Psychotherapy. Collected Works,* Vol. XVI. 1954.

———. *Psychological Types. Collected Works,* Vol. VI (in preparation). Alternate source: English translation, *Psycho-*

---

* *The Collected Works of C. G. Jung,* translated by R. F. C. Hull, are published by the Bollingen Foundation (Bollingen Series XX) in the United States of America by Pantheon Books and in England by Routledge and Kegan Paul.

logical Types, by H. G. BAYNES. London and New York, 1923.

———. "A Study in the Process of Individuation," *The Archetypes and the Collective Unconscious. Collected Works,* Vol. IX, Part I. 1959.

———. "Synchronicity: An Acausal Connecting Principle," *The Structure and Dynamics of the Psyche. Collected Works,* Vol. VIII, 1960.

———. "The Unconscious as a Multiple Consciousness," section 6 of "On the Nature of the Psyche," *The Structure and Dynamics of the Psyche. Collected Works,* Vol. VIII. 1960.

———. "Wotan," *Civilization in Transition. Collected Works,* Vol. X. 1964. Alternate source: English translation by BARBARA HANNAH in *Essays on Contemporary Events.* London, 1947.

KRONFELD, A. See under HOVORKA, O. VON.

LAPORTE, J. *Le rationalisme de Descartes.* Paris, 1945.

LE COQ, A. VON. "Die buddhistische Spätantike in Mittelasien: Die manichäischen Miniaturen, II Teil," *Ergebnisse der kgl. preuss. Turfan-Expedition.* Berlin, 1923.

LEISEGANG, HANS. *Die Gnosis.* 2d ed. Leipzig, 1924.

LEROY, MAXIM. *Descartes, le philosophe au masque.* Paris, 1929.

LÖWITH, KARL. "Das Verhältnis von Gott, Mensch und Welt in der Metaphysik von Descartes und Kant," *Sitzungsberichte der Heidelberger Akad. der Wiss., Phil.-hist. Klasse,* Transaction 3. 1964.

MARITAIN, JACQUES. *Le songe de Descartes.* Paris, 1932.

MIGNE, JACQUES PAUL (ed.). *Patrologia Latina.* 221 vols. Paris, 1844–64.

MILHAUD, G. *Descartes savant.* Paris, 1921.

MOGK, E. *Germanische Religionsgeschichte und Mythologie.* Leipzig and Berlin, 1927.

NIETZSCHE, FRIEDRICH. *Thus Spake Zarathustra.* Modern Library edition. New York.

NINCK, MARTIN. *Wodan und germanischer Schicksalsglaube.* Jena, 1935.

PAULI, W. "Die Einfluss archetypischer Vorstellungen auf die

Bildung naturwissenschaftlicher Theorien bei Kepler," in C. G. JUNG and W. PAULI, *Naturerklärung und Psyche* (Zurich, 1952). English translation by PATRICIA SILZ, "The Influence of Archetypal Ideas on the Scientific Theories of Kepler," in C. G. JUNG and W. PAULI, *The Interpretation of Nature and the Psyche*. Bollingen Series LI. New York and London, 1955.

PAULY, AUGUST FRIEDRICH VON. *Pauly's Realenclopädie der classischen Altertumswissenschaft.* Edited by GEORG WISSOWA. Stuttgart, 1893——.

PLATZECK, E.-W. *Raimund Lull, sein Leben—seine Werke: Die Grundlagen seines Denkens.* 2 vols. Düsseldorf, 1962.

POINCARÉ, HENRI. *Wissenschaft und Methode.* Leipzig and Berlin, 1914.

POLIVKA, G. See under BOLTE, J.

PUECH, H. C. "Der Begriff der Erlösung im Manichäismus," *Eranos-Jahrbuch 1936.* Zurich, 1937.

QUIRING, HEINRICH. "Der Traum des Descartes," *Kant-Studien, Philosophische Zeitschrift,* XLVI, No. 2. 1954–55.

RITTMEISTER, J. "Die mystische Krise des jungen Descartes," *Confinia Psychiatrica,* Vol. IV. 1961. Posthumously published, with additions by A. Storch.

RÖD, WOLFGANG. *Descartes: Die innere Genesis des cartesianischen Systems.* Munich and Basel, 1964.

ROSSI, PAOLO. *Clavis Universalis: Arte mnemoniche e logica combinatoria da Lullio a Leibniz.* Milan, 1960.

SCHÖNENBERGER, STEPHEN. "'A Dream of Descartes': Reflections on the Unconscious Determinants of Science," *International Journal of Psycho-Analysis,* Vol. XX. 1939.

SEBBA, G. *Bibliographia cartesiana: A Critical Guide to the Descartes Literature, 1800–1960.* Archives Internationales de l'Histoire des Idées, Vol. V. The Hague, 1964.

SIRVEN, J. *Les anneés d'apprentissage de Descartes, 1596–1628.* Paris, 1925.

STOCK, HYMAN. *The Method of Descartes in the Natural Sciences.* New York, 1931.

STORCH, A. *Nachtrag zur heutigen Beurteilung von Descartes.* See under RITTMEISTER, J.

SUDHOFF, KARL (ed.). *Historische Studien und Skizzen zur Natur- und Heilwissenschaft.* Berlin, 1930.

—— and MATTHIESSEN, WILHELM (eds.). *Paracelsus . . . Sämtliche Werke.* 14 vols. Munich, 1922–32.

WAERDEN, B.-L. VAN DER. *Einfall und Ueberlegung: Drei kleine Beiträge zur Psychologie des mathematischen Denkens.* Basel and Stuttgart, 1954.

WHITEHEAD, A. N. *Science and the Modern World.* New York, 1948.

WISDOM, J. O. "Three Dreams of Descartes," *International Journal of Psycho-Analysis,* Vol. XXVIII, Pt. 1. 1947.

YATES, FRANCES. *Giordano Bruno and the Hermetic Tradition.* London, 1964.

Psychological Aspects in Early Hasidic Literature

Siegmund Hurwitz
Translated by Hildegard Nagel

I. Introduction

A *Festschrift*, PUBLISHED IN 1944 by the Hebrew University in Jerusalem on the occasion of Professor Hugo Bergman's sixtieth birthday, included a short study by Gershom G. Scholem, Professor of Jewish Mysticism at that university, in which, among other matters, he referred to the very original and till then unknown concept of *qadmut-ha-sekhel* in the Hasidic writings of the so-called Maggid of Meseritz.[1] Here Scholem reached the conclusion that this concept—*qadmut-ha-sekhel*—comes close to that of the unconscious in modern psychology.

In the later years of the nineteenth century Ahron Marcus, a pupil of the Hasidic Rabbi of Radomsk, had already concerned himself with this problem. In an extensive study of the relation between certain concepts in Jewish literature and the philosophy of Leibniz, Schelling, and particularly Eduard von Hartmann, Marcus claimed that these concepts corresponded to the ideas of a preconscious or an unconscious.[2] He cited, among other sources, a little-known work by the Hasidic Rabbi Shneur Zalman of Ladi (1743–1813),[3] in which are found some strange, hitherto unknown concepts, namely, *qadmut-ha-sekhel* and *sekhel-ha-neelam*, which Marcus—

1. G. Scholem, *Ha-bilti moda we-mussag qadmut-ha-sekhel be sifruth ha-hassidith* ("The Unconscious and the Concept *qadmut-ha-sekhel* in Hasidic Literature") (Jerusalem, 1944).
2. Ahron Marcus, *Hartmanns induktive Philosophie im Chassidismus* (Vienna, 1888).
3. Shneur Zalman of Ladi, *Likkute Torah*, cit. Marcus.

perhaps basing himself on Fichte's idea of an "unconscious region" and Schelling's concept of a "preconscious"—has translated rather freely as "preintelligence" and the "unconscious."

Marcus investigated Kabbalistic as well as Hasidic literature. He tried to prove that a work by the Moroccan-Jewish scholar Hayim ben Atar (1696–1743) contained certain ideas which anticipated the concept of the unconscious as developed by Eduard von Hartmann about a hundred years later. His main purpose was to raise the question of priority and to decide it in favor of ben Atar.[4] However, the passages of ben Atar which he selected and in part translated into German are so unclear and confused that all attempts to explain them satisfactorily proved unsuccessful. In fact, it seems to me that even a partial explanation would be a hopeless task.

Although it was not possible to substantiate examples of any concept of the unconscious in Kabbalistic literature, there have been discovered, in the writings of Shneur Zalman of Ladi, a representative leader of the Hasidic movement, the emergence of certain ideas which are very close to the present-day conceptions of the unconscious.

Scholem has succeeded in showing that this concept—the *qadmut-ha-sekhel*—is by no means an original creation of Shneur Zalman of Ladi, but already appears in the older Hasidic writings of Rabbi Dov Baer of Meseritz. In the article referred to above, Scholem has assembled the pertinent passages contained in R. Dov Baer's works and painstakingly put them together, without, however, adding any psychological interpretation or elucidation. But what interests us here is less the historical sequence than the nature of these concepts, which have such interesting correspondences to the views of modern psychology.

As is well known, many writers and philosophers have evinced a kind of presentiment or intuitive awareness of the

---

4. Hayim ben Atar, *Or ha-hayim* ("The Light of Life"), *cit.* Marcus, *op. cit.*, p. 102. See also Scholem, *op. cit.*, p. 2.

existence of a preconscious or unconscious which precedes human consciousness, which forms a kind of dark psychic background to the bright foreground of conciousness. So Kant speaks of a "field of dark or obscure mental contents" (*Vorstellungen*).[5] Similar ideas are not difficult to point out in Leibniz, Schelling, and others.

About the middle of the eighteenth century these vague intuitions and speculations began to take more definite form and thereafter led to the true scientific "discovery" of the unconscious. That such ideas, among others, should also turn up in Kabbalistic-Hasidic writings seems to me significant and by no means an accident. For Hasidism is that movement which took over the heritage of mediaeval Jewish mysticism—of the Kabbalah—whose dominant concepts revolved around the focal points of God, the world, and the soul, and their interrelationship.

It seems improbable that Eduard von Hartmann, whose work on the unconscious first appeared in 1869,[6] or his perhaps even more important predecessor, C. G. Carus, had knowledge of the teachings of the Maggid of Meseritz, which were written in Hebrew and have not even yet been translated. The texts themselves should be important both from the standpoint of the history of the psychology of the unconscious and for an interpretation of the symbol content of mystical texts. With these ends in view I have tried to translate the quotations cited by Scholem as literally and faithfully as possible, with special attention to their meaning. Now and then, making use of the original text, I have quoted some passages at greater length.

To those unfamiliar with this material, these texts naturally present all kinds of difficulties. But even for those who have some access to the Kabbalah and to Hasidic mysticism they provide riddles enough. It is true that by a certain empathy one can come closer to their atmosphere, their mood, and

5. I. Kant, "Vom Erkenntnisvermögen," in *Anthropologie*, Vol I.
6. Eduard von Hartmann, *Philosophie des Unbewussten*, 3d ed. (Berlin, 1871).

their spirit; but without a particular psychological exposition and interpretation, important passages remain incomprehensible, especially—as is often the case—when they keep to symbolic language.

My study is based, on the one hand, on the psychology of C. G. Jung; on the other, on the results of Scholem's modern critical research on the Kabbalah. To Professor Scholem I am greatly indebted for his help and for much information, given both orally and in writing. I am grateful to Dr. Isaiah Tishby, of Jerusalem, for his valuable advice. The urge to undertake this work I owe above all to Professor Jung. His knowledge of religious psychology and his researches into the history of symbols have given me the key which opened the way into the strange and problematical world of Jewish mysticism.

II. THE GREAT MAGGID AND HASIDISM

HASIDISM is a Jewish religious revivalist movement which arose in eastern Europe at the beginning of the eighteenth century and encouraged a deeply rooted, truly religious feeling about life to find an outlet.[1]

From its birthplace in Poland this movement spread to Romania, Russia, and Lithuania, taking on a different coloration in each country. The great economic privation of the Jews at the beginning of the eighteenth century, as well as their widespread lack of political rights and protection, helped to provide a fertile ground for all sorts of mystical movements and heretical sects. Another factor was the inability of Talmudic studies—conditioned largely by thinking processes and able in some degree to satisfy rational consciousness—to open the way to any *religious* experience. As a result, especially in the combative early period of Hasidism,

1. S. A. Horodezky, *Religiöse Strömungen im Judentum. Mit besonderer Berücksichtigung des Chassidismus* (Bern and Leipzig, 1920); M. Buber, *Die chassidischen Bücher* (Berlin, 1927), and *Die Erzählungen der Chassidim* (Zurich, 1949); W. Rabinowitsch, *Der Karliner Chassidismus, seine Geschichte und Lehre* (Tel Aviv, 1935).

the study of the law and its commentaries is given relatively little place, and individual prayer gains particular importance.

Hasidism is one of those highly important mystical movements which in part existed alongside, and in part in secret or even open opposition to, the official concept of Judaism. It was defended as passionately as it was attacked by its more rational opponents, the *Mitnagdim.*

A central idea, which can be traced through the whole of Hasidism, is the unity of God and Nature. A typical proponent of this concept is the Maggid of Meseritz. According to him, "all things visible in the whole are vestures of the Godhead." Indeed, he even goes so far as to say that "God clothes himself in the very lowest levels of being, even in bad things." Therefore man must seek to grasp the inwardness of things, not the outer appearance, for all "the inner is God." [2]

Rabbinical Judaism centers its *Weltanschauung* in the "Law" or "Torah." In addition to the *written* law (*Torah she-bikhtav*), that is, the five books of Moses, there is also the teaching transmitted *orally*, the Talmud (*Torah she-be-al peh*). According to the Pharisaic view, the two Toroth were delivered to the Jewish people simultaneously, at the time of the Covenant between God and Israel on Mount Sinai. The binding character of both teachings, and their actualization by the individual and the collective, constitute the real starting point for the idea of Israel as the chosen people. The Talmud in its two sections, the Mishnah and the Gemarah, forms a kind of running commentary on the Torah by the learned scribes of five centuries. The study of the Torah and still more that of the Talmud occupies a large place in Rabbinical Judaism up to the present time. The Rabbinical ideal is therefore represented by the Scriptural scholar (*talmid hakham*). In Hasidism, on the other hand, the religious experience of the individual is put in the foreground. The direct confrontation of man with God, his being called by God, and the direct dialogue between God and man are the expressions of this deeply religious attitude. Hence it is not the scholar but

2. Horodezky, *op. cit.,* pp. 76 ff.

the Hasidic "holy one," the "*zaddik*," the "mediator," who as the ideal figure has put his stamp on the whole Hasidic movement. Here it does not so much matter what the *zaddik* teaches but what he himself is, how he lives, what kind of personality he has.

A pupil of the Great Maggid said: "Before I went to the Great Maggid and preacher of Meseritz, I studied eight hundred Kabbalistic books, but when, after all this, I came to the holy preacher, I perceived I had not really learned anything as yet." Another pupil reports that he had not sought out his teacher to learn about the Torah but to see how he fastened his bootlaces.

This stress on personalities and their individual attitudes was a step forward for Hasidism but at the same time entailed a danger. For it turned out that the exaggerated overvaluation of certain *zaddikim* led to a cult of Hasidic leaders and the founding of whole dynasties of *zaddikim* who were celebrated by the masses as miracle-workers, healers, and supermen, until finally their elevation went to their heads. And therewith began the decay and downfall of this movement.

The two streams—Hasidism and Rabbinism—are the outer expression and reflection of an inner spiritual development which was fated to flow in two opposite directions. Sometimes it is the more rational orientation which dominates consciousness, while everything irrational is repressed and falls into the unconscious. Then again, almost like a dynamic force of nature, there follows a breakthrough of irrational and, above all, mystical ideas which for centuries influence and shape consciousness itself. The two streams have fundamentally the same point of departure, namely, the Talmud. The rational movement is connected mainly with the sections of the Talmud that deal with religious law—the so-called Halakhah—and leads from there, by way of the so-called Rabbinism and the mediaeval religious philosophy of Maimonides, to modern orthodoxy. The irrational movement has its starting point, for the most part, in the similes, legends, myths, and, in general, the storytelling sections of the Talmud—the so-called Aggadah. From there it leads to the Jewish Apocalypse and the Jewish Gnosis and reaches its highest point in the Kabbalah. From here it goes on to the different, partly heretical, Messianic movements and finally to Hasidism. The conflict evidenced in the development of Judaism is naturally not confined to the spiritual history of the Jews. It can also be seen, for example, in mediaeval Christianity, where the more rational Scholastic theology of the Dominican Thomas Aquinas and the deeply introverted Franciscan mysticism of Bonaventura stand in strong contrast to each other. But in Judaism the opposites are more sharply contrasted and the tension between them is greater. The reason for this may be that the Jewish people entered upon the process of developing a culture relatively early and as a result was also confronted with the problem of the opposites, namely, the opposites of spirit and nature. The polarity in Judaism's spiritual development is perhaps most marked in the second half of the sixteenth century, at which time the learned and astute thinker Rabbi Joseph Karo wrote a super-commentary on Rabbi Jacob ben Asher's *Book of Turim*, as well as the *Shulhan arukh*, a detailed compendium of ritual law, while his most important pupil, Moses Cordovero, became one of the greatest intuitive-speculative mystics of the circle of Safed Kabbalists.[3] In spite of often coming danger-

3. The emergence of the unconscious opposite can be observed not only in a spiritual movement but frequently also in single individuals. Thus R. Joseph Karo is not solely a master of rabbinical dialectic. His mystical side shows clearly in his dream-diary, *Maggid mesharim* (Vilna, 1879), in which he describes his visionary experiences. H. L. Gordon has undertaken to explain Karo's inner experiences from the standpoint of psychopathology, but his psychological interpretations bypass the essential (H. L. Gordon, *The Maggid of Caro* [New York, 1949]). See also S. Hurwitz, "H. L. Gordon: The Maggid of Caro," *Schweiz. Zeitschrift f. Psychologie*, IV (1951).

It is certainly no accident that the most impassioned opposer of Hasidism, the Gaon Elijah of Vilna, was most deeply impressed by the Kabbalah and left behind him, among other things, several volumes of a commentary on the *Zohar*. Nor was the author of the *Summa theologica* an exclusively rationalistic thinker. On the contrary, his hymns and "sequences" show the depth of a real religious feeling.

ously close to heresy, neither Kabbalah nor Hasidism was expressly antinomistic. Their position was similar to that of alchemy, which, to be sure, often moved on the edge or borderline of official Christianity but never broke with it directly.

The founder of Hasidism, who became a legendary figure, was Rabbi Israel Baal Shem, the "Master of the Good Name," called Baalshem, or "Besht," for short (1700–1760). Tradition says that he withdrew for seven years into the solitude and seclusion of mountain and forest in order to seek God. His most important pupil was R. Dov Baer of Meseritz (*ca.* 1704–72).[4] It is told of him that he learned from his teacher "the language of birds and trees." Of the life of this Dov Baer—or, as he is also called, the Great Maggid (which means "preacher")—we have only scanty reports. He was born a few years later than the Baalshem in Lokaczy in Volhynia. As was usual at the time, he graduated from a Talmud school and then turned to the study of the Lurianic Kabbalah. He soon acquired a reputation as an important Talmudic scholar and profound Kabbalist. He began his career as a teacher in the village of Torczyn. Then he took up the calling of a wandering preacher and as such was active in various cities such as Koretz, Dubno, and Meseritz, where he preached penitence, asceticism, and spiritual change. His intensive studies and many self-chastisements finally undermined his already weakened health, so that he became very ill. Persuaded by his many friends, he made up his mind to go to the Baalshem, who was famous for his miracles and healing art. Hasidic tradition describes the meeting of the Maggid with the Baalshem most impressively and has embellished it with many legends. According to one version, the Baalshem demanded that his pupil interpret a difficult passage from *Ets hayim*

---

4. M. Buber, "Der Grosse Maggid und seine Nachfolge," in *Die chassidischen Bücher*; S. Dubnow, *Geschichte des Chassidismus* (Berlin, 1931) and *Weltgeschichte des Jüdischen Volkes* (Berlin, 1928), Vol. VII.

159 Psychological Aspects in Early Hasidism

("Tree of Life"), a work by the Kabbalist Hayim Vital; but the master rejected the Maggid's interpretation, which was limited to the literal meaning of the words, not because it was incorrect but because it omitted the "soul." As soon as the Baalshem began to expound the deeper meaning, the whole house was filled with light.[5] From this time on the Maggid remained with the Baalshem. He became his most gifted pupil and later his successor. His meeting with the master led to a profound *inner* transformation. The learned Talmudist became a true mystic. His ascetic attitude changed too and gave place to a positive yea-saying. After the Baalshem's death, the Maggid went to Meseritz, and, as a result, this city became the center and pilgrim goal for the whole Hasidic movement. The Maggid died in the year 1772, at a time when the conflict with the opposition had reached its highest point.

R. Dov Baer is one of the most important and profound mystics inside the Hasidic movement.[6] In contrast to the Kabbalists, who always tried to maintain the esoteric character of their teachings, his heart's desire was to bring Hasidism to the people, and for this purpose he sent his pupils as emissaries to the Jewish communities. As a result of his active propaganda, Hasidism spread very fast and soon gained a great following.

The Great Maggid left behind no written records. But his pupils wrote down his lectures and expositions of the Torah.[7] In this way a number of collections of notations were made and preserved:

   5. M. Buber, *Die Erzählungen der Chassidim*, pp. 193 ff.
   6. G. Scholem says of the Maggid of Meseritz (*Major Trends in Jewish Mysticism* [Jerusalem, 1941; New York, 1946]): "If one studies the writings of Rabbi Baer of Meseritz, the most important follower of the Baal Shem and the real organizer of the movement, one sees immediately, that in them the old ideas and conceptions, all of which duly make their appearance, have lost their stiffness and received a new infusion of life by going through the fiery stream of a truly mystical mind."
   7. A. Z. Aescoli-Weintraub, *Introduction à l'étude des hérésies religieuses parmi les Juifs: La Kabbale, le Hassidisme* (Paris, 1928).

a. *Maggid debarab le-Jaaqob o likkute amarim* ("Reporters of His Words to Jacob, or Selections from His Talks"). Koretz, 1781, and Berdichev, 1808, the latter edition with the approbation of R. Levy Isaac of Berdichev. The book is not to be confused with the work of the same title *Likkute amarim* or *Tanya*, written by a pupil of the Maggid, Shneur Zalman of Ladi. *Maggid debarab le-Jaaqob* was assembled by another pupil of the Great Maggid, Solomon of Lusk, who says in his Foreword that the master had commissioned him to write down his teachings and to publish them at a later time.[8]
b. *Or ha-emeth o imre zaddikim* ("Light of Truth or Words of the Just"). Shitomir, 1890.[9]
c. *Or Torah* ("Light of the Torah"). Koretz, 1804. Based on a manuscript written by R. Isaiah of Dunayewzy. A collection of sermons by the Great Maggid.

Fragments of lectures and sayings of the Maggid are found, along with other material, in the following work:

d. *Likkute yeqarim* ("Precious Collection"). Lemberg, 1792, and Koretz, 1804. The book contains quotations from "four men who walked most excellently along the paths of God," namely, the Baalshem, Dov Baer of Meseritz, R. Mendel of Przemyslany, and R. Michel of Zloczow. The author is R. Meshullam Feibush of Zbaraz, who in his youth had been acquainted with the Great Maggid.

---

8. The photocopy of the Lublin edition of 1927, which I have before me, has a quite different pagination from that of the first edition used by Scholem. The page numbers here refer to the Lublin edition.

9. Dubnow, whose ideas on Hasidism are one-sidedly rationalistic and often unfair and therefore must be very carefully evaluated, holds this book to be a forgery, but in my opinion without sufficient proof (Dubnow, *Geschichte des Chassidismus*, I, 148, n. 2). Scholem is convinced of the authenticity of this work (G. Scholem, *Ha-bilti moda we mussag qadmut-ha-sekhel be sifruth ha-hassidith* ["The Unconscious and the Concept *qadmut-ha-sekhel* in Hasidic Literature"] [Jerusalem, 1944], p. 3).

161 Psychological Aspects in Early Hasidism

Other sayings of the Great Maggid are to be found scattered among the works of Zeev Wolf of Shitomir,[10] Elimelech of Lisensk,[11] and Nahum of Chernobyl.[12]

As I have mentioned before, the aim of this work is to investigate certain psychological concepts of the Great Maggid and a few of his followers and to point out their background. Our concern will be with those ideas which are related to the concept *qadmut-ha-sekhel*. For the better understanding of the texts I will begin by saying that, in agreement with Scholem, I believe that the concept *qadmut-ha-sekhel* must be equated with the unconscious. To support this theory I shall quote all those passages in *Maggid debarab le-Jaaqob* and *Or ha-emeth* in which the expression *qadmut-ha-sekhel* occurs.

Since these texts interest us primarily from the psychological standpoint, we will evaluate them as the statements of a human being whose consciousness shows a definite structure. We will begin by investigating the conscious standpoint of the author. On the other hand, we must also look at these texts as manifestations of this man's unconscious, which modifies and shapes his consciousness. This psychological approach, oriented toward the unconscious psychic background, requires a special method of text interpretation, having much in common with the interpretation of other contents of the unconscious.

The psychological method of interpreting dreams, images, or texts involves certain difficulties. For in order to understand the real meaning of a dream, image, or text, we generally make ourselves familiar with the context. In the case of a dream, we get the context by a consideration of the dreamer's association to the dream images. In this way light is thrown on the often obscure passages and they are brought closer to

10. Zeev Wolf of Shitomir, *Or ha-meir* ("Shining Light") (Koretz, 1798).
11. Elimelech of Lisensk, *Noam Elimelech* ("The Bliss of Elimelech") (Warsaw, 1881).
12. Nahum of Chernobyl, *Meor einayim* ("Light of the Eyes") (Slavuta, 1798).

our understanding. This method of clarification, enrichment, and extension or amplification has been prescribed and used by C. G. Jung. It can be employed whenever and wherever the object is to make unconscious contents accessible to understanding. In our case the author's associations are not obtainable, since he never explains his images and symbols precisely. It is true that the Great Maggid speaks very frequently in his lectures about "wisdom" or "discriminating reason." But these in the main have already become psychological concepts and are the expressions of a rational consciousness. The symbol, which is the adequate expression of the irrational, remains relatively in the background. Indeed, one often has the impression that, though these symbols are certainly current and familiar to the Maggid, they have lost much of their immediate vitality. Yet we are less concerned with interpretating and explaining the Maggid's psychological concepts than we are with understanding his symbols. Since the Maggid's other writings do not help us much, it seems preferable to go back directly to those sources which were not only known to the author but from which he actually starts. In these writings the images and symbols still emerge in their original freshness and distinctness. These writings are, first of all, the *Book Bahir*, from the early period of the Kabbalah, and, next in line, the chief work of the Kabbalah, the *Zohar;* of some importance also is the late Kabbalistic literature stemming from the Lurianic movement.[13] The symbolism of the *Bahir* and the *Zohar* is not

13. The quotations from the *Zohar* cited in this study have been directly translated from the original Aramaic text, using the editions of Rom (Vilna, 1882) and Reuben Margulies (*Sefer ha-Zohar* [Jerusalem, 1940–46]). For comparative purposes I have also used the often faulty translations in English (*The Zohar*, translated by Harry Sperling and Maurice Simon [London, 1931–34 and 1949]) and in German (*Der Sohar: Das Heilige Buch der Kabbala*, translated from the original text by Ernst Müller [Vienna, 1932]). I was also greatly assisted by the outstanding work contributed by the school of Scholem, *Mishnath ha-Zohar* ("Textual Passages from the *Zohar*"), arranged according to subject and translated into Hebrew by P. Lachower and Isaiah Tishby, with explanations, Introduction, and text variations by Isaiah Tishby (Jerusalem, 1949).

163 *Psychological Aspects in Early Hasidism*

expounded by the Maggid, since he obviously assumes it to be familiar. By returning to these sources, we shall be able to reconstruct an objective context.

An exclusively rationally oriented consciousness may at first find such a method open to question. But we must bear in mind that Hasidic mysticism cannot be regarded as a unique historical development, a single fruit which only once ripened spontaneously on the tree of Jewish religion. Such a point of view not only leaves historical continuity out of consideration; it also does not do justice to a psychic phenomenon such as Jewish mysticism. For Hasidism is only one phase of Jewish mysticism, the beginnings of which reach back to the Talmudic period. During this same period there existed important—though by no means yet clarified—interrelations with pagan-Christian Gnosticism, Manichaeism, Neoplatonism, and alchemy. To me the psychological explanation for this is that beyond the area of our personal consciousness we find ourselves in an unknown dark region in which we meet with the more ancient strata of the human soul. Out of these deeper realms of the collective unconscious stem the strange images and symbols which are often incomprehensible to us. The assumption of a collective unconscious is neither a foggy speculation nor a heuristic principle. It is the recognition of an empirical fact which has long been demonstrated and confirmed. And, as archaic images and symbols which correspond strikingly with the symbols of Gnosticism and mediaeval alchemy are often found in the spontaneous manifestions of the unconscious of modern people, so Kabbalistic symbols can be traced in the dreams, visions, and phantasies of modern Jews.

The situation in regard to the Hasidim of the eighteenth century was undoubtedly clearer, since with them the Kabbalistic tradition was completely self-evident and alive. Kabbalistic works were studied for centuries on end; manuscripts were copied and, after the introduction of printing, were constantly reprinted in new editions. The first printing of the *Zohar* took place in Mantua and Cremona during the middle of the sixteenth century. Since then there have been not less than eighty known editions, the last appearing in 1945. Another outstanding Kabbalistic work, mentioned above, is the *Book Bahir,* the origin of which is obscure and which has come down to us through the thirteenth-century circle of mystics in Provence. It was printed for the first time in the year 1651 and was reprinted as recently as 1883. The work *Shaareh orah,* by the Spanish Kabbalist Joseph Gikatilla (*ca.* 1300), was printed over and over again between 1560 and 1880. It was not until the so-called emancipation of the Jews in the nineteenth century—that is, their gaining equal civil and political rights, which led to the disappearance of the ghettos and the breaking-up of their outer collective—that the long historical continuity was interrupted. But the emancipation could not cut the lines of connection with the spirit and the unconscious traditions. These values have sunk into the unconscious, but in certain constellations of fate they emerge as mysterious changelings or split-off pieces of the personality, or, erupting into the field of consciousness, they may uncover an unconscious, profoundly religious problem.

One peculiarity of our texts will continue to occupy us in many ways. The author of *Maggid debarab le-Jaaqob* discusses phenomena of whose expressly psychic character he himself can have no doubt. This is shown clearly by the whole context in which the passages are embedded. Consciousness and the unconscious—thought and prethought, as he terms them—are, according to his conception, psychic conditions or processes which stand in reciprocal relation to each other. Hence it is not surprising that the Great Maggid employs his own psychological terminology. It enables him to characterize his subject as what it is: a psychological event, i.e., a happening in the soul.

But, along with these psychological concepts, the author employs other designations; he introduces philosophical terms and finally has recourse to mystical symbols, which he uses to bring closer to us, to describe, and to interpret phenomena like the conscious and the unconscious. And that brings us to

165 *Psychological Aspects in Early Hasidism*

the real kernel of the problem that we must try to answer. How can we explain the fact that the Great Maggid speaks to us in a language that is at once theological-mystical, abstract-philosophical, and conceptual-psychological when the questions he deals with are apparently neither theological nor philosophical but exclusively psychological? How does he come to introduce symbols stemming from Jewish mysticism which have an expressly numinous character? Does he use this symbolic language because for him the Kabbalistic symbol is something familiar and living and is especially well fitted to give expression to a state of things of which he is halfway conscious and for which he lacks the adequate psychological means of expression? If this is the case, we should have to ask a further question: Why does the Great Maggid not confine himself to the purely symbolic? What makes him add to this a psychological language of his own creation? Does he perhaps make use of philosophical and psychological concepts because the symbol no longer satisfies his rational *consciousness?* But in that case the extensive use of mystical symbolism is difficult to understand.

We will begin by stating the question, without anticipating its answer. The following discussions are at bottom no more than a series of amplifications which result from the very statement of the problem, even when they often appear somewhat far-fetched. In order not to overburden this complicated subject, material not directly related to our problem has been omitted.

III. Consciousness and the Unconscious

(*Sekhel* and *qadmut-ha-sekhel*)

Text Passage 1

The force of intelligence [*habanah*] has its seat in the heart—corresponding to the saying "The heart is intelli-

gent"—for there it receives [its content or influence] from the uppermost level, [i.e.] the unconscious [*qidmat-ha-sekhel*].
(*Maggid debarab le-Jaaqob*, p. 18a)

Commentary

THIS TEXT shows how the Great Maggid makes use of different kinds of terms for one and the same concept. Insofar as he speaks of the "uppermost level," he is moving entirely within the world of traditional Kabbalistic concepts. In applying to this level the term *qadmut-ha-sekhel*, he creates a new and hitherto unknown psychological concept, the concept of the unconscious. So here the Kabbalistic symbol and the psychological concept are juxtaposed and made interchangeable. Therefore, to understand the text, we are forced to examine both symbol and concept more closely. We must become acquainted with the meaning and the content of the particular symbol and also with the etymological meaning and the content of the concept he has originated. So, for the better understanding of our texts, we shall begin with a brief account of the historical development of the Kabbalah and of a few of its basic contents.[1]

Kabbalah means "transmittal, tradition." Originally every transmittal was termed Kabbalah. But in the course of time the term acquired an increasingly particular meaning, and since about the period of the thirteenth century it has been understood as referring to the mystical-esoteric tradition of Judaism.

Mystical currents can be traced in Judaism as far back as the Talmudic period. It is said of many teachers, for example of Rabbi Akiba, that they had "trod the *pardes*," that is, had

---

1. Cf. especially A. Franck, *Die Kabbala oder die Religionsphilosophie der Hebräer* (Berlin, 1922); D. H. Joel, *Die Religionsgeschichte des Sohar* (Berlin, 1918); and G. Scholem, *Die Geheimnisse der Schöpfung* (Berlin, 1935), *Major Trends in Jewish Mysticism* (Jerusalem, 1941; New York, 1946), and *Die jüdische Mystik in ihren Hauptströmungen* (Zurich, 1957).

devoted themselves to mystical vision. The speculations of these early mystics circled around two focal points: Creation mysticism devoted itself to the Genesis myth of Creation (*maaseh bereshith*), while throne mysticism focused upon the prophet Ezekiel's vision of the Chariot Throne of God (*maaseh merkabah*). Meditation and inward vision were practiced, especially in the smaller mystic circles and in the conventicles of "those who descend to gaze on the *merkabah*" (*yorde merkabah*).

Between the third and sixth post-Christian centuries there appeared a darkly oracular book in Hebrew, the "Book of Creation" (*Yetsirah*). It already contains a complete account of the divine primal numbers, the so-called Sefiroth. The Kabbalah attained its first bloom during the twelfth century, in Provence, in the circle of Abraham ben David of Posquières and Isaac the Blind. In this period the "Book of Splendor" (*Bahir*), whose origins are completely obscure, gained general attention. Somewhat later, in the city of Gerona, in northern Spain, a new Kabbalistic center gathered around Azriel and Nachmanides. Abraham Abulafia developed his own technique of mystical contemplation. His pupil Joseph Gikatilla, in his book *Shaareh orah*, wrote the first systematic work on the symbolism of the Sefiroth. In Spain also, at the end of the thirteenth century, appeared the chief work of the older Kabbalah, the "Book of Radiance" (*Zohar*), which for nearly three centuries was given a position of canonical dignity and validity along with the Bible and the Talmud. After the Spanish tragedy of 1492 the Kabbalah experienced a second blooming in Palestine. But there the Safed movement, led by Isaac Luria and his followers, gave the older Kabbalah what was really a new shape. The Kabbalah had a decisive influence on the heretical movement known as Sabbatianism, and especially on Hasidism, which became the true inheritor of the Kabbalah. To be sure, the spiritual content of the Kabbalah was modified in many respects, and the mystical movement lost its expressly esoteric character.

Jewish religious philosophy—from Saadia to Maimonides—tried again and again to free the Jewish concept of God of all mystical traits. The God-image of the Kabbalists is mystical in nature. It appears to them, much as it did to the Gnostics, in the great symbols and primal images of the human soul.[2]

Like most Gnostic systems, from Satornilos, Basilides, and Valentinian to Markion, the Kabbalah differentiates between an absolute, unknowable Nothing, called the "Infinite" (*en Sof*), and a multiplicity of its manifestations in which the Hidden God—the ἄγνωστος θεός—reveals himself and becomes visible.[3] *En Sof* lies outside space and time; it is the undivided, self-enclosed being of God, inaccessible to the meditation or the cognition of men.[4] And the most intensive efforts of the Kabbalists are directed toward grasping and encompassing the nature of this mystic Nothing in ever new paradoxical images. *En Sof* is the "most closed of all things," "the beginning of every beginning which is not yet a beginning"; it has "form and no form," and so forth.[5]

From out of this state of hiddenness *en Sof* emerges in a drama of intradivine development. But the inner event has a correspondence in the realm of created beings. What man experiences *inwardly* as a manifestation of God emerging from the primal state of inaccessibility appears to him *out-*

---

2. G. Scholem, "Kabbalah und Mythus," *Eranos-Jahrbuch 1949* (Zurich, 1950).

3. Cf. the differentiation between God and divinity. Of the latter Eckhart says: ". . . its simple nature is formless of form, beingless of being, and thingless of things" (Fr. von Pfeiffer, *Meister Eckhart* [Göttingen, 1906], II, 497, 34 ff.).

4. Jacob Boehme says: "For one cannot say of God that he is this or that, evil or good, that he has differences within himself: for He is in Himself nature-less, as well as affect- and creature-less. He has no inclination toward anything, for there is nothing before Him toward which He could incline, whether evil or good: He is himself the bottomless void [*Ungrund*] without any will as regards nature or creature except as an eternal nothing. . . . He is the Nothing" (Jacob Boehme, *Von der Genaden-Wahl* [Leipzig, 1924], Chap. I).

5. G. Scholem, *Reshith ha-kabbala* ("The Beginnings of Kabbalah") (Jerusalem, 1949), pp. 176 f.

wardly as a cosmogony. Here we meet with an idea, also current in Hermetic philosophy, that everything above corresponds to something below—or in modern terms, that everything inner corresponds to an outer something. So for the Kabbalists—to give only one example—the Exodus from Egypt is indeed a historical fact, but, at the same time, this outer event refers to an inner one, namely, to an inner exodus from the inner slavery to an inner freedom.

The inner life of the self-unfolding, self-differentiating, and self-revealing God becomes visible in various aspects, which in the Kabbalah are described as powers, degrees, words, roots, radiations, or as primal numbers (Sefiroth).[6] There has been no lack of attempts to relate this evolution of God to Gnostic Neoplatonic concepts of emanation, particularly as they occur in Plotinus and Proclus. But the Sefiroth do not really represent mediating elements between the bright, good realm of light of the spirit and the dark, evil realm of matter, although the Sefiroth theory has certain relations to the Valentinian gnosis and its doctrine of archons.[7] According to many Kabbalists the Sefiroth exist only in the minds of men.[8] Seen from the human standpoint, it is in them that the undifferentiated God unfolds himself and becomes accessible in his different aspects to human meditation and cognition. Seen from *en Sof*, these differences do not exist; there is only "the one stream of divine life," for it is said of the *en Sof:* "They

---

6. The name Sefirah has no linguistic connection with the Greek *Sphaira* but derives rather from the Hebrew root *Sfr*, which means "to count, add up, give an account of." The term used in Hebrew for "number," however, is not *sefirah* but *mispar*, which is also derived from the stem *sfr*. *Sefirah*—in contradistinction to *mispar*—does not mean number as an instrument of counting but number as idea, number as such or as a spiritual principle of structure. It is in this sense that Azriel of Gerona calls the Sefiroth "potentialities of all reality that is definable in numbers" (Azriel of Gerona, *Perush esser sefiroth;* cf. G. Scholem, art. "Kabbala," *Encyclop. Jud.*, IX, 27 ff., 33 f.).
7. Scholem, *Reshith ha-kabbala*, pp. 104 f.
8. I. Tishby, *Mishnath ha-Zohar* (Jerusalem, 1949), pp. 104 f.

are He, and He is they." [9] And the *Bahir* says that the *en Sof* is "One in all His names." [10]

In the classical arrangement of the Kabbalah the ten Sefiroth are as follows:

en Sof
kether (1)

binah (3)   *hokhmah* (2)
din (5)   *hesed* (4)
                 tifereth (6)
hod (8)   *netsah* (7)
                 yesod (9)
                 malkuth (10)

Nothing
crown (1)

intelligence (3)   wisdom (2)
stern judgment (5)   mercy (4)
                 beauty (6)
                 (compassion)
majesty (8)   lasting endurance (7)
                 foundation (9)
                 kingdom (10)

Generally the crown (*kether*) was held by the Kabbalists to be the first manifestation of the *en Sof*. This *en Sof* is the mystical "primal nothingness" or the "nothing" of the Kabbalists, out of which all the other Sefiroth emanate.

Many Kabbalists sometimes introduce another Sefirah, namely *daath* or knowledge, which forms a balance between the two polar opposites of *hokhmah* and *binah*:

binah (2)   *hokhmah* (1)
                 daath (3)

---

9. *Zohar*, III, 70a.
10. *Bahir*, § 96. Psychologically this means that the collective unconscious is, to begin with, a completely undifferentiated totality which, however, from man's viewpoint appears in a wealth of archetypal figures and images.

These three Sefiroth represent not only three different aspects of the Godhead as it unfolds itself but, beyond this, three stages in the development of all things: in the beginning they are hidden in the divine wisdom, they become manifest in discriminating reason, and they can become knowable in the knowledge of God.

Now for the Maggid of Meseritz the "highest degree" was not *kether* but the succeeding Sefirah, *hokhmah*. This conception probably found its way into Hasidism under the influence of the late Kabbalistic trend stemming from Isaac Luria. This was all the more likely because in Hasidism the old Kabbalistic symbols are no longer strictly differentiated or held separate from one another. Thus under certain conditions well-defined attributes are transferred from *en Sof* to *kether* and from *kether* to *en Sof*.

Out of divine wisdom unfolds the Sefirah *binah* ("discriminating reason or intelligence"). This corresponds to the "intellectual power" (*habanah*) mentioned in our text, for which there is an etymological basis (*habanah-binah*).[11] For both words derive from the root *bin*, which originally had the meaning of "divine, separate." In its figurative sense it also means "to perceive," and in the so-called causative (*hiphil*) form it means, above all, "to distinguish, to understand." Hence the noun *binah* also means "understanding, comprehension, intelligence" and clearly carries the original meaning of discrimination and separation between two opposites. Like every Sefirah, *binah* evolves out of the preceding Sefirah, in this case *hokhmah*. In this way the two has sprung from the one, which is its polar opposite. Insofar as this developmental process is carried out in the Sefirotic world, it is an event in the divine realm. But according to the Kabbalistic conception, this happening within the Godhead has an exact correspondence in a parallel process within the human soul. Thus the unfolding of the *binah* out of the *hokhmah* is a divine and, at the same time, a human process. It is for this reason that

11. J. Grasowsky, *Milon shimushi le-safa ha-ivrith* (Tel Aviv, 1937).

our text says that the force of intelligence receives its influence or its content from the *hokhmah* in the heart of the human being.

The heart is the central point of the circulation of the blood and consequently the real center of vegetative life. It pushes the blood into the peripheral organs and sucks it back again. According to the ancient Jewish conception, blood is the carrier of the so-called "blood-soul" or is even identical with it.[12] Therefore it is said: "For out of it [the heart] are the issues of life."[13] But in Biblical and Talmudic literature the heart is also held to be the source of all the activities of the soul. It is the seat of sensation, feeling, emotions, and affects. Joy, sorrow, anxiety, sympathy, despair, fear, and anger come from the heart. But thoughts and concepts also stem from the heart, and so it becomes the real seat of understanding and knowledge. A "wide" heart, an encompassing heart, means the same as an encompassing understanding. The phrase "an understanding heart"[14] means a heart that is possessed of understanding and insight and that strives for knowledge. The Midrash says: "The kidneys give counsel, the heart judges, and the tongue speaks."[15] According to the Talmud, the heart is also the seat of the impulse toward evil, which is found between the two chambers of the heart.[16]

In our text, which is based on a quotation from the Talmud,[17] the heart is above all the place where the *habanah* or *binah* comes into being. Here the separation of *hokhmah* and *binah* is consummated. This gives the heart the character of a comprehensive and superordinate totality. The Kabbalah sometimes calls it the king of the organs (*mlk*), and indeed in a double sense: on the one hand as the superordinate central

---

12. Lev. 17:14: "For it [the blood] is the life [*nefesh*, 'soul'] of all flesh."
13. Prov. 4:23.
14. Prov. 15:14: "The heart of him that hath understanding seeketh knowledge: but the mouth of fools feedeth on foolishness."
15. *Midrash rabba ad Levit.*
16. *Talmud Babyl. Tractate Berakhot,* 61a.
17. *Ibid.*

173 Psychological Aspects in Early Hasidism

organ, on the other as a connecting middle member between brain and liver.[18]

In the *Bahir* the word "heart," which carries the number value 32, is brought into relation with the "thirty-two hidden paths of wisdom," mentioned in the *Book Yetsirah*, which represent the spiritual foundations of the world.[19]

In the manuscript copy of Isaac the Blind's commentary on the *Book Yetsirah*, dating from the beginning of the thirteenth century, the heart appears as the seat of the Sefiroth: "And all the higher potencies are given, that they may be meditated upon. For every potency [issues] [20] from a potency above it, and they are given [or transmitted] in the *heart* [21] of him who prays, that he may meditate, meditate as far as the infinite [as far as *en Sof*]."[22] The potencies correspond to that which the Kabbalah later designated as the Sefiroth. In this text the Sefiroth appear in the heart of the meditator and are thus characterized as a kind of psychic reality that can be the object of meditation and contemplation.

The Maggid of Meseritz has given the Sefirah *ḥokhmah*—or rather that which corresponds to it in the human sphere—an extremely striking and original designation, namely, that of "preconscious" (*qadmut* or, in another read-

18. This concept is based on a play on words. In the word *melek* (*mlk*) the *l* forms the center between *m* and *k*. These letters are at the same time the initials of the words:

$$\begin{aligned} m\textit{oah} &= \text{brain} \\ l\textit{eb} &= \text{heart} \qquad mlk = \text{king} \\ k\textit{abed} &= \text{liver} \end{aligned}$$

So one can say that, just as the letter *l* represents the connection between *m* and *k*, so the heart (*leb*) is the connecting center between brain (*moah*) and liver (*kabed*) and therewith the king of these organs.

19. According to the *Bahir* (§ 43, p. 76) "heart refers to the number 32" (since its numerical value is 32), namely, the "thirty-two hidden paths of wisdom" by means of which, according to the *Book Yetsirah*, the world was created.

20. According to the Vatican MS. reading: "fills itself."

21. My italics.

22. MS. Abraham Graziano (at Hebrew Union College, Cincinnati), cit. Scholem, "Der Begriff der Kawwana in der alten Kabbala," *Monatsschrift für Geschichte und Wissenschaft des Judentums* (1934), pp. 496 ff.

ing, *qidmat-ha-sekhel*). In order to understand this concept, we must examine its etymology more closely.

The Hebrew noun *sekhel* is already used in the Bible with the meaning of "having insight or understanding, behaving wisely, or making with skill" (Isa. 44:18; Jer. 9:23). *Sekhel* is translated differently, by different authors, as "understanding, insight, or reason."[23]

The corresponding Arabic term *aql* is likewise translated by most Arabic scholars as "intellect, understanding, reason." All the other expressions which the Maggid also uses for *sekhel*, as *binah* ("intelligence"), *habanah* ("power of understanding"), and *mahashabah* ("thinking, idea") are close to the concepts of reason, understanding, intellect. But in our text it can hardly be solely a matter of what one usually designates psychologically as intellect, that is, directed thought.[24] This in my opinion would be a completely inadmissible narrowing of the concept. The term *sekhel* can, it is true, also mean "intelligence, reason" (*ratio*); but just as often it corresponds much more to what one would call spirit (*nous*) in contrast to matter (*hylē*) and to conscious thinking, or even simply consciousness.

The nouns *qadma*, *qidma*, *qadmut*, and *qadmuta* have as their primary meaning "origin,"[25] "earlier state."[26] In their verb form they mean, above all, precedence in time.[27] Accordingly, *qadmut* or *qidmat-ha-sekhel* would mean a kind of thinking, conceiving, or consciousness which preceded the actual thinking, conceiving, or consciousness of the moment. This kind of thinking is termed by A. Marcus—somewhat

---

23. J. von Hammer, *Encyclopädische Uebersicht der Wissenschaften des Orients, aus sieben arabischen und türkischen Werken übersetzt* (Leipzig, 1804); A. Weiss, "*Führer der Unschlüssigen*": *Deutsche Uebersetzung* (Frankfurt a.M., 1845).

24. C. G. Jung, *Psychological Types*, trans. H. G. Baynes (London and New York, 1926).

25. Gesenius-Buhl, *Hebräisches und arabisches Handwörterbuch über das A.T.* (Leipzig, 1910).

26. Grasowsky, *op. cit.*

27. S. M. Laser and H. Torczyner, *Deutsch-hebräisches Wörterbuch* (Berlin, 1927).

arbitrarily—as "preconsciousness." In contrast to this, the concept *qadmut-ha-sekhel* implies a later thought, idea, or consciousness that not only follows the *qadmut-ha-sekhel* in time but is also dependent upon it. Moreover, this kind of thinking is related to a central point, as will be seen still more clearly in the following passage.

Even these few statements are evidence enough to allow us to assume it probable that the concepts *sekhel* and *qadmut-ha-sekhel* refer to the conscious and the unconscious.

Text Passage 2

A thought [*mahashabah*] . . . is comprehensible to oneself, but to others not comprehensible. But the unconscious [*qadmut-ha-sekhel*] is not even comprehensible to oneself. Therefore it says in the verse "the hidden is God's, the revealed is ours," even that name of God: YHWH our God.

(*Maggid debarab le-Jaaqob*, p. 22a)

Commentary

Here the Great Maggid introduces a new term, *mahashabah*. The primary meaning of *mahashabah* is "thinking," but it can also mean "what is thought" and thence a "plan, intention, project." The expression derives from *hashob*, which is equivalent to "thinking" but also means "to count" and "to calculate." It is clearly a purposeful and directed activity related to the person of the thinker and is, as such, conscious. In the same way, the closely related term *binah*— discriminating consciousness—implies in this context a conscious activity, insofar as an act of becoming conscious is possible only through the perception and differentiation of opposites. It is therefore not far-fetched to equate the concept *sekhel*, and also *binah* and *mahashabah*, in our text with conscious thinking, conscious conceiving, in short, with consciousness as such, while *qadmut-ha-sekhel,* as that which precedes consciousness, is taken to correspond to the unconscious.

The unconscious—as our text says—is not comprehensible to oneself. Indeed we can say nothing whatever about the unconscious directly; it is for us simply the unknown. It is accessible to us only indirectly through its effects upon the sphere of consciousness, which make it possible to try to "translate" its image-language into the conceptual language of consciousness. This gives a special significance to the statement in our text that the unconscious belongs to a "hidden," that is, a divine, realm, but consciousness to one that is "revealed," that is, human.[28]

Text Passage 3

When there comes to the Hasidic holy one [*zaddik*] one of the seven thoughts out of the unconscious [*qadmut-ha-sekhel*], then he should hold on [to this thought] and free it [from its sensual disguise or imprisonment] . . . for it is in Israel's power to lead everything back to *hokhmah,* the source of Israel.

(*Maggid debarab le-Jaaqob,* p. 22a)

---

28. This passage is contained in a wider context which gives a pronounced mystic interpretation to the familiar verse (Deut. 29:29): "The secret things belong unto the Lord our God: but those things that are revealed belong to us . . ." (*ha-nistaroth le YHWH elohenu, we ha-nigloth lanu*). The author of the *Maggid debarab le-Jaaqob* asks himself, among other things, why in this verse the phrase *we ha-nigloth* ("*and* the revealed") contains the last two letters, the *waw* and the *he,* of the four-letter name of God YHWH—the so-called tetragram—while, on the other hand, *ha-nistaroth* ("*the* secret things") contains a *he* but not, as one would expect, also a *yod.* If so, the complete tetragram would have expressed the totality of the divine and the human realms. The omission of the final letter *yod* in this verse is explained by the author as meaning that the *qadmut-ha-sekhel*—which corresponds to the *yod*—is beyond the grasp of mankind. Consequently the tetragram is not complete, either. For further discussion of tetragram symbolism, see pp. 210 ff.

Commentary

This passage is difficult to interpret. It begins by saying that thoughts from the unconscious can fall into a man's mind. In ordinary speech we say that such thoughts "pop up" or "fall into" one's head. Now whether—keeping to this image—they pop up from "below" or fall from "above," in either case these thoughts or sudden ideas come from a psychic level which lies outside our consciousness.

Here "the seven thoughts" obviously mean seven kinds of thought of differing quality. These seven thoughts constitute an inner unity, for they are not spoken of as simply seven but as "the" seven thoughts. This implies that we have before us a very definite, delimited unity, a kind of septet. In order to explain these seven thoughts, I want to refer to a later passage of the *Maggid debarab le-Jaaqob*, where it says:

> All thoughts in their entirety in the seven ways of being [modes] correspond to the seven days of the Building, so, for example, to love, fear, etc. On every level there are good and— God preserve us from them—evil [thoughts]. The seven evil ones would also bring the seven peoples back to life. When, therefore, an evil thought enters a man, he should search out exactly what level [side] it belongs to. He should say to himself: "What have I done, that I have taken a part of the world of thoughts and thrown it on the place of dirt?" Therefore he ought to humble himself and lead this thought back to the level of "nothingness." [29]

Here the seven thoughts of the text are brought into connection with the seven lower Sefiroth. The division of the ten Sefiroth into an upper group of three and a lower group of seven has been found as early as the Kabbalistic circle in Gerona. While the three upper Sefiroth (*kether, hokhmah,* and *binah*) are called the "Sefiroth of the world" (*Sefiroth shel olam*), the seven lower Sefiroth, from *hesed* to *malkuth*, represent the "Sefiroth of the Building" (*Sefiroth shel bin-*

---

29. *Maggid debarab le-Jaaqob*, p. 25a.

yan). The latter also correspond to the seven days of Creation, hence the designation "days of the Building." This has nothing to do with the separate days of the week but refers to their cosmic archetypal image, that is, to the First Days, which in their totality represent the prototypal week.

The seven thoughts or contents from the seven lower Sefiroth are regarded in this passage under the aspect of a certain moral or ethical symbolism and are called love, fear, etc. These contents ascend up to the "highest level," *hokhmah*, and from here are transmitted through the *binah*.

From the standpoint of moral evaluation, these thoughts could be separated into good and evil. It appears that here the Maggid of Meseritz was thinking of certain conceptions of evil which had acquired central importance in the *Zohar* and in the Kabbalah in general. There, to be sure, disparate answers had been given to the old Gnostic query, *unde malum*, whence the evil? One of the most widespread conceptions—obviously shared by the Maggid—is to the effect that the divine realm of light of the bright pure Sefiroth is opposed by an equally dark, demonic countersphere, consisting of evil, impure Sefiroth. That is the Kabbalists' "other side" (*sitra ahra*). A man should therefore determine whether the thoughts or ideas arising out of the unconscious issue from the bright or the demonic realm.[30]

The emerging thought is now to be set free—literally "pulled away"—from all the residues of sensual nature in which it is still caught. This is obviously a process of abstraction, of extracting or "pulling out" something. According to

---

30. Quite possibly, in referring to the seven thoughts, the author of the *Maggid debarab le-Jaaqob* had also in mind the ancient Midrashic tradition which says that there are "seven things" which existed before the creation of the world. As related in the *Pirke Rabbi Eliezer*, cit. Micha ben Gorion, *Die Sagen der Juden* (Berlin, 1935), pp. 19 f.: "Seven things were created before the world was created, and they preceded the Creation by two thousand years. These were: the Scriptures, the Throne of His Glory, the Garden of Eden, and Hell, penance, the highest temple and the Messiah. But the Name of the Messiah shone even before the sun was there." Earlier, in the *Talmud Babyl. Pesakim*, 54a, the seven appear in a different sequence.

Maimonides, abstraction represents a kind of thinking by which essential characteristics are differentiated from the unessential.[31] According to Jung, abstraction is

> the drawing out or isolation of a content (e.g., a meaning or general character, etc.) from a connection, containing other elements, whose combination as a totality is something unique and individual, and therefore inaccessible to comparison. Singularity, uniqueness, and incomparability are obstacles to cognition; hence to the cognitive tendency the remaining elements, though felt to be essentially bound up with the content, must appear irrelevant.[32]

Our text speaks of a process of abstraction by which the "sensuous part" of a concept's content is to be withdrawn. As we have stated, the nature of abstraction consists in a differentiation between the essential and the unessential residues of a sensuous character, that is, those elements which are directly connected with an object perceptible to the senses; it is this differentiation which constitutes the premise for a conscious cognition. Thinking restricted to the concrete object is a primitive way of thinking, always related to sense perceptions and bound to the thing perceived. Abstract thinking, on the contrary, is a thinking "freed" and separated from the sensuous object.[33]

The meaning of our passage could therefore be expressed, in brief, about as follows: The idea or conscious concept gained by the process of abstraction has its source in preconscious thinking, in the unconscious.

IV. Sefiroth Symbolism

IN THE FOLLOWING PASSAGE we meet with further symbols that have their source in the world of Kabbalistic concepts.

31. S. J. Bombach, *Versuch einer systematischen Darstellung der Erkenntnislehre des Maimonides* (Tarnov, 1935).
32. Jung, *Psychological Types*, p. 520.
33. *Ibid.*, p. 533.

Text Passage 4

What exists in singularity has its source in that which is common [to all], that is, in the unconscious alone. This is the hylic *yod*, who manifests himself in a human being into whose consciousness or cognition something suddenly falls, after he has been pondering with his intelligence on things that were hidden from him till now. That which suddenly falls into him came to him as an influence from the unconscious [*qadmut-ha-sekhel*]. Therefore there is contained in the letter *beth* of the word *bereshith* [with which, namely, the Creation story of Genesis begins] the possibility of all the words that follow. For this reason *beth* has a point in the center [*dagesh lene*]. In the *Zohar* this is called the [Primordial] Point in the Palace, for the [letter] *beth* is called the Palace of all letters. But these [letters] exist in a hylic form of being, hence the [Primordial] Point in the center [of the letter *beth* and the Palace] refers to the *yod*, which is *hylē*, primal matter, unconscious [*hokhmah*].

(*Maggid debarab le-Jaaqob*, p. 40b)

Commentary

In this passage we meet with a number of highly significant mystical symbols, like Primordial Point, Palace, and hylic *yod*, whose meaning is important for the understanding of our text. Kabbalistic tradition has long been familiar with the coordination of the separate four letters of the revealed name of God, YHWH, the so-called tetragram, with the different Sefiroth. While the *yod* corresponds to the Sefirah *hokhmah*, the first *he* is associated to the Sefirah *binah*. One might even say that there exists a kind of mystical identity between the letters of the alphabet and the Sefiroth, since they give symbolic expression to the same things. So the Hebrew letter *yod* has the shape of a point; hence the designation "point" or "Primordial Point" (*nequda*). Speculations in regard to the Primordial Point are mentioned in many sections of the

181 Psychological Aspects in Early Hasidism

Zohar, and the knowledge of them is taken for granted. From these speculations we arrive at the following juxtapositions:

sekhel (consciousness)	*qadmut-ha-sekhel* (the unconscious)
binah	*hokhmah*
Two	One
Palace	Point
he	*yod*

According to the so-called *gematria*—a part of the ancient mystery of numbers which in later times was adopted and widely disseminated by the Kabbalah—a letter of the alphabet can always be replaced by the number value which corresponds to it, because letter as well as number—or, what is the same thing, the Sefirah—expresses the essential nature of a thing, and therefore each can stand for the other. Words possessing the same number value (*isopsephia*) show an essential inner relationship or mystical identity.[1]

The arithmetical value given to the letter *yod* by the method of *gematria* is 10. The Primordial Point *yod* is in itself an indefinite and indefinable something, out of which *in potentia* all things can come into being.[2] As starting point for the development of every creature it is, to be sure, on the one hand the One; but, since it already contains and includes in

---

1. In the number speculations of the Gnostics—in particular of the Ophites—we repeatedly find the familiar equation: Christ (*mashiach*) = serpent (*nahash*), both words having the number value 358. The arithmetical value of a particular name of God, namely, Elohim, and of *ha-tewa* ("nature") is the same, that is, 70. Hasidic writings refer repeatedly to this relationship, which expresses the inner unity, or mystical identity, of this particular aspect of God (*Elohim*) and nature.

2. Cf. also *Codex München* 47, *cit.* G. Scholem, "Eine unbekannte mystische Schrift des Mose de Leon," *Monatsschrift für Geschichte und Wissenschaft des Judentums* (Berlin, 1927), p. 114: "Yod is the Primordial Point which emanates in all directions." In the speculations of the Gerona school, i.e., those of Azriel and Nachmanides, the emanation is also thought of as a development of the Primordial Point to a line and of the line to a plane.

itself the germinal form of the ten Sefiroth, it also represents the Ten and therewith the final point of development.

Concerning the Primordial Point, the *Zohar* says:

In the beginning (Gen. 1:1), when the will of the King began to take effect, he engraved signs into the heavenly sphere [that surrounded him]. Within the most hidden recess a dark flame issued from the mystery of *en Sof*, the Infinite, like a fog forming in the unformed, enclosed in the ring of that sphere, neither white nor black, neither red nor green, of no color whatever. Only after this flame began to assume size and dimension did it produce radiant colors. From the innermost center of the flame sprang forth a well out of which colors issued and spread upon everything beneath, hidden in the mysterious hiddenness of *en Sof*. The well broke through and yet did not break through the ether [of the sphere]. It could not be recognized at all until a hidden, supernal point shone forth under the impact of the final breaking-through. Beyond this point nothing can be known. Therefore it is called *reshith*, beginning—the first word [out of the ten] by means of which the universe has been created.

It is written: "And they that be wise shall shine as the brightness of the firmament; and they that turn many to righteousness, as the stars for ever and ever." (Dan. 12:3). The Most Mysterious struck its void, and caused this point to shine. This "beginning" then expanded, and made for itself a palace for its honor and glory. There it sowed a sacred seed, which was to generate for the benefit of the universe and to which may be applied the Scriptural words "the holy seed is the stock thereof" (Isa. 6:13).[3]

It reads almost like a Gnostic cosmogonic myth, when, out of the bottomless infinite (*Ungrund*),[4] in which, to begin with, all the opposites lie mixed together in misty indefiniteness and nondifferentiation, the various pairs of opposites evolve. The first to appear are fire and water, for, as the

---

3. Scholem, *Die Geheimnisse der Schöpfung* (Berlin, 1935), pp. 45 ff., translation of *Zohar*, I, 15a (*Sitre Torah*). See also Scholem, *Zohar: The Book of Splendor* (New York: Schocken Books, 1949), pp. 27 ff.

4. The term *Ungrund* stems from Jacob Boehme and represents a literal translation of the word *en Sof*. Boehme became acquainted with the Kabbalah through Dr. Balthasar Walter.

original fire "assumes size and dimension," a well springs up from within the fire itself. Obviously, what we have here is a kind of fiery water or watery fire—a concept similar to that of the alchemists, who also used to call the *aqua permanens* "ignis noster," or vice versa.[5] The further differentiation of the infinite is represented by the appearance of the shining colors. The increasing tension of opposites then leads to a sort of breakthrough out of the infinite, and the Primordial Point and the Palace appear as new forms.

Already in the *Zohar* and, later, more frequently in the Kabbalistic writings of Isaac Luria, the Primordial Point is given the mystical appellations of "father" (*abba*) or "father

---

5. Concepts regarding the Primordial Point are given much space also in Islamic mystical literature. This may be connected with the fact that the Koran, like the Bible, begins with the letter *beth*, which is likewise written in Arabic with a point (ﺐ). In a work written between 1246 and 1318 it is said: "All secrets of God are in the heavenly books, their content in the Koran, that of the Koran in the first sura, that of this sura in the first verse, that of this verse in the first letter, that of this letter in the point beneath it (ﺐ)" (Franz Dornseiff, *Das Alphabet in Mystik und Magie* [Leipzig, 1922], p. 134). In alchemy, too, we find similar speculations concerning the Point. C. G. Jung says: "The centre of nature is 'the point originated by God' (Mus. herm., 1678), the 'sun-point' in the egg (Consilium Coniungii, 1566). This, a commentary on the Turba says, is the 'germ of the egg in the yolk' (Ruska: Turba). Out of this little point, says Dorn in his 'Physica Genesis,' the wisdom of God made with the creative Word the 'huge machine' of the world (Theatr. chem., I). . . . For the 'most perfect form is round, because it is modelled on the point. . . .' The point symbolizes light and fire, also the Godhead in so far as light is an 'image of God' or an 'exemplar of the Deity.' This spherical light modelled on the point is also the 'shining or illuminating body' that dwells in the heart of man" (C. G. Jung, *Mysterium Coniunctionis, Collected Works*, XIV [1963], pp. 45–47). Similar concepts are found also in Heinrich Khunrath (*Vom hylealischen Chaos*), who represents Sapientia in the form of the "salt-point" and in John Dee (*Theatr. Chem.*), who says that all things originated from the point and the monad (*cit.* Jung, *Aion, CW*, IX, Pt. II [1959], pp. 220 f.).

NOTE: *The Collected Works of C. G. Jung*, translated by R. F. C. Hull, are published by the Bollingen Foundation (Bollingen Series XX) in the United States of America by Pantheon Books and in England by Routledge and Kegan Paul. The *Collected Works* will hereafter be referred to as "*CW*."

of the All," while the Palace is described as mother (*imma*).[6] The *Zohar* says of this:

> Let there be light. [Literally: Let life become!] Everything that has come to be came into being in the mystery of this "become." The word *yehi* (YHY), "become," points by the letters *yod* and *he* (YH) to the mystery of the union of father and mother [the upper creative forces, called "Primordial Point" and "Palace"]. Then the word *yehi* repeats the letter *yod*, thus returning to the Primordial Point [out of which everything has come to being] and so [like the germ resembling a point in an embryo] forms a new beginning, from whose extension [and development] something different comes to pass: Light.[7]

Similarly in the *Zohar, Idra rabba*:[8]

> As the Ancient One, whose name be blessed, took on a form, he shaped everything in male or female form. In another form things could not exist. Therefore the first beginning of development, which began with *hokhmah*, was at once male and female, namely *hokhmah* as father and *binah* as mother.

In our text the next Sefirah, *binah*, corresponds to the symbols mother and Palace (*hekhal*). The *Bahir* texts already speak of two mothers, the upper (*imma ilaa*) and the lower (*imma tataa*), namely, *binah* and *malkuth*. The two Sefiroth are in their essence closely related, so that the symbols of the one are often accounted valid for the other. And both are spoken of as the upper or the lower Shekhinah.[9] A kind of mystical identity between them stems first of all from the fact that both correspond to the letter *he* of the tetragram, the first and the second *he* of the name of God, YHWH. We will return to this subject later.

In addition to the relation of *binah* to the letter *he*, we can

---

6. Similarly in the *Bahir*, § 74d, where *binah* is designated "mother" (in other passages also as "world mother").
7. *Zohar*, I, 15a.
8. *Zohar*, III, 290a.
9. A parallel to this is the Gnostic conception of a double *sophia*, one at the beginning and a second on the edge of the *plērōma*, though here the first *sophia* corresponds to the *hokhmah* and not to the *binah*.

185 Psychological Aspects in Early Hasidism

also trace certain mystical connections with the letter *beth*, the second letter of the Hebrew alphabet. As *aleph*, the first letter, represents the masculine principle, *beth* represents the feminine.[10] The shape of *beth* corresponds to a house open in front, whence probably the name *beth* or *bayit* ("house") for this letter. According to the interpretation of Rabbi David abu Simra, this *beth* is formed from a *daleth*, ד, and a horizontal *waw*, ו, whose combined numerical value is 10, showing that, like the *yod*, the *beth* contains the ten Sefiroth.[11]

According to the *Tikkune Zohar*, *beth* corresponds to the *binah*, while the point inside it (*dagesh lene*) represents the *hokhmah*.[12]

According to the *Zohar* the Primordial Point (*reshith*) and the "house" (*bayit*), which has now become a Palace, unite, and from their union springs a new and third word.[13] For a strange mystical fusion of the words *reshith* and *bayit* (status constr. *beth*) results in the word *bereshith*, "primordial beginning," the first word of the Bible, by which the world-creating activity of the self-revealing God is first manifested.

Another Kabbalistic interpretation of the Creation myth is derived from a translation of the first verse, "In the beginning God created heaven and earth" (*bereshith bara elohim et ha-shamayim we et ha-arets*), when, by an odd turn to the mystical, this comes to be translated "*With* the beginning God created heaven and earth"—a translation that in fact does not conflict with the Hebrew text, since *bereshith* can just as well mean "with the beginning" as "in the beginning." But since *reshith*—"the beginning"—signifies the Primordial Point and therewith the *hokhmah*, one could also say: "With wisdom God created, etc." Perhaps the Biblical exegist of the *Zohar* may have thought here of the paraphrasing Aramaic translation of the Bible, the Targum, in which the Genesis passage is altered to say: "With wisdom God created heaven

10. *Zohar*, I, 30a.
11. David abu Simra, *Magen David* 4.
12. *Tikkune Zohar*, Introduction.
13. *Zohar*, I, 15b.

and earth" (*be-hokhmah bra elohim yat shamaya we yat ara*).[14]

The letter *yod*, as it says in our text, is hylic in nature. It obviously represents a sort of matter. This must mean that the *yod* forms a sort of spiritual *hylē* or spiritual matrix out of which the *he* crystalizes. This highly paradoxical concept of a spiritual matter or a hylic spirit recalls the old alchemical myth of the spirit in matter. We find this idea among the most diverse Kabbalists, for the problem of *hylē* occupied alchemists, Kabbalists, and philosophers of religion alike. And insofar as *yod* is identical with the *hokhmah* and the *qadmut-ha-sekhel*, a hylic character belongs to it also. From here extend some interesting lines of connection with certain religious concepts, which we shall discuss briefly at this point.

Even in the pre-*Zohar* period, in the Kabbalistic circle of Gerona, the identity of *hokhmah* and *hylē* was a common concept.[15] On the other hand, the concept of a spiritual matter was a basic idea of the Neoplatonically oriented religious philosopher Solomon ibn Gabirol. After him, Maimonides concerned himself above all with the problem of the hylic nature of the intellect. His speculations seem to me of interest in the elucidation of this concept and will therefore be briefly presented.

The main desire of Maimonides was to achieve a synthesis between the teachings of Judaism and the philosophy of Aristotle.[16] His picture of the universe is essentially Aristotle's view of nature, though colored throughout by Neoplatonic ideas. His concepts not only opened new paths to Jewish religious philosophy, but their influence extended to the Christian mysticism of Meister Eckhart as well as to the Kabbalah. It was above all his conception of the nature of proph-

14. Possibly the logos speculations of Philo and the Alexandrian philosophers play a part here. Cf. Bousset-Gressmann, *Die Religion des Judentums im späthellenistischen Zeitalter* (Tübingen, 1926).
15. I. Tishby, *Perush ha-aggadoth le Rabbi Azriel* ("Commentary on the *Aggadoth* of R. Azriel") (Jerusalem, 1945).
16. A. Stöckel, *Grundriss der Geschichte der Philosophie* (Mainz, 1919).

ecy and the theory of the so-called "active intellect" which assumed importance for the trend which is usually termed "prophetic Kabbalah."

It is particularly in the theory of the "active intellect" that Maimonides shows himself to be a follower of Aristotle's psychology. Aristotle distinguished between the passive and the active intellect. The passive intellect (νοῦς παθητικός) is a passive, "possible," intelligence subordinate to the "material" principle. It is to begin with a kind of *tabula rasa* and a capacity for passive reception of cognitions. This passive intellect is in itself a state of possibility. It requires a stimulus from an intelligible object. The active intellect (νοῦς ποιητικός) is an active intelligence, subordinate to the "formal" principle. In the Aristotelian conception this *intellectus agens* comes to men from without (θύραθεν).

Since the passive intellect can "become all things" and, on the other hand, the active intellect "effects all things," the two relate to each other as potentiality to actuality. The active intellect grasps objects of sensory perception, abstracts from them their sensory and individual particularities, and in this way creates a so-called intelligible form of cognition. This cognition is then transmitted to the passive intellect, whereby it is first enabled to recognize the nature of sensory objects. The conceptual cognitions of the active intellect are imparted to the passive intellect, provided the latter is prepared to take them in. Through this intervention of the active intellect the passive intellect is led from the state of potentiality into that of actuality, and the capacity for cognition becomes "actualized."

Maimonides has combined this theory of the active intellect with the Neoplatonic theory of emanation in order to explain the beginning of the world: from God the "unmoved Mover" first emanated a highest intelligence; then from this, through further radiation, there emanated a second; from the second came a third, and so forth. Upon this ladder of Creation the ten intelligences are the real mediators between God and mankind. These intelligences or "immaterial intellectual spirits" (*sekhel ha-nibdal*) represent a kind of bodiless spirits, who also guide the nine planetary spheres. For, like the spheres of the day and the fixed stars, the seven heavenly spheres also have their own intellectual spirit to guide and move them. Above our sublunary world presides the tenth intelligence, which is called "effective intelligence" or "active intelligence" (*sekhel ha-poel*).[17]

Here Maimonides, like Abraham ibn Daud and the Islamic Aristotelians, adopts the theory of the peripatetic Alexander of Aphrodisias, who had already seen the active intellect as something outside the human soul and had elevated it to a universal cosmic principle—a kind of cosmic intellect.[18] Aside from this concept, the *intellectus agens* (*sekhel ha-poel*) of Maimonides coincides very nearly with the active intellect of Aristotle. Yet Maimonides lacks an exact corresponding term for the passive intellect. On the other hand, he introduces two new concepts which are closely related to Aristotle's νοῦς παθητικός: the hylic and the acquired intellect. The hylic intellect (*sekhel ha-hyulani*) is similarly a latent, potential understanding. Through the sum of individual experiences the human being attains an ever increasing number of "acquired" concepts, and the hylic intellect finally comes to be an acquired intellect (*sekhel ha-niqna*). The more a man succeeds in moving out of the hylic into the acquired intellect, the greater is the possibility that he can attain access to the higher intellectual spirits of the planetary spheres.[19]

It might seem at first glance that Maimonides' concept of the hylic intellect could be thought of as identical with the concept in our text. But the two concepts do not coincide at all points. Here the religious philosopher and the mystic go different ways. For to the latter the hylic intellect is not something exclusively passive and receptive. Paradoxically,

17. Maimonides, *Guide to the Perplexed*, II, 4, 5, 12.
18. J. Gutmann, *Die Philosophie des Judentums* (Munich, 1933).
19. R. J. Z. Werblowsky brought it to my attention that the expression "acquired intellect" (*intellectus acquisitus*) is also found in the writings of Arabic Aristotelians.

there is also ascribed to it a potential or latent activity of its own.

It would lead us too far to investigate more closely these controversial trains of thought. What seems to me of essential importance in the present context is the fact that the Great Maggid pointed to the same religious-philosophical problem of the opposites and that this provides us with an additional insight into the phenomena of *sekhel* and *qadmut-ha-sekhel*.

V. THE SYMBOLISM OF NUMBERS AND NAMES

Text Passage 5

[A man] should consider that he is, as it were, the tool of a craftsman. When such a one strikes the stone with a hammer, it is not the hammer [itself] that wants to strike the stone, for then it would be separated from the craftsman. Even so, the unconscious [*qadmut-ha-sekhel*] flows into consciousness, and, so, too, [man] was created, and all his limbs are his tools.

(*Or ha-emeth*, p. 76b) [1]

Commentary

THIS QUOTATION points above all to the fact that consciousness is dependent upon and conditioned by the unconscious. Consciousness is the hammer that carries out the movement. But behind what is moved stands the mover, and behind the effect is the effector as *causa movens*. The impulses move from the unconscious into consciousness, which receives its contents from the unconscious. Hence consciousness is to a great extent dependent upon the unconscious, while the unconscious has its own law.

1. The page number refers to the Husyatin edition (1899).

Text Passage 6

A wise man understands, thanks to his experience, [how to guess or recognize] the thoughts of the King from his motions. There is also a level of the Son, whose Father is, as it were, the unconscious [*qadmut-ha-sekhel*]. Everything the Son wills, the Father has thought [before]. . . . Even in practical works there is an unconscious [*hokhmah*]; when, for instance, we see the practical work of a craftsman, we understand that the craftsman is wise [*hakham*]. This shows that, in the vessel, wisdom exists in a hidden way. But thought presupposes an unconscious [*qadmut-ha-sekhel*] which makes thought think. [Even] for him with insight it is impossible to grasp it. For the unconscious can be grasped only through consciousness. Thought, however, is based on the consonants, which are the vessels of creation. But the unconscious is higher than the consonants, and the vessels cannot hold it, hence [the saying]: "Wisdom comes from the 'Nothing.'"

(*Or ha-emeth*, p. 15b)

Commentary

IN THIS PASSAGE the relation of the unconscious to consciousness is depicted as that of father to son, much as it is in certain alchemical treatises.[2] Here, too, there is frequent reference to the concept that everything manifested in consciousness has previously existed latently in the unconscious.

The craftsman who carries out a practical task is called wise (*hakham*). This goes back to Biblical terminology, where *hokhmah* means primarily "skill, workmanship." This original meaning still shows through in our text. The skilled worker or *hakham* is a wise man just because his work exists in his *hokhmah*, that is, in his unconscious conception. But the emergence of unconscious contents into consciousness

2. C. G. Jung, *Psychology and Alchemy*, *CW*, XII (1953), pp. 317, 329.

presumes certain impulses within the unconscious which form the actual stimulus toward greater consciousness.

Even for "him with insight"—the Hebrew text here uses the term for "initiated" (*maskilim*)—it is not possible to understand the unconscious directly, since it is just in regard to it that he begins by being unconscious. But he can gain access to it by means of its effects upon his consciousness.

Cognition is first made possible by the consonants,[3] which are really the instruments which first made God's Creation possible. The concept of the great importance of the letters or consonants of the Hebrew alphabet is very old and is part of the earliest Kabbalistic heritage of ideas. This is already evident in the oldest Kabbalistic work, the *Book Yetsirah*.[4] According to its conception, the twenty-two consonants of the Hebrew alphabet have more than a merely profane meaning. They also possess hidden mystical powers which give them a unique double aspect. Like everything on earth, they, too, have their heavenly correspondence. The *Zohar* says in several places that the divine primal image and the earthly reflected image are related to each other like male and female. According to another interpretation, the alphabet includes letters with expressly male or female character. The *waw* or the *yod* belong to the first, the *beth* and the *he* to the second. Cordovero said that the pronouncing of a particular letter will awaken the essential nature which it embodies. This will ascend to heaven and there unite with the corresponding element of the heavenly letter to become one bodiless spiritual being.

The consonants constitute the actual structural elements from which the different words and names are composed. These, then, represent nothing other than the sum of the single consonants of the alphabet in their countless number of

3. In Hebrew, on the contrary, vowels do not in general play an important part. They were used in writing only very late, by the so-called Massoretes, and are still omitted in printed works or manuscripts.

4. *Sefer Yetsirah* ("The Book of Creation") (Mantua, 1562); L. Goldschmidt, *Das Buch der Schöpfung* (Frankfurt a.M., 1894).

variations and combinations. The creative power of single letters or of whole words is a very ancient concept in the mysticism or magic of many peoples. According to the Kabbalistic conception, the letters of the alphabet have issued out of the divine nature itself. The Talmud says [5] that God created heaven and earth, that is, the whole universe, with the help of the alphabet, and according to the *Book Yetsirah* the ten primary numbers and the twenty-two letters of the alphabet together form the "thirty-two hiddens paths of wisdom," those mystical powers by which the whole world was created.

According to the *Zohar*, "the letters of the divine name contain the secret of the Torah. The Torah begins with a *beth*, which is followed by an *aleph*, and this expresses [the fact] that the world was created by the power of these letters. *Beth* refers to the feminine and *aleph* to the masculine principle, and the two, so to speak, lead the group of twenty-two letters." [6]

The letters, as spoken consonants or written signs, form the building-stones of speech and writing, whereby human language enters into a correspondence with the language of God. In human language the single consonants are, to begin with, of purely material nature. But at the same time they also partake of an expressly spiritual character, since they simultaneously, in the combinations of the consonants, give form to divine names and words. In this way they come to represent actual creative potencies. This is what gives the spoken or written word its own creative force. The strange double aspect of the consonants, as both profane and mystic, material and spiritual entities, makes them the mediators between the upper and the lower, the divine and the earthly realms—the bridge on which divine and human speech find a meeting place.

The divine names formed by the consonants are themselves

5. G. Scholem, art, "Yetsirah," *Encyclop. Jud.*, VIII, 103 ff.
6. *Talmud babyl.* (Vilna ed.), *Tractate Berakhot*, 55a.

closely connected with the different Sefiroth; indeed, as the carriers of divine essences, they are really identical with them. That is why, in the *Book Bahir*, the Sefiroth are designated as names or words (*ma-amarim* = λόγοι) and why God, too, has no definite name before He becomes manifest in the Sefiroth.[7] It is only as God emerges from the nameless abyss of nothingness that He to a certain extent loses his anonymity and becomes namable and so can be spoken of. Hence the name is the carrier of the essential being; the knowledge of the name means knowledge of the secrets of the name's possessor. Here we meet with some very strange relationships to actual magic; and, indeed, we can never draw a clear line between magic and mysticism.

A belief in the magic power of letters and names (thaumaturgy) is present in all peoples. In accordance with it, the name of God, YHWH, is said to have been inscribed upon the rod with which Moses divided the waters of the Red Sea.[8] One of the mystics, Phineas ben Yair, has said that the prayers of the Jewish people are not granted on earth because it has lost the knowledge of the spoken four-letter name of God but that, in the Beyond, God will again make his name known to the people.[9] The knowledge of the name also bestows on the knower secret, magic powers; he attains the mastery of spirits and demons. According to one legend, the demon-lord Asmodeus was bound with a chain and seal ring, upon which was engraved the name of God.[10] The dread of God's holy names (*shemoth, azkaroth*) was so great that any manuscript in which they were miswritten or marred was considered unusable and kept in a special chamber,[11] while the names

---

7. "Before the Holy One, may He be praised, created the world, He was, and His name was hidden in Him" (*Zohar hadash*, 40).
8. *Pesiqta* (ed. S. Buber), 140a.
9. *Midrash shoher tob*.
10. *Talmud babyl. Tract. Gittin*, 68a.
11. Franz Dornseiff, *Das Alphabet in Mystik und Magie* (Leipzig, 1922), p. 135.

themselves were encircled by a sort of temenos.[12] Erasing or correcting such manuscripts was forbidden.

Like the individual letters, words possess a special creative force; they can even animate dead matter. We find a distinct echo of this concept in the tales about the Golem, which were largely influenced by Kabbalistic ideas. *Golem* originally meant "embryo; dead matter." It is unformed and lifeless raw material. Text passage 4, above, designates the *hokhmah*, too, as *hylē*, raw material, *golem*, and in text passage 5 it is referred to directly as *prima materia* (*homer rishon*). The Golem of classic legend is a sort of homunculus. He is shaped from a lump of clay and brought to life by a label on which is written the name of God; this is placed under his tongue. Another legend has him brought to life by writing on his forehead the Hebrew word *emeth* ("truth")—that mystic word containing the first (*aleph*), the middle (*mem*), and the last (*tau*) letters of the Hebrew alphabet. The erasure of the first letter changes the word *emeth* to *meth*, that is, "death"; and when this erasure is accomplished, the Golem again becomes a lifeless image.[13]

According to another legend of the early Middle Ages, the

---

12. Dornseiff (*ibid.*, p. 143) presents an interesting parallel in Islamic literature. In a late Tunisian manuscript of the *Thousand and One Nights* there is a story about the Brahman Padmanaba: "There are two kinds of talismans, the Kabbalistic and the astrological. The first, which is the best kind, brings about its wonderful effects by means of letters, words, and prayers; the other is powerful because of the countereffects taking place between the planets and all metals. I use the Kabbalistic talismans; they were once revealed to me by the great god Vishnu, who is lord of all the pagodas of the world." The Brahman says further: "Know then, my son, that the letters are connected with the angels, every letter is ruled by an angel; and if you ask me what an angel is, I will answer you: It is a ray of an outflow of the virtues of the Almightiness and the qualities of God. The angels which dwell in the earthly and in the heavenly world rule those who abide in our earthly one. The letters form the words, then the words the prayers, and it is the angels who, designated by the letters and assembled in the written and spoken words, work the wonders at which ordinary men are amazed."

13. G. Scholem, art. "Golem," *Encyclop. Jud.*, VII, 501 ff.; M. Grünwald, art. "Golem," *Jüd. Lexikon*, II, 1200 f.

195 Psychological Aspects in Early Hasidism

Golem is roused to life by the reciting of certain creative words during a circumambulation. If these are spoken backward and the circumambulation is carried out in the reverse direction, the Golem again becomes lifeless matter.[14]

In later legends the Golem is created by the High Rabbi Loew in Prague. For his creation three persons must be present. While the clay from which the Golem is made embodies the earth, the three persons represent the other elements: fire, water, and air. The animation is brought about by seven circumambulations, during which those words of the Creation story are recited by means of which God gave man a living soul.[15] Returning the Golem to his original state is effected, in the Prague legend too, by the repetition of the circumambulation, with the same words spoken backward.[16] The close connection between such magic practices and *Yetsirah* mysticism should not be overlooked.

After this brief digression into the field of letter and number symbolism, I should like to summarize its relation to the interpretation of our text as follows. Conscious thinking or conceptualization is brought about by means of the letters of the alphabet, which, as the elements of thought, are the containers of all things of the spirit. Wisdom, however, as unconscious thinking and conceiving, is higher than the letters. For the letters, as elements of *conscious* thought, are unable to encompass the *unconscious* thought of the *hokhmah*.

The last sentence of text passage 6 contains an allusion to the well-known verse in Job 28:12, which here undergoes a totally new and different interpretation. The familiar transla-

---

14. R. Joseph ben Shalom ha-Ashkenazi of Barcelona says, in speaking of the *Yetsirah* mysticism underlying the Golem legends: "The creative and destructive ordering of the world are the same, only in reverse succession" (*cit.* Scholem, art. "Golem," *Encycl. Jud.*, VII, 503). The backward reading or recitation of sentences has a magical effect: by this means the consummated magic becomes ineffective.

15. Gen. 2:7.

16. Micha Joseph ben Gorion, *Der Born Judas* (Berlin, 1934), pp. 700 ff.

tion of this verse is: "But where shall wisdom be found? and where is the place of understanding?" But in our text, since the word "where" (*me-ayin*) in Hebrew has also the meaning "nothing," a typical inversion into the mystical retranslates the verse to "Wisdom is found in the Nothing." [17] This method of elucidation and interpretation of words, as well as the endeavor to track down allegorical or mystical meanings, is already to some extent found in the Midrash, a collection of myths, fables, and legends gathered during the course of several centuries. But it is particularly characteristic of the homiletic literature of the Kabbalah and of Hasidism.[18]

Text Passage 7

The difference between the *hokhmah* and the other hypostases consists in [the fact] that the latter are conditioned by time . . . , which is not the case with the *hokhmah*. This is the *prima materia*, which puts on forms and takes them off. . . . Continuously and without interruption she [*hokhmah*] expends the life-force downward and receives fullness [influx] from above, without interruption even for a moment, eternally and beyond comprehension. So, for example, the consonants of thinking flow continuously out of the unconscious [*qadmut-ha-sekhel*], that is, without interruption; and in every moment of time other conso-

---

17. Prof. I. Tishby, Jerusalem, drew my attention to the fact that this mystical interpretation of the verse in Job was already known in the pre-Zoharian exegesis and later became a common possession of Kabbalistic literature.

18. Also "Hasidic exegesis, like traditional Jewish exegesis in general, is an exegesis of *words*. Every word of the *sacred* scripture is essential. It has its own hidden but yet accessible meaning as word. Yet the word is not regarded as absolute, dissociated from its context of ideas. However, the relation between a word and the context of ideas is of a different kind from that which would seem exclusively correct according to our logically discursive thinking. Thus the first word of the Bible, *bereshith*, is given an exegesis of its own. Yet everything that can be said about this word is related to the Creation, about which the word *bereshith* has something to say" (Lazar Gulkowitsch, "Das kulturhistorische Bild des Chassidismus," in *Acta et Commentationes Universitatis Tartuensis* [Tartu, 1938], p. 100).

nants emerge out of the unconscious, which draws off [their sensual encasement or clothing] and sends them on to thought. Then it [the unconscious] draws forth others [consonants] and without interruption sends them further, though this [process] cannot be understood.

(*Or ha-emeth*, p. 42a)

Commentary

THE OPPOSITE CHARACTER of consciousness and the unconscious is here expounded with particular impressiveness. While consciousness is temporally conditioned, the unconscious is something that exists outside the category of time. Our consciousness always orients itself according to time and space by perceiving things in juxtaposition and in succession. The unconscious, on the other hand, possesses the quality of spacelessness and timelessness, in which the past, the present, and the future exist and operate simultaneously, side by side.

The unconscious represents a sort of raw primal matter. The Hebrew word for it—*homer rishon*—interestingly enough corresponds exactly to the alchemical term *prima materia*. A synonym for the concept is *golem*, which means "raw material, matter, clay, or excretion." [19] Similarly, alchemical treatises say of the *prima materia:* "in stercore invenitur." [20] The consonants flow from this primal matter into consciousness in a constant stream. Here they "coagulate," take on a fixed form, and now constitute the elements of human speech.

If we now briefly summarize all that our texts have said about the *qadmut-ha-sekhel*, we shall find that that which these texts call *qadmut* or *qidmat-ha-sekhel* has a double meaning. Within the human realm it represents a primary thinking, conceiving, or consciousness which precedes intel-

19. Isa. 10:6, 29:16.
20. C. G. Jung, *Symbolik des Geistes* (Zurich, 1948), p. 124. (English translation, *The Spirit Mercury* [Analytical Psychology Club of New York, Inc., 1953], p. 32.) This paper will be included in the *Collected Works,* Vol. XIII, as "The Spirit Mercurius."

lect, reason, conscious thinking or conceiving. This to a certain degree seems to show that this concept does in fact correspond to what modern psychology calls the unconscious.

But, in another way, as divine wisdom, *qadmut-ha-sekhel* belongs also to the Sefirotic and hence to the divine realm. In this case it assumes the character of transtemporality. It is chaotic, undifferentiated raw or primal matter, a kind of *hylē*, but of a spiritual character. As Primordial Point it is the center and starting place for the development of the Sefiroth. It is related to the Father and, as wisdom, likewise to the world-creating logos. In this way these mythical images correspond to the archetypal concepts also found in alchemy and natural philosophy.

VI. Coniunctio Mysticism

THE FOLLOWING PASSAGE is probably the most interesting and illuminating in regard to the concepts of the unconscious held by the Maggid of Meseritz. It brings us to the central problem of the Kabbalah, that of the symbolism of the *coniunctio*. I shall first of all try to show the archetypal background of these concepts. For this purpose, however, it will be necessary to draw upon a still greater number of amplifications.

Text Passage 8

If a man has difficulties with something, then he begins to think about it. As a result, [something] falls like lightning into his consciousness as a sudden stimulus, and so some idea comes to him. But this comes to him from the unconscious [*qidmat-ha-sekhel*], which is the *hokhmah*. [But] it is not the unconscious [itself] which fell like lightning into his consciousness; rather, that aspect under which suddenly something occurred to him is called fundament [*yesod*]. Herein is the mystery of the union of the unconscious [*qadmut-ha-sekhel*]—namely the *hokhmah*—and consciousness—namely the *binah*, [i.e.] of father and mother. By this is meant the union in the higher hypostases, in which the male bestows his influx upon the female. Here, too, occurs a union of the unconscious, namely the *hokhmah*, with consciousness, namely the *binah*.

(*Or ha-emeth*, p. 70a)

Commentary

OUR TEXT BEGINS with what seems the self-evident statement that a man in a conflict situation who thinks about his problem will receive sudden ideas from the unconscious. Freud, as is well known, used the ideas suggested by dream contents and introduced the technique of so-called free association.[1] Jung expanded this method and developed it into "amplification," at the same time stressing that the original image must be held intact in order to prevent the unlimited spread of active associations.[2] Both methods proceed from the assumption that the "ideas that come into one's head" represent a manifestation of the unconscious. According to the Great Maggid, the sudden insight or—what is the same in Hebrew—the invention, is that which comes to men from the unconscious. The text makes it clear that it is not the whole unconscious which invades the field of human consciousness but only certain concepts or aspects, as, for example, the aspect *yesod*.[3]

This is possible because, according to the Kabbalistic conception, each single Sefirah always includes all the others. So it is said in the *Zohar:* "Every Sefirah includes at the same time also the principles of all the others, except that in each single Sefirah a certain principle appertaining particularly to

---

1. Sigmund Freud, *Introductory Lectures on Psychoanalysis. Complete Works*, Vol. XV (London, 1963), Chap. VII, pp. 106 ff.
2. C. G. Jung, "The Relations between the Ego and the Unconscious," *Two Essays on Analytical Psychology*, *CW*, VII, (1953), *passim*.
3. Cf. the Kabbalistic Tree of Life, p. 170.

itself seems to predominate."[4] Hence the *hokhmah*, along with all the other aspects, also includes the aspect *yesod*. When the *yesod* of the *hokhmah* enters the *binah*, it acts as a sort of mediating agent through which the Sefiroth *hokhmah* and *binah* achieve a union. So the text leads logically into what it terms the "mystery of the union."

But what does this union signify, and what constitutes the mystery that surrounds it? We must begin by saying that the union of *sekhel* and *qadmut-ha-sekhel*, or of *hokhmah* and *binah*, represents an aspect of the central problem of the union of opposites as such. We therefore cannot avoid entering more deeply into this problem in order to reach a psychological understanding of the text's content by a study of its archetypal background.

What we have here is in truth a very special kind of "mystery." Not only Kabbalah and Hasidism, but also alchemy, have regarded the union of the opposites and their synthesis into a totality as an essential concern. Terms like *coniunctio oppositorum, mysterium coniunctionis, hieros gamos*, and, in the Kabbalah, "sacred copulation" (*zivvug ha-qodesh*) show just how much this union was felt to be a numinous suprapersonal event. The alchemist either finds the opposites already differentiated as such within the so-called *prima materia*, or they are mixed up with each other in a primal chaos. In the latter case they must be separated by a long and often repeated process of distillation or transformation whereby they can finally be reunited on a higher plane in a unified whole. The same problem of the opposites runs through the entire Kabbalah. But here, in contrast to alchemy, the unconscious contents are not projected into unknown matter; they are located within the divine realm of the Sefiroth.

The Sefiroth theory of the Kabbalists very early included the pairs of opposites such as day-night, light-darkness, above-below, right-left, male-female, white-red, good-evil, etc. According to Jung, the "factors which come together in

4. *Tikkune ha-Zohar*, 47.

the *coniunctio* are conceived as opposites, either confronting one another in enmity or attracting one another in love."[5] The intensity of the tension of opposites is demonstrated in the polar opposition of the symbols of life and death. *Hesed* and *din* correspond to the flowing waters of love and mercy and the dark fire of stern judgment, while *netsah* and *hod* are said to be "inseparable friends." *Hokhmah* and *binah* sometimes appear in personified form and constitute a male-female pair of opposites. Already in the *Zohar*, *hokhmah* is called "father," and *binah* "mother" or "world mother." So it says:

As the Ancient One—may his name be praised—took a form, he shaped all things in the form of male and female. In another form things cannot exist. Therefore, too, the first beginning of the development which began with *hokhmah* was at once male and female, namely, *hokhmah* as *father* and *binah* as *mother*, from whose union everything else originated.[6]

Another male-female pair of opposites is formed by *tifereth* and *malkuth*. They, too, represent the masculine (*duqrah*) and the feminine (*nuqbah*) principle. Designations like "bridegroom and bride," "king and queen," or "*matronita*," the "saint and the Community of Israel,"[7] and—in conformance to alchemy—the recourse to cosmic symbols, like sun-moon or heaven-earth, show that these pairs of opposites possess a definitely suprapersonal character.[8]

According to a strange concept, whose development can be traced particularly in the Lurianic Kabbalah, the original unity and wholeness of the hermaphroditic primal man has

5. C. G. Jung, *Mysterium Coniunctionis*, CW, XIV (1963), p. 3.
6. *Zohar*, III, 29a.
7. The phrase "Community of Israel" (*Knesseth Israel*) is not meant to refer to the Jewish people but rather to its heavenly or archetypal prototype.
8. Jung points out (*Mysterium Coniunctionis*, p. 6) that the "elevation of the human figure to a king or a divinity, and on the other hand its representation in subhuman theriomorphic form, are indications of the *transconscious* character of the pairs of opposites. They do not belong to the ego personality but are supraordinate to it. . . . The pairs of opposites constitute the phenomenology of the paradoxical *self*, man's totality."

been torn apart, with the result that the harmony of the Sefirotic world has been disturbed. The Kabbalah explains this situation in part as follows: The feminine part—represented by the Shekhinah—of the primal man, *adam qadmon*, who forms the totality of the Sefiroth, has been split off and in this way divided into his male-female opposites. One of the grandest and deepest conceptions taken by Hasidism from the Kabbalah is the doctrine that, just because of this split, God needs man, whose task it is to reunite the riven opposites within the divine personality itself. From this point of view the exile of the Jewish people receives a deep and special meaning. For this exile of the people corresponds in the "upper world," so to speak, to an exile of the Shekhinah, who went into exile with them (*galuth Shekhinah*). The return of the Jewish people from exile therefore means, in Jewish mysticism, the redemption of the Jewish people; it is above all an earthly image and likeness of an inner-divine drama of redemption, of the homecoming of the Shekhinah to God. So it is said in the *Zohar:*

It is told: "And the evening and the morning were the first day [one day]." For there is no night without a day and no day without a night, and they are called one only because of their being joined in a unity. So also the Holy One, may He be praised, is named as one with the "Community of Israel" [i.e., the Shekhinah] but not so when they are separated from each other. But because at the present time the "Community of Israel" is in exile, it cannot, so to speak, be called one. But when will it be called one? Then, when Israel will return from banishment and the Community of Israel to its place, in order there to unite with the Holy One, praised be He; that is the meaning of the verse (Zech. 14:9): "In that day shall there be one Lord, and his name one." But one without the other is not called one.[9]

So, while the man needing redemption strives to restore the disturbed world order (*tikkun ha-olam*),[10] he is at the same

---

9. *Zohar*, III, 93a.
10. G. Scholem, *Ra-ayon ha-geulah be-Kabbala* ("The Idea of Redemption in the Kabbalah") (Jerusalem, 1946).

time working toward the redemption of God and his union with the Shekhinah, and thus toward the restoration and realization of the wholeness of God.

The union of the opposites into a totality is therefore one of the high aims of the Kabbalah. We read in the *Zohar:* ". . . when they [the masculine and the feminine] unite, they look as if they were one body. From this we learn: the masculine by itself is like only one part of a body, and the feminine also. But when they join together as a whole, then they appear as one *real* body." And again: "The *matronita* united herself with the king. From this, *one* body resulted. Thence comes the blessing of this day. Therefore we know: what is only masculine or only feminine is called only part of the body. But no blessing rules over a faulty or incomplete thing, but only over a complete place, not over one that is divided, for divided things cannot long endure or be blessed." [11]

The earthly correspondence to the "higher" man (*adam ilaa*) or primal man (*adam qadmon*) is the similarly bisexual first human being (*adam ha-rishon*). He, too, originally contained the masculine and the feminine and so formed a totality.[12] As the *Zohar* says: "The first man consisted of masculine and feminine, for it is said: 'and God said, Let us make man in our image, after our likeness.' Therefore he was created male and female and was divided only later." [13] In the Genesis exegesis of the *Zohar* a similar concept is expressed:

In the same mystery in which heaven and earth were created, man also was created. Of the first it is said [Gen. 2:4]: "These are the generations of the heavens and of the earth." Of man it is said [Gen. 5:1]: "This is the book of the generations of Adam." There it says: "in the day that God created man." Of man it is said: "Male and female created he them, in the day when they were created." Therefore an image (*dioqna*) which does not

11. *Zohar*, III, 296a.
12. That is why it says: "In the moment that man was created, the whole world was completed, the upper and the lower world. For all things are contained in man" (*Zohar*, I, 48a).
13. *Zohar*, II, 55a.

contain male and female is not a higher [heavenly] picture. This we have already ascertained in the secret tradition. Come and see, in a place in which male and female are not united, the Holy One, blessed be He, will not take up his dwelling place. And blessing prevails only in a place where male *and* female are present. It is said [Gen. 5:2]: "And [He] blessed *them*, and called *their* name 'man' [*adam*]," for even man is only called [man] when male and female are united in him.[14]

As was said earlier, the aspect *yesod* entered the *binah* from the *hokhmah* and led to the "mystery of the union" of the two Sefiroth. It is again *yesod* that brings about the union of *tifereth* and *malkuth*. It has already been pointed out that the Sefiroth taken as a whole are frequently represented in the image of primal man (*adam qadmon*), while taken singly they represent the different members of his body. Hence *yesod*, as the spiritual principle of procreation, is associated to the phallus, while *netsah* and *hod* correspond to the testicles. It is *yesod* that "sends forth blessings for the union of the holy king with the *matronita*, and in this way blessings are distributed to all the worlds."[15] So *malkuth*, too—in reference to the familiar simile in Isaiah 58:11—is described as a "watered garden" (*gan rave*)."[16] In the highly dramatic description in the last chapter of the *Zohar* of the death of Rabbi Simon ben Yochai, he reveals, shortly before his death, that the deepest of all mysteries is the union of the holy king with the *matronita*,

for all the sap, strength and force of the whole man's body are gathered there [in *netsah* and *hod*] and all the "hosts" [*Sabaoth*] which have their source in them pass through the opening of the sexual organ [*yesod*]. That is why they are called "hosts" [corresponding to the two names of God, YHWH-Sabaoth and Elohim-Sabaoth, which correspond to the two Sefiroth *netsah*

---

14. *Zohar*, I, 55b.
15. *Zohar*, III, 62a.
16. *Zohar*, I, 141a. Cf. also Knorr von Rosenroth, *Kabbala denudata*, I, p. 240, 4: "quod Malchuth vocetur gan rave, hortus irriguus Jesch. 58, 11 quando jessod in Ipsa est, eamque adimplet atque irrigat aquis supernis."

and *hod*]. But *tifereth* is YHWH, hence the name YHWH-Sabaoth. The male member itself is the outermost of the whole body and is called *yesod*. It is the element [degree] that gives joy to the woman, for the whole desire of man is toward woman. By means of *yesod* he [*tifereth*] penetrates the woman at that place which is called Zion. . . . And the *matronita* receives blessing only through the trinity, namely *netsah*, *hod*, and *yesod*. And she has joy and receives blessing in that place which is called the "lower all-holiest." For it says [Ps. 133:3]: "There YHWH commanded the blessing." Of this [the all-holiest] there are two degrees, an upper and a lower. Therefore, since only the High Priest who approaches from the side of love has permission to enter there [in the all-holiest of the temple, hence the lower degree], so only he may enter the upper place [the all-holiest of the *matronita*, the upper degree] who is called love [*hesed*]. [By this is meant *tifereth* in its aspect of *yesod*.] When he enters the all-holiest, the *matronita* is blessed in that place which is called Zion. But "Zion" and "Jerusalem" are [also] two degrees; one corresponds to love, the other to stern judgment.[17]

These concepts of the *coniunctio* are found throughout the Kabbalah and greatly influenced Hasidism. It is just in this regard that Hasidic theories show their widespread dependence on the trains of thought found in the *Zohar*.[18]

Yesod's entering the *binah*—as our text says—would mean psychologically that the generative and creative principle of the unconscious has entered consciousness. Hence *yesod* belongs to both realms and so to some extent forms a bridge or mediator between consciousness and the unconscious.

Now the text describes this *coniunctio* as a union of the *partsufim* ("figures"). The theory of the *partsufim* is already alluded to in the *Zohar*, but not till the Lurianic Kabbalah did it really achieve development and formulation. While in the

17. *Zohar*, III, 296a.
18. So, to give only one example from Hasidic literature, the Maggid of Chernobyl (*Meor enayim*) says: "The 'Community of Israel' longs constantly for the Holy King and incites him by this longing to unite with it. For only the 'Community of Israel' and the 'Holy One, may He be praised,' together form a unity, for one without the other cannot be called a whole."

earlier Kabbalistic theories the Sefiroth represented aspects or modes of being in which God reveals himself, in the Lurianic Kabbalah they become mere structural principles of every form of created life and fall more and more into the background. The *partsufim*, or figures, have a much more expressly personified character than the Sefiroth, so that the split in the divine personality goes still further than in the Sefiroth theory. Here *kether* comes to be the "long-suffering" (*arikh anpin*) or the "ancient Holy One" (*atiqa qaddishah*); *hokhmah* and *binah* become "father" (*abba*) and "mother" (*imma*); the six following Sefiroth make up the configuration of the "impatient one" (*zeir anpin*) or of the "holy king" (*malkah qaddishah*), while *malkuth* represents the "feminine side" (*nuqbah zeir*) of the "impatient one."

The ten Sefiroth, as we have said, are arranged in pairs of opposites which either attract or repel each other. Within the decad two pairs of opposites have a very special inner relationship: *hokhmah-binah* and *tifereth-malkuth* (or, in Lurianic terminology, *abba-imma* and *zeir-nuqbah*) form two male-female pairs of opposites which are distinguished from the other Sefiroth pairs. The duality of these two pairs of opposites points psychologically beyond a simple opposite to a dual oppositeness, so that really two conjunctions result which are mutually related to each other. To understand this, we must go still further into the symbolism of the *Zohar*, though it should be stressed that a Kabbalistic symbol never means anything clearly defined or precise but, like every symbol, is something manifold and evanescent which can be interpreted differently according to its place and context.

The *Zohar* always describes *binah* as well as *malkuth* with feminine symbols. At times *binah* in relation to *malkuth* is termed the "higher mother" or "higher Shekhinah," while *malkuth* is called "lower mother" or "lower Shekhinah." [19] Other feminine symbols, too—as, for example, the Garden of Eden—are used for both *binah* and *malkuth*. So it is said that

19. *Zohar*, I, 247b.

"*Waw* (= *tifereth*) is the son created by *yod* and *he*, who are father and mother." [20] In a commentary of Psalm 19 which gives a mystical interpretation of the word *amr* ("word"), it is said that *aleph* is a symbol for the father and *mem* for the mother, while *resh* ("head") designates the firstborn son (*tifereth*).[21]

In this way two conjunctions result, which, because of their inner relationship, cross each other to form the following pattern:

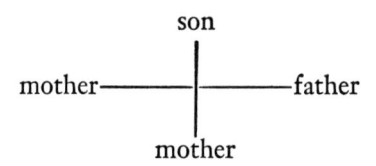

```
           son
            |
mother —————+————— father
            |
          mother
```

On the other hand, *malkuth* is also called "daughter" in relation to *hokhmah* and *binah*. "She [*malkuth*] is sometimes called daughter and sometimes sister, and here she is called mother. And in fact she is all these. Who penetrates into this mystery has attained precious wisdom." [22]

As the daughter of *hokhmah* and *binah*, *malkuth* is also the sister of *tifereth*.[23] In that case we arrive at the following configuration:

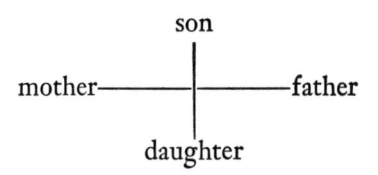

```
           son
            |
mother —————+————— father
            |
         daughter
```

The *Book Bahir* [24] already speaks of *malkuth*—in reference to the well-known Midrashic analogy to Canticles III, 11—as

---

20. *Zohar*, I, 28a.
21. *Zohar*, I, 247b.
22. *Zohar*, II, 100b.
23. Cf. von Rosenroth, *Kabbala denudata*, I, p. 70: ". . . frater est tipheret, quia ille modus est frater mensurae malchuth."
24. *The Book Bahir* (Vilna, 1883), p. 7b, § 43.

at once mother, daughter, and sister.[25] This results in a union of the son with mother-daughter-sister. The parallels to alchemy, which also calls the union of *rex* and *regina* a *hieros gamos* of brother-sister or son-mother, are not accidental. To me, however, it seems not so much a case of dependence or mutual influence as of the independent spontaneous emergence of a symbol that was constellated in alchemy and Kabbalah alike.[26] The archetypal motif which—however veiled—is at the bottom of this incest situation cannot be overlooked. Yet the incest motif should not be misinterpreted by taking it in the literal sense. For the whole context shows clearly that we have before us the primal image of the sacred marriage (*hieros gamos*) and that the incest component points to that union with one's own being which, from time out of mind, has been felt to be a supranatural or numinous event. Indeed, alchemy calls it an *opus contra naturam*.[27]

Here we can enter only very briefly into the archetypal background which underlies the *coniunctio* symbolism. For anything further we must turn to the various studies of C. G. Jung and his school[28] on the subject of so-called mandala symbolism. However, for the better understanding of our text, it is important to mention that the simple as well as the dual *coniunctio* are symbols for that which one usually calls human wholeness. This psychic totality contains, on the one hand, the conscious part of the psyche, and, on the other, the unconscious. When this totality of the personality is constellated, very definite symbols or groups of symbols emerge in the unconscious.

25. August Wünsche, *Midrash schir ha schirim* (Leipzig, 1880).
26. C. G. Jung, *Psychology and Alchemy*, *CW*, XII (1953), pp. 220, 317, 396, and *The Practice of Psychotherapy*, *CW*, XVI (1954), p. 227, n. 29.
27. R. Israel of Rushin, a great-grandson of the Great Maggid, says of such incestuous unions that they are permitted only in the "upper worlds"; the "lower worlds" cannot tolerate them.
28. C. G. Jung, "Concerning Mandala Symbolism," *The Archetypes and the Collective Unconscious*, *CW*, IX, Pt. I (1959), p. 355; Erich Neumann, *The Origins and History of Consciousness* (Bollingen Series XLII) (New York, Pantheon Books, 1954).

209 Psychological Aspects in Early Hasidism

In a dual *coniunctio* the two pairs of opposites intercross each other and in this way form a quaternity. The psychologem of the intercrossed conjunctions was for the first time described and psychologically interpreted by Jung. As he has demonstrated, these symbols are not a matter of contrivance or invention by the human intellect, nor of alchemical or Kabbalistic speculations, but rather of a true primal image, or what Jung has termed an archetype. The archetype of the intercrossed *coniunctio* he has described as the "marriage-quaternio." [29]

Symbols such as the *coniunctio* and the *quaternio* appear in modern people, too, and indeed spontaneously during the individuation process, in which there is a gradual lessening of the distance between the conscious and the unconscious. The end goal of individuation—psychic totality—is expressed in the symbols of wholeness.

Jung says of these symbols that they

have the character of "wholeness" and therefore presumably *mean* wholeness. As a rule they are uniting symbols, representing the conjunction of a single or double pair of opposites, the result being either a dyad or a quaternio. They arise from a collision between the conscious and the unconscious and from the confusion which this causes (known in alchemy as "chaos" or "*nigredo*"). Empirically, this confusion takes the form of restlessness and disorientation. The circle and quaternity symbolism appears at this point as a compensating principle of order, which depicts the union of warring opposites as already accomplished.[30]

It has already been suggested that the Kabbalah likewise contains archetypal symbols like the *coniunctio* and the *quaternio*, as shown in the single as well as the double *coniunctio* of the Sefiroth. The assumption that this has to do with an archetypal pattern is supported and even confirmed by other related material found in the Kabbalah. For we meet with the same results when we turn to the letter and number symbol-

29. Jung, *The Practice of Psychotherapy*, p. 222.
30. Jung, *Aion*, *CW*, IX, Pt. II (1959), p. 194.

ism of the name of God. This leads us to a short discussion of the long-drawn-out mystical speculations upon the so-called tetragram, which appear over and over again in Kabbalistic writings, particularly in the *Zohar*.

The four-letter revealed name of God consists of the letters Y H W H: *yod, he, waw,* and *he*. We have already pointed out that masculine and feminine qualities are often ascribed to the letters of the Hebrew alphabet. The *yod* has an expressly masculine meaning. Its number value is 10, corresponding to the ten Sefiroth, which, as the Primordial Point, it contains in itself as a germ (see above, p. 181).

The *he*, on the other hand, is already characterized as feminine by the *Book Bahir*. Its number value is 5. It is related to the soul, which, according to many Kabbalists, consists not of three but of five parts—a concept already known at the time the *Zohar* was written.[31]

The letter *waw* of the tetragram has again an expressly masculine character. Its number value is 6, and it is related to the six directions of space.[32] That is also why *waw* represents the center of the Sefiroth when they are thought of as a

---

31. As said by Azriel of Gerona (*ca.* 1200).
32. "They said to him [namely, to R. Amora]: 'What is the meaning of *waw?*' He answered: 'The world is sealed up in six directions.' They said: 'But is *waw* not a single [letter]?' He answered them: 'And is it not written [Ps. 104:2]: "Who coverest thyself with light as with a garment"?'" (*Bahir*, § 21). Scholem writes on this passage: "This verse is obviously a well-established proof of the doctrine of the six directions, and here the knowledge of this function is already taken for granted. It is employed in this way also in section 55. It refers to cosmogonic concepts which later were translated into mystical letters. A good explanation of the motif is given in *Zohar* II, 164b, where it says concerning Ps. 104:2: 'This verse they have interpreted to mean that God, as he created the world, covered himself with that primal light and so created heaven. . . . And he stretched out the heavens like a tent and from it made the letter *waw*.' In the whole Kabbalah since *Bahir*, 'heaven' counts as a spatial symbol which manifests itself in the central Sefirah (*tifereth*) and is symbolized in the *waw* of the tetragrammaton. On the basis of its shape, *waw* was regarded as the prototype of extension into space" (Scholem, *Das Buch Bahir: Ein Schriftdenkmal aus der Frühzeit der Kabbala auf Grund der kritischen Neuausgabe* [Leipzig, 1923], p. 26).

group, for "the third letter, *waw*, designates those six Sefiroth which follow the three upper ones. It is the mystery of the union of all the Sefiroth, the upper and the lower: it ascends up to *kether* and descends down to *malkuth*. All are united with it, from above, from below, from right, and from left. *Waw* itself is called the 'middle line.' " [33]

The Kabbalistic literature of every period is full of speculations regarding the tetragram, i.e., the relations of the four numbers to one another and to the Sefiroth in particular. Whereas the *yod* is associated with the Sefirah *hohkmah*, *binah* is symbolized by the first *he*, and the sixth Sefirah, *tifereth*, by the *waw*, while the second *he* is attached to the lowest Sefirah, *malkuth*.

A differentiation between an upper and a lower *he* is already found in the mystic number speculations of the *Book Bahir*.[34] The two *he*'s are often designated as the two "mothers," the first or upper *he* corresponding to the *binah* or "higher" mother, and the second or lower *he* to the "lower" mother. The two *he*'s are also called the two Shekhinoth.

33. "Litera tertia, Waw, denotat sex illas Sephiras, quae tres supremas sequuntur, Estque mysterium unionis omnium Sephirarum, superiorum et inferiorum: et ascendit usque ad Kether, descendit usque ad Malchuth: omnesque eidem adhaerent, quaedam supra, quaedam infra, quaedam ad dextram, quaedam ad sinistram; ipsa autem vocatur linea media" (Knorr von Rosenroth, *Kabbala denudata*, I, p. 494).

34. "When R. Amora's students asked him the meaning of the separate letters, he answered: 'Actually the sequence [in the Hebrew alphabet] should have been *gimmel he* [instead of *gimmel daleth he*].' 'And why is it written *gimmel daleth*?' He said to them: '[Inasmuch as] they are interchangeable [namely, with the *he*], the *gimmel* can become *he* at its head [by a line], *daleth* by a splinter.' 'And what signifies this *he* [namely, that *he* into which these letters change themselves]?' He replied to them, 'The *upper* and the *lower he*' " (*Bahir*, § 20). Scholem remarks: "This passage of the *Bahir* is probably the oldest in which this terminology for the two *he*'s appears. Previously one meets only with the 'first' and the 'last' *he*. The new term shows plainly that here further-reaching mystical thoughts are already in the background: the 'upper' *he* is the *he* that corresponds to the 'upper' Shekhinah, and in the same way the 'lower' *he* is that corresponding to the 'lower' Shekhinah" (G. Scholem, *Das Buch Bahir: Ein Schriftdenkmal* . . .).

As father and mother, the *yod* and the *he* engender the *waw*, which, as *tifereth*, is the son of both. "It is said of God: 'And God created'; that means that father and mother created the son; for it says 'God created Jerusalem,' that is, the *waw* which is the son, who was created by *yod* and *he*, who are father and mother." [35]

Yod, *he*, *waw*, and *he*—or, respectively, *hokhmah*, *binah*, *tifereth*, and *malkuth*—constitute an inner unity or totality:

We have learned that the upper *he* was moved by the love of an inseparable companion, namely *yod*, and brought forth the *waw*. As *waw* came into being, he brought his companion with him. Then came *hesed* [love, mercy] and separated them, and roots sprang out of the Highest. Branches spread and grew, and the lower *he* was created. The branches spread higher and higher till they joined with the upper tree, and the *waw* was united with the *he*. Who accomplished this? *Hesed*. But the union of *yod* with the upper *he* is brought about not by *hesed* but by *mazal* [fortune or fate]. So *yod* is joined with *he*, *he* with *waw*, *waw* with *he*, and *he* with all, and the whole forms a unity whose parts can never be separated. But whoever effects a separation between them, so to speak lays waste the world.[36]

The myth of the separation and exile of the Shekhinah corresponds here to a kind of rending-asunder of the name of God. According to a passage in the *Zohar*, it is the demonic Lilith who steps between the two *he*'s of God's name and in this way hinders the union of *yod* with the first *he* and of *waw* with the second.[37] Hence in the mystical alphabet speculations of the *Zohar* the return from exile of the Shekhinah and her union with the Holy King correspond to the unity and wholeness of the divine name. In this sense Zechariah 14:9, "in that day shall there be one Lord, and his name one," is given an expressly mystical interpretation.

At a later time (*ca.* 1600) Abraham Hacohen Herrera, in particular, concerned himself with the symbolism of the tet-

35. *Zohar*, I, 28a.
36. *Ibid.*
37. *Zohar*, I, 27b.

ragram. Herrera (Irira) was a pupil of Israel Sarug's; and Sarug, though he had not studied with Luria, showed a very similar Kabbalistic trend. Herrera's work *Puerto del cielo* ("Gate of Heaven") was written in Spanish. A manuscript copy is still extant. It was first translated into Hebrew (*Shaar ha-shamayim*) and excerpts from this, taken for a Latin compendium, were included in Knorr von Rosenroth's *Kabbala denudata* ("Porta Coelorum"). Herrera says of the tetragram: "This is the reason why the real name [of God] has four letters, three different and one taken twice: the first *he* emanates directly from the *yod*, the other *he* indirectly from the *waw*."[38]

It would lead us too far afield to discuss here the difference between emanation by *via directa* and *via conversa*. Most important in this connection is the fact that Herrera took note of two conjunctions, namely of *yod* and *he primum* and of *waw* and *he alterum*. The idea is strongly emphasized by his terming the two *he*'s "wives" (*uxores*).

The tetragram contains four letters, of which three differ from one another. The two *he*'s are, so to speak, identical, while *yod* and *waw* are different. But on the other hand, the two *he*'s also differ, namely, as an upper and a lower *he;* while a very close relationship can also be seen between *yod* and *waw*.[39] From the psychological standpoint this paradox of identity and difference can be explained by the fact that both identity and difference are present. The identity between the two *he*'s is more pronounced and the differences less; the

38. "Et haec est causa, quod nomen essentiale habeat quatuor literas, tres diversas, & unam bis sumptam: Primum emanavit à Jod, via directa, & alterum à Vav, via conversâ & reflexâ" (R. Abraham Cohen Herrera [Irira], Lusitano "Porta coelorum. In quo Dogmata Cabbalistica philosophice proponuntur et cum Philosophia Platonica conferuntur," in *Kabbala denudata*, I, Diss. VI, Chap. VIII, 4, p. 116.)

39. There are, for example, a whole series of verbs (*verba primae yod*) in which a direct change of the *waw* to *yod*, or the reverse, can take place. This exchange of sound, as that from *yod* to *waw*, can also be observed in parallel Arabic forms (Hebr. *yalad*, causative *hiwaled* = Arab. *wâlada*) (see Gesenius-Kautzsch, *Hebr. Grammatik* [Leipzig, 1902]).

identity between *yod* and *waw* is less emphasized and the differences more prominent. In this way two conjunctions result, in which the differences between the male partners, and the identity between the female partners, are in the foreground. This results in an image which corresponds completely with the Sefirotic *quarternio:*

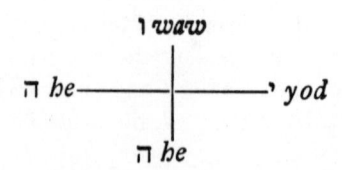

```
              ו waw
              |
  ה he ———————+——————— ׳ yod
              |
              ה he
```

In his *Mysterium Coniunctionis* Jung points repeatedly to the fact that the divine name YHWH represents a double union of two male and two female elements, which form a kind of quaternity. Referring to the Herrera passage quoted above, he has stressed the completely archetypal background of these concepts. According to him, the duality of the two *he*'s in the tetragram results because "*yod* and *vau* are masculine, and the feminine *he*, though doubled, is identical and therefore a single unit. To that extent the essential Name is a triad. But since *he* is doubled, the Name is also a tetrad or quaternity." [40]

The question why difference preponderates in the male elements and identity in the female elements of the *quaternio* is answered by Jung as follows:

The doubling of the feminine *he* is archetypal, since the marriage *quaternio* presupposes both the difference and the identity of the female figures. This is true also of the two masculine figures, as we have seen, though here the difference usually predominates—not surprisingly, since these things are mostly products of the masculine imagination. Consequently the masculine figure coincides with man's consciousness, where differences are practically absolute. Though the feminine figure is doubled, it is so little differentiated that it appears identical.[41]

40. Jung, *Mysterium Coniunctionis*, p. 430.
41. *Ibid.*

215 Psychological Aspects in Early Hasidism

From the psychological standpoint these various paradoxes have always to do with the central problem presented in our text passage—the problem of the *coniunctio* mystery and its symbolism. This is shown us by an important passage in the *Zohar* which offers various mystical interpretations of Proverbs 1:8: "My son, hear the instruction of thy father, and forsake not the law of thy mother." According to the interpretation of R. Eleazar, "father" and "mother" refer to the Holy One (*tifereth*) and the Community of Israel (*malkuth*); according to R. Yehudah, on the contrary, they refer to *hokhmah* and *binah*; while a third interpretation, by R. Yitzchak, says: "Both interpretations mean one and the same thing." [42]

Another aspect of the *coniunctio* problem which emerges from the mystic letters of the tetragram is the problem of the three and four, or the triad and the tetrad. The peculiar vacillation between triad and tetrad is the expression of a particular set of problems which assumes this form in both Kabbalistic and alchemical literature.

The three represents an expressly masculine number. It signifies the masculine, active, fiery, spiritual. The four, on the other hand, represents the feminine, passive, watery, physical. The problem of which is most worth striving for—the masculine or the feminine, the spirit or the body, triad or tetrad—betrays the existence of an uncertainty which, according to Jung, points to an "as well as," for—as he puts it—"the central ideas are ternary as well as quaternary." [43]

The symbols of the three and the four have a very special importance in the Kabbalah also. The Sefiroth tree consists of three triads—an upper, a middle, and a lower—and of three so-called pillars—a right, a middle, and a left: one pillar for every three Sefiroth. The *Zohar* says that the Ancient of Days consists of three heads that are all alike.[44] Expressly

42. *Zohar*, II, 85a.
43. Jung, *Psychology and Alchemy*, p. 26.
44. *Zohar*, III, 288a.

quaternary symbols are also frequently met with in the Kabbalah. The tetrad was already related to the tetragram by Herrera, who said that the tetragram had the quality of a real *quaternitas*, a concept mentioned earlier by the Christian Kabbalist Johannes Reuchlin. For Herrera all quaternian concepts depend upon the tetragram;[45] he speaks of "quaternions." The *quaternius* is for him a "numerus perfectus," for it contains "primum parem, nempe 2. & primum imparem & totum denarium 1. 2. 3. 4." From this he concludes: "ad hoc nomen Tetragrammati etiam applicantur sequentes Quaterniones."[46] There follow whole series of quaternities, like the four winds, the four rivers of Paradise, the four archangels, etc. His ideas are obviously based on much older concepts found in the *Zohar*.[47] There it says:

For Michael, Gabriel, Nuriel, and Raphael govern the four elements, water, fire, air, and earth, of which each has four faces. Sin, corruption, anger, and wrath are related to the *white* gall or lung which forms a plexus, to the *red* gall of the liver, whose redness comes from Mars, to the *green* gall, which is [also] connected with the liver and which is the sword of the angel of death and of which it is said [Prov. 5:4] that 'her end is bitter as wormwood, sharp as a two-edged sword,' and to the *black* gall, which is related to Lilith and governed by Saturn.[48]

The four primary colors[49] in the *Zohar* are presumably related, on the one hand, to the four planets, Jupiter, Mercury, Mars, and Saturn, which represent the four "corners of the world,"[50] and, on the other, to the four stages of the alchemical opus, which proceeds from the *nigredo* to the

45. Abraham Herrera, "Porta coelorum," in *Kabbala denudata*, Chap. VIII, p. 147.
46. *Ibid.*, p. 145.
47. Similarly, also, Knorr von Rosenroth: "omnis enim quaternio dependentiam habet a quatuor literis tetragrammati."
48. *Zohar*, III, 227b.
49. Sometimes black takes the place of the blue color; so, for instance, *Zohar*, I, 71b.
50. E. Bischoff, *Die Mystik und Magie der Zahlen* (Berlin, 1920), p. 202.

albedo and through the *citrinitas* to the *rubedo*, though sometimes the *viriditas* takes the place of the *citrinitas*.[51] In our quotation these four colors correspond to four different kinds of gall, obviously related to the humors of Hippocrates. Similarly, in the Genesis exegesis of the *Zohar*, the darkness which, it says, "lay on" *tehom* contains a black, a white, a red, and a green fire.

In certain *Zohar* passages [52] the four elements, the four points of the compass, the four principal metals, etc., are connected with one another, so that a quaternion results, such as is also known to alchemy: [53]

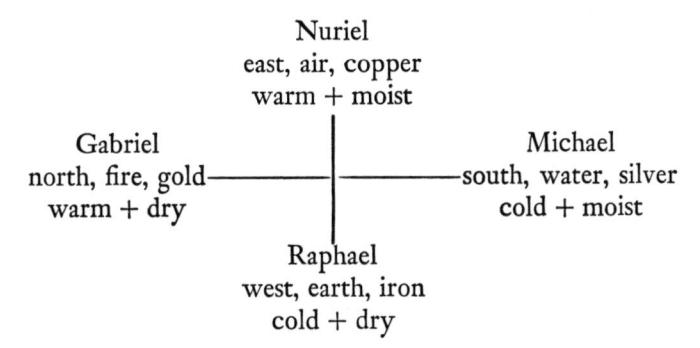

```
                    Nuriel
              east, air, copper
                warm + moist
                      │
Gabriel               │                Michael
north, fire, gold ────┼──── south, water, silver
 warm + dry           │          cold + moist
                      │
                    Raphael
              west, earth, iron
                 cold + dry
```

We also find the same uncertainty or vacillation between the three and the four or the seven and the eight. Scholem has pointed out that "most of the old Kabbalists knew three different worlds, the upper, the middle, and the lower," while

---

51. Jung, *Psychology and Alchemy*, p. 219.
52. For example, *Zohar*, II, 23b.
53. A very similar quaternion pattern is found in Moses de León's *Sheqel ha-qodesh*, as also in *Codex München* 47, which, according to G. Scholem, must be accounted as a fragment of an early work of Moses de León. In the latter there is, in addition, reference to four principal vowels and to the four standards of camp organization (Num. 2:3), as well as to the four letters of the tetragram YHWH, which last are called the four basic elements of the spiritual world (*arba yessodeth elyonim*) (G. Scholem, "Eine unbekannte mystische Schrift des Mose de Leon," *Monatsschrift für Geschichte und Wissenschaft des Judentums* [1927], pp. 116 ff.).

the later Kabbalists afterward postulated the so-called four-world theory.[54]

The four is sometimes in the strange situation of being apparently left out altogether. The cornerstone (*ewen shetiyah*) which, as the rock Moriah, served as Isaac's sacrificial altar and later as the altar for burned sacrifices in Solomon's temple, and which is called the center of Jerusalem and the world, consists of water, fire, and air. The fourth element, the earth, is apparently lacking, but, according to the *Zohar*, this cornerstone was hurled by God into the earth and buried. In the tetramorphic vision of Ezekiel, which since the beginning of Jewish mysticism has been the starting point for Kabbalistic meditations and speculations, there are three theriomorphic figures—a lion, an eagle, and an ox—while the fourth and disparate element is a man.[55]

The fourth has the further peculiarity of sometimes appearing doubled. We have already mentioned the doubling of the *he* in the tetragram. Or, as something apart, the fourth is directly opposite the triad, in which case the triad and the one unite to form a quaternity. The *Zohar* says:

At the time that the Lord unites with the *matronita*, a messenger comes from the south and cries: Awake, ye heavenly hosts, and unfold the banner of love in honor of your Lord! Then one of the leaders of the heavenly host—his name is Bo-el ["God is in him"]—stands up. In his hand are four keys which he took from the four ends of the world. On one key is engraved the sign *yod*, on another key the sign *he*, and on the third key the sign *waw*. And he lays them under the Tree of Life. These three keys, which are marked with the three signs, become one. After they have united, there comes to them that other key [namely,

54. G. Scholem, "Eine unbekannte mystische Schrift des Mose de Leon," p. 118.

55. In Jewish ornamentation the fish triad and the four fishes are often used together as a Messianic symbol; see Rahel Wischnitzer-Bernstein, *Gestalten und Symbole der jüdischen Kunst* (Berlin, 1935), pp. 123 and 135. The vacillation between three and four, or between seven and eight, can be followed as far as the symbolism of ritual; the most ancient Jewish cult symbol is the seven-branched candlestick. An eight-branched candlestick is used at the Feast of Chanukah.

the fourth, with the sign *he*] and unites itself with these others which are the union of the three, and all orders and companies [of angels] come to these two keys [namely, the three that united into one, and the fourth], and they all enter the garden [Eden], and all express the unity [of God] even as it happens below.[56]

Speculations of this kind are found throughout Kabbalistic literature, including those mystical speculations on the Hebrew letter *shin*,[57] which consists of three heads on three beams, and which many Kabbalists assert formerly had four heads, one of which was subsequently lost.[58]

After this digression let us return to the symbolism of the four letters of the divine name YHWH. The first two letters, *yod* and *he*, form the divine name YH, already exemplified in the Bible and to which, since the very earliest times, mystical powers have been ascribed. Hence the Talmud says that God consummated the whole Creation with these two consonants, since the word "let there be" (in Hebrew *yehi*, YHY) contains these two letters. According to an old Talmudic *aggadah*, "this world was created with *he* and the future world with *yod*." [59]

56. *Zohar*, I, 133b.

57. The phylacteries (*tefillin*) have a three-headed *shin* on the right side of the prayer cap (*tefillin shel rosh*), which is worn on the forehead, while the left side bears a four-headed *shin* (*Schulḥan arukh, Oraḥ ḥayim*, §§ 32, 42). Magen Abraham, in his commentary on this passage, points out that the four-headed *shin* is "more estimable" than the three-headed. Otherwise Halakhic literature, such as *ha 'manhig* by R. Abraham ben ha-Yarchi of Lunel and *Orhoth hayim* by R. Aaron ben Jacob ha-Cohen, adds little toward the elucidation of this ritual symbolism.

58. The close connection between the quaternity and the deity has been known since time out of mind and points to an archetypal character, evidenced in the syncretic Judeo-Hellenistic name *tettrassyah* or *tettrossyah* ("God is the four") of the early mystical Hekhaloth text, in the Gnostic name Barbelo (*be arba eloah* = God is in the quaternity, namely, Father, Son, Sophia, and Primal Man), and by the names Barbariel and Ἀρβαθιάω of the Egyptian papyri.

59. *Talmud Babyl. Tractate Menakhot*, 29b: "An exposition by R. Yehudah ben Ileai: Those are the two worlds which the Holy One, praised be He, has created, the one with the *he*, the other with the *yod*. I had not known whether the future world with *yod* and this world

The *Zohar* speaks in one passage of four variants of God's name YHWH:

So he [David] played on the harp in four ways: a simple song designated by Y, a double song designated by YH, a threefold one by YHW, a fourfold by YHWH. And these are the ten signs which David fashioned, corresponding to ten kinds of psalms. But they increase again to 72 faces according to the reckoning of these ten letters.[60]

The connection between the letters four, ten, and seventy-two seems somewhat strange to begin with. But Johannes Reuchlin, the humanist and Kabbalah student, had already attempted to derive the tetractys of the Pythagoreans from the tetragram. When we look at the four different names of God in an ascending pattern conforming to the Pythagorean tetractys, we obtain the following picture: [61]

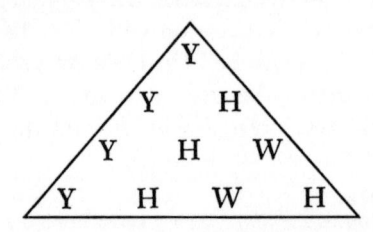

```
        Y
      Y   H
    Y   H   W
  Y   H   W   H
```

Here the *four* letters of the divine name YHWH form a Greek delta, whose number value is also 4. But at the same time the diagram contains *ten* letters. We reach the same end sum if we write the four letters in the so-called πληρωματικός or *plene* orthography (*be milim*) of number mysticism, that is, as they are pronounced. *Yod* + *he* + *waw* +

---

with *he*, or this world with *yod* and the future world with *he*. Therefore it is said [Gen. 2:4]: 'These are the generations of the heavens and of the earth when they were created.' But one should not read *be hibaram* [as they were created] but rather *be-he baram* [with *he* He created them]." Similarly in the Midrash of the alphabet by R. Akiba, *cit.* August Wünsche, *Aus Israels Lehrhallen: Kleine Midraschin zur jüdischen Ethik, Buchstaben- und Zahlensymbolik* (Leipzig, 1909).

60. *Zohar*, III, 227b.
61. Ernst Müller, *Der Sohar* (Vienna, 1932), p. 167, n.

he = ten letters. If we now replace the letters of the tetractys by their corresponding number value—*yod* = 10, *he* = 5, *waw* = 6, and *he* = 5—we arrive at the number 72. This again may be connected with the seventy-two-letter name of God.[62]

The close connections between tetrads and decads can be traced in Jewish as well as in non-Jewish literature. The concept of the number ten as a kind of unity is already found in the Old Testament, which, along with the ten plagues, tells of the Ten Commandments on Sinai and the ten horns of Daniel's apocalypse. In the Midrash we find God's ten miracles of the sea and the ten categories of angels. The Pythagoreans held in the highest esteem the *teleios arithmos* ("perfect number"), namely the square of $1 + 2 + 3 + 4 = 10$. It is described as a sacred number "in the formula of the oath sworn by the tetractys, the powerful and mysterious decad, source and root of eternity."[63] Aristotle, too, calls the decad the "number of completeness" because the numbers of the first decad are used to form all other numbers.

According to an old Talmudic tradition, *ten* things were created on the first day of Creation: heaven and earth, *tohu-wa-bohu*, ("waste and void"), light and darkness, wind and water, the measure of the day and the night. Heaven and earth—for it is said in the Scriptures: "In the beginning God created heaven and earth." *Tohu-wa-bohu*—for it is said: "And the earth was a *tohu-wa-bohu*." Darkness—for it is said: "And darkness was upon the face of the deep." Light—for it is said: "And God said, let there be light." Wind and water—for it is said: "And the Spirit of God moved upon the face of the waters." Day and night—for it is said: "And the evening and the morning were the first day."

---

62. Abraham ibn Ezra, *Yesod mora* ("Foundation of the Fear of God"), Chap. II, cit. Ernst Müller, *Abraham ibn Ezra, Buch der Einheit* (Berlin, 1921); see also Müller, *History of Jewish Mysticism* (Oxford, 1946).

63. Léon Brunschvicg, *Le rôle du Pythagorisme dans l'évolution des idées* (Paris, 1937).

It has been transmitted that *tohu* is the green line that surrounds the whole world and from which darkness enters the world.[64]

The number speculations of the *Book Yetsirah* place great stress upon the unity and completeness of the number ten. The "thirty-two secret paths of Creation" consist of the three primary decads and the twenty-two letters of the Hebrew alphabet. It says of the primary numbers that they are *belimah*, that is, separate entities which together form a unity, since "their end is joined to the beginning and their beginning to the end."[65]

The decad and its relation to the tetrad are also contained in the Gnostic theory of aeons. According to Irenaeus, the Gnostics taught that

> Moses, at the very beginning of the Creation story, already indicated the mother of all things, since he says: "In the beginning God created heaven and earth." Since—they say—he speaks of these four, God and the beginning, heaven and earth, he has expressed their fourfoldness. But in order to show also what is invisible and hidden in them, he says: "And the earth was without form and void." The second quaternity, however, as the issue of the first, he has spoken of by naming the "deep" and the darkness in which are the water and the Spirit moving above it. Then he is also mindful of the decad and names the light, day and night, the firmament, evening and morning, land and sea, plants, and, as the tenth, wood. So by these ten names he has proclaimed the ten aeons.[66]

Philo calls the quaternion the "cause and source of the most perfect decad."[67]

---

64. *Talmud Babyl. Tractate Hagiga*, 12a. According to M. Friedländer, "Tohu, the green circle surrounding the world" represents the "Ophitic diagram" (M. Friedländer, *Der vorchristliche Gnostizismus* [Göttingen, 1898]). Cf. H. Leisegang, *Die Gnosis* (Leipzig, 1924), pp. 160 f.
65. The *Book Yetsirah* (Mantua, 1562).
66. Irenaeus, *Haer.* I. 18. 1, *cit.* M. Friedländer, *op. cit.*, pp. 112 f.
67. Philo, *De mundi opif.* I. 10.

223 Psychological Aspects in Early Hasidism

Johannes Reuchlin in his *De verbo mirifico* relates the decads to the ten Sefiroth, while Agrippa of Nettesheim connects the ten Sefiroth with the *decem nomina mystica* of the Church Father Hieronymus.[68] With Jacob Boehme, too, the decad plays a considerable role. According to him, the ternarius and the septenary of the nature- or well-spirits stem from the abyss (*Ungrund*), which corresponds to the *en Sof* of the Kabbalah.

Moses Cordovero speaks of the decad as a perfect number, for "the number which contains everything is the ten, and no other besides. Everything which goes beyond the ten returns again to the unit." [69]

Jewish number mysticism, in all its various forms, whose beginnings can be traced back to the Talmudic period and which reached its full flowering in the mediaeval Kabbalah, employs a whole series of different ways of counting, in which numbers are substituted for letters or whole words, or certain numbers are substituted for other numbers. By the usual or "great" numbering (*mispar gadol*) the first letter of the Hebrew alphabet corresponds to 1, the second to 2, and so forth, while the last five letters are used for the hundreds. Counting by the square root of words is carried out by replacing the square root of a given word or letter by another method of calculation, that of letter-square-root numeration, namely, the sum of the squares of the single letters of a given word.

There exists a form of counting, the so-called "progressive" counting, in which the letter is replaced, not by a number, but by a progressive summation of the sums of the numbers in a series. Since, for example, the sum of the first five numbers of the series $1 + 2 + 3 + 4 + 5 = 15$, the number value of 15 also accrues to the five. On the other hand, the sum of the first four numbers gives $1 + 2 + 3 + 4 = 10$. Con-

---

68. Hieronymus, *Marcell. epist.* 136. III.
69. Moses Cordovero, *Pardes rimmonim* ("Pomegranate Garden"), cit. J. Molitor, *Philosophie der Geschichte oder Ueber die Tradition* (Münster, 1857).

sequently, the fourth letter, *daleth,* whose number value is 4, also symbolizes ten. The habitual substitution of the number value of the name for the name itself is called, in number mysticism, the "method of the face or the front side" (*panim*). The method of combination, on the other hand, by which the four at the same time symbolizes the ten, is termed the "union of the fours." The procedure itself is usually designated the "method of the back side." At times there is mention of the "mystery of the back-side union of the fours" (*sod rebua ahurim*) or simply the "mystery of the back side" (*sod ahurim*).[70] According to Albertus Magnus, the *anthropos,* which for him represents a sort of world soul (*anima mundi*), contains the *four* elements which together form a decad.[71]

As we have seen, the number ten, or decad, contains the tetrad; indeed it has actually originated in the tetrad. Like the quaternity, the decad represents a unity or totality—to be sure, a unity on a higher plane. Here we meet with highly significant lines of connections with contemporary alchemy, for the *denarius* (decad) "forms the *totius operis summa,* the culminating point beyond which it is impossible to go except by means of the multiplication. For, although the *denarius* represents a higher stage of unity, it is also a multiple of 1 and can therefore be multiplied to infinity. . . ."[72]

It may seem that with our excursion into the realm of *coniunctio* mysticism and Kabbalistic number symbolism we have touched upon a field only distantly related to our problem. Yet these very ideas provide the archetypal foundation without which it is impossible to have a truly deep understanding of Hasidic mysticism. The union of the opposites, the resulting wholeness represented by the quaternity or, on a higher level, by the decad, are the symbolic expression of the totality of the human being that includes not only consciousness but also the unconscious.

70. S. A. Horodezky, art. "Gematria," *Encyclop. Jud.,* Vol. VII.
71. Jung, *Psychology and Alchemy,* p. 222.
72. Jung, *The Practice of Psychotherapy,* pp. 304 f.

That is why the union of opposite aspects is of vital concern to Gnosticism, Kabbalah, alchemy, and to mysticism in the widest sense. We meet with this concept very early in Jewish literature, but only in Jewish mysticism did it acquire its distinctive character. In the Midrash, a vast collection of myths, tales, and legends, it is fire (*esh*) and water (*mayim*) that have to be united so that heaven (*shamayim*) may come to be.[73] As is well known, the mystical reinterpretation of the Song of Solomon as the union of God with Israel saved it from being relegated to the Apocrypha at the time the Old Testament was canonized.[74]

Naturally, this concept of the *coniunctio* is not a matter of "inventions" or attempts at rational explanations but of a primal motif or collective image which is part of the culture of every people at certain stages of the development of consciousness. In other words, it is what Jung has called an archetype. The numinous character of the union of opposites is accentuated when it is transposed to the divine sphere, since the union of the conscious and the unconscious now also represents the union of *hokhmah* and *binah*. The archetype of the *coniunctio*—like every archetype—is the kind of universal concept that can be understood only as a manifestation of the collective unconscious. When even noted scholars like August Wünsche find the symbolism of the *coniunctio* obscene and blasphemous and go so far as to make statements

---

73. The same in *Zohar*, II, 164b: "At first the light was on the right and the darkness on the left. What did the Holy One then, blessed be He? He mixed them together and out of this made the heavens." Similarly in the *Bahir*, § 102: "And why is it called 'heaven'? Because it is circular in shape like a head, and that teaches that water is at its right and fire at its left and it in the middle, and that [means the word for heaven] *shamayim*: out of fire [*esh*] and water [*mayim*]."

74. The prophets' image of the Divine Marriage belongs here also, as was pointed out by Dr. Rivkah Schärf Kluger ("Das Bild der Gottesehe bei den Propheten des A.T." [ms.]). [Translator's note: This paper appeared as "The Image of the Marriage between God and Israel as It Occurs in the Prophets of the Old Testament, especially Ezekiel XVI," in *Spring 1950* (Analytical Psychology Club of New York, Inc.). At present out of print.]

like "Kabbalistic literature, especially the *Zohar*, celebrates the cohabitation of king and queen in expressions that verge on the shameless and violate decency and morality to the utmost,"[75] this only demonstrates an unfortunate lack of understanding of the symbolic content of these texts.[76]

As long as psychic contents are unconscious, they usually appear in projected form. As inner factors they remain unknown to us, but they present themselves to us in outer objects.

In the terrestrial realm, for instance—as we said above—it is fire and water that unite and form heaven. Looked at from this standpoint, alchemy's acceptance of the Star of David enclosed in a circle as the "philosopher's stone" or the *filius philosophorum* is easily understood. This symbol (☆), as alchemy conceives it, represents the union of fire (△) and water (▽); the surrounding circle refers to the totality and infinity of *en Sof*, which contains and encompasses the united opposites. Kabbalist and alchemist alike experienced the union of opposites in the form of cosmic projections, as the union of Sol and Luna. Terrestrial and cosmic projection might be termed the allegorical plane. As a further development this

---

75. August Wünsche, art. "Kabbala," *Realenencyclopädie für protest. Theologie*" (Leipzig, 1898), p. 673.

76. E. Bischoff expresses himself similarly: "This image (of the union of *tifereth* and *malkuth*) seems particularly offensive, in that Biblical phrases referring to God (his entry into Jerusalem, Zion, etc.) are related to this mystical sexual act of *'tifereth,'* since *'tifereth'* is in any case thought of as a manifestation form or revelation potency of God" (Erich Bischoff, *Die Elemente der Kabbala* [Berlin, 1920], I, 230). Equally astray are the speculations of M. D. Langer, who is largely influenced by Blüher's and Freud's lines of thought. He completely overlooks the suprapersonal backgrounds of the *coniunctio* concept, i.e., the underlying archetype of the union of the opposites (D. M. Langer, *Die Erotik in der Kabbala* [Prague, 1923], pp. 140 f.). In contrast, Arthur Edward Waite has shown a considerably greater understanding of the symbol content of Jewish mysticism (A. E. Waite, *The Holy Kabbala* [London, 1929]). Here I will not go into the extremely fantastic ideas of Israel Regardie, which represent a pseudo-scientific medley of analytical psychology, Kabbalah, and magic practices (I. Regardie, *The Middle Pillar* [Chicago, 1945], and *The Philosopher's Stone* [London, n.d.].

union takes place on the mystical plane. The mysticism of the Song of Solomon sees it as a union of God and Israel, the Christian variant as that of Christ and Ecclesia; and, since the time of Bernhard de Clairvaux, it has been thought of as the union of Christ and the soul. We cannot enter more closely here into the more important differences between the concepts of Jewish and non-Jewish mysticism. As we saw, in the Kabbalah this event is moved into the Sefirotic sphere and so into the sphere of the divine. Scholem is right when he says:

> But while in other instances the Kabbalists refrain from employing sexual imagery in describing the relation between man and God, they show no such hesitation when it comes to describing the relation of God to himself, in the world of the Sefiroth. The mystery of sex, as it appears to the Kabbalist, has a terribly deep significance. This mystery of human existence is for him nothing but a symbol of the love between the Divine "I" and the Divine "You," the Holy One, blessed be He, and his Shekhinah. The ἱερός γάμος, the "sacred union" of the King and Queen, the Celestial Bridegroom and the Celestial Bride, to name only a few of the symbols, is the central fact of a whole chain of divine manifestations in the hidden world. *In God* there is a union of the active and the passive, procreation and conception, from which all mundane life and bliss are derived.[77]

This union *in God* constitutes "the true unity of God, which lies beyond the diversity of His various aspects. . . ."[78] In psychological terms, this would point to a process occurring for the most part in the unconscious. Consciousness plays a part insofar as it reflects the unconscious processes in symbols or images. Thus these symbols represent a reflection of the unconscious in consciousness. In contrast to alchemy, which projected the unconscious into unknown matter, the Kabbalah remains in the world of the spirit. This fact is important because it explains many difficulties which impede the understanding of Kabbalistic treatises. In addition it offers an expla-

---

77. G. Scholem, *Major Trends in Jewish Mysticism* (New York, 1941), p. 227.
78. *Ibid.*

nation for the outspoken, often overobtrusive, sex symbolism in the Kabbalah, which becomes the more pronounced, the more purely spiritual the realm in which its concepts move.

Now, it seems as if the Great Maggid, passing beyond the allegorical and mystical planes, had reached a higher level, which may be described as psychological. For it is clearly evidenced by the whole pattern of connections in our texts that the Great Maggid possessed an intuitive awareness that this *coniunctio* took place in the depths of the human soul. We have already pointed out that, in our first text passage, the separation of *hokhmah* and *binah*, of the unconscious and the conscious, occurred in the human heart. It is the man who reflects who receives ideas from the unconscious. It is indeed man who holds the center of the stage. The transition to a deeper psychological understanding is already clearly shown in the Sefiroth mysticism of the Kabbalah: the Sefiroth as the foundation of all existence not only form the facets of God's being; they are also the structural elements of the human psyche.[79] So the wisdom and discriminating intelligence of God correspond to the wisdom and discriminating intelligence of man. To be sure, with the Great Maggid the "union of the higher hypostases" is less in the foreground than the *coniunctio sekhel–qadmut-ha-sekhel*. And yet the archetypal model is not lost sight of, and the relationship of the *coniunctio sekhel–qadmut-ha-sekhel* to that suprapersonal happening is completely apparent.

So one could say that the development of human consciousness out of the unconscious appears, from the human standpoint, as a reflection or refraction of the unfolding of divine intelligence (*binah*) out of divine wisdom (*hokhmah*). In this way the human soul has bestowed on it the dignity of becoming the mirror of an intradivine drama of development,

---

79. According to Scholem, "there is something in the human soul which corresponds to the Sefirah *hokhmah*" (G. Scholem, *Ha-bilti moda we-mussag qadmut-ha-sekhel be sifruth ha-hassidith* ("The Unconscious and the Concept *qadmut-ha-sekhel* in Hasidic Literature") (Jerusalem, 1944), p. 5.

Text Passage 9

When one or another clever idea enters a man's consciousness, this certainly originates in the world of thought. But what is it that brings the thought into his consciousness? It is something hidden, altogether unknown, it is the Crown, it is called the Nothing and the unconscious (*qadmut-ha-sekhel*).

(*Or ha-emeth*, 77a)

Commentary

THIS QUOTATION is of particular interest because here the symbol *hokhmah* is replaced by *kether* or *ayin*, that is, by the mystical primal Nothing. However, it is not only characteristic of the Great Maggid, it is typical of Hasidism in general, that under certain conditions aspects of *kether* or *ayin* are transferred to *hokhmah*. Yet such an obliteration of the boundary lines of Kabbalistic symbolism is found not only in the Great Maggid but quite generally in Hasidic writings.

VII. THE UNCONSCIOUS—DREAM—PROPHECY

THE FOLLOWING PASSAGE is taken from *Or ha-meir*, the work of one of the Great Maggid's students, Zeev Wolf of Shitomir,[1] the so-called Maggid of Shitomir.

Text Passage 10

I heard from the Great Maggid—may his memory be a blessing for us in our life in the Beyond—in relation to what the wise

1. R. Zeev Wolf of Shitomir, *Or ha-meir* ("The Shining Light") (Koretz, 1708), chapter on "*Rosh hashana*," p. 38a. I owe Professor Scholem special thanks for a letter telling me of this textual passage.

men told [*Talmud Tractate Berakhot*]: "As he woke early in the morning, a verse came to him." That is the "small prophetic vision." The question now is: Often our eyes see a dream. In the dream a quotation [comes] to us in the midst of sleep. When sleep flees, this verse comes to us immediately upon awaking. [But] this is as yet no proof that it is a case of a "small prophetic vision." And he [the Maggid of Meseritz] explained the meaning of the passage "as he woke early in the morning, a verse came to him" as follows: He pressed forward as far as the unconscious [*qidmat-ha-sekhel*] which had caused the thought [*mahashabah*]. The unconscious is something primordial that contains much more light and power than the level of [conscious] thought. But the human being reaches the level of the unconscious only after he has freed himself from [the bonds of] the senses. He must think of himself as if he had no more connection with this world. [Then] he becomes united with the innermost [reaches] of his thought and the height of his divine nature, so that he no longer perceives his own self. This is a proof that he has pressed forward as far as the unconscious. But such a one can, if he will, raise himself above the sensuality of the world, be it by night or by day. That is [according to the Maggid of Meseritz] the meaning of the passage "as he woke early in the morning, a verse came to him." That signifies that he pressed forward to the unconscious at any time and whenever he would, freeing himself from sensuality during the day [also] and not only when he awoke in the early morning. That is the "small prophetic vision," for the concretized thought does not come from phantasy [imagination] but is like a "small prophetic vision." But for this one needs a testing of consciousness and a careful pondering and consideration.

(*Or ha-meir*, p. 38a)

Commentary

A STUDY OF THIS PASSAGE shows us first of all that it consists of three layers that are related to one another. First comes a quotation from the Talmud. Then follows a commentary on this verse, which is not from the Talmud, and finally a special

231 Psychological Aspects in Early Hasidism

interpretation which the Maggid of Shitomir has taken from the Maggid of Meseritz.

The quotation itself runs: "Rabbi Johanan said: If someone rises early in the morning and a verse occurs to him, that is a 'small prophetic vision.'" It is worth noting that this verse is taken from the *Tractate Berakhot*.[2] It is contained in one of the longer chapters of the treatise, which is devoted to a detailed examination of the nature and significance of dreams. The quotation continues: "Rabbi Johanan says further: three dreams are fulfilled, namely, the dream in the morning, the dream a friend dreams about you, and the dream that contains its own meaning." Although our verse itself has no real connection with dreams, the whole context in which it is set shows clearly that a connection exists. The commentator on this verse obviously knew there must be a connection between an early-morning dream and an early-morning remembrance of a Biblical verse, for he expressly says that this verse first occurred in the dream. When the dreamer awakes early and obviously is still influenced by the immediate impression of the dream occurrence, he remembers the verse which entered his consciousness out of the region of dream. Such a thought from the unconscious is designated by the commentator as a "small prophetic vision." The sense of a close relation between dream and prophecy has been alive in Judaism since the earliest times. Already in the Bible we read the familiar saying: "If there be a prophet among you, I the Lord will make myself known to him in a vision, and will speak to him in a dream."[3] The same *Tractate Berakhot* from which the above quotation is taken calls the dream the "sixtieth part of prophecy."[4] And the Midrash says: "The

2. *Talmud babyl.* (Vilna) *Tractate Berakhot*, 55b. The same verse is found verbatim also in *Berakhot*, 57b. Here Rashi, in his commentary on the passage, interprets the phrase "awaking early" (*hishkim*) as "when one rises from one's couch."

3. Numbers 12:6.

4. *Talmud babyl. Tractate Berakhot*, 57b. Maimonides comments on this passage in *Guide to the Perplexed:* "Such a comparison of quantity could not take place between two things that are of a different nature" (*Moreh nebukim*, II, 36).

dream is the unripe fruit fallen from the tree of prophecy."[5]

The *Zohar*, in commenting on Genesis 46:2 ("And God spake unto Israel in the visions of the night . . .") discriminates between vision and dream, saying that a dream is more precise than a vision and can explain what is dark in a vision.[6] That is why our commentator calls the dream a "small" prophecy or prophetic vision, in contrast to a genuine prophecy.

Maimonides in particular has repeatedly spoken of the close connection between dream and prophetic vision. He explains the nature of prophecy by saying that the emanation or radiation proceeding from God "is transmitted by the mediation of the active intellect, first to the thinking faculty and then to the imagination of man. In this state man reaches the highest degree of perfection possible to him as a human being."[7] For Maimonides, prophecy is closely connected with his theory of *intellectus agens*. When this "intelligence" streams into the human soul, it may act upon either a man's imagination or his intellect. In the first case he will become an oracle or a dreamer, in the latter, a learned man or a scientist. But when both imagination and intellect are involved, he will become a prophet.[8] According to Maimonides, the dream is a kind of pre-stage of actual prophecy, for the prophets "see prophetic visions in a dream, in a vision of the night, or by day if they fall into a deep sleep."[9] But even in the waking state a prophet may experience dreams and visions, especially if he is able to withdraw himself from the sense impressions of the external world.[10]

Now the Maggid of Shitomir carries the elucidation of the verse in question still further, by giving it a truly mystical

5. *Midrash bereshith rabba*, 17, 7; 44, 19.
6. *Zohar*, I, 149b.
7. Maimonides, *Moreh nebukim* ("Guide to the Perplexed"). Also *Mishneh Torah*.
8. Maimonides, *op. cit.*
9. *Ibid.*
10. Philipp Bloch, *Charakteristik und Inhaltsangaben des Moreh Nebuchim* (Leipzig, 1908), pp. 35 ff.

interpretation. He, too, calls the dream thought a "small prophetic vision," but only if it emanates from the sphere of the *qadmut-ha-sekhel*. Only if the dreamer can penetrate the depths of the unconscious proper can the thought be called prophetic. Therefore the Great Maggid interprets the phrase "early rising" (*hishkim*) as "penetrating into and on" into the *qadmut-ha-sekhel*. In order to attain this self-immersion, one must withdraw so far from the "sensuality" of the outer world that it loses its significance. Thus the inner world acquires more and more importance. In psychological terms, this is a process of active introversion. It also explains why one is able "at any time and whenever he wishes" to penetrate to the *qidmat-ha-sekhel* also "during the day, not only on waking early in the morning."

Turning away from outer reality must by no means be interpreted here as a flight from the world. It means neither a negation of life nor a devaluation of the here and now. For the Maggid, the withdrawal from the "sensuality" of the world signifies an introspective self-submergence. For, as he says in another place, "a man should gradually detach his ego from his body till he has passed through all the worlds and has become one with God, till he disappears entirely out of the bodiless world."[11] Thus self-detachment is the prerequisite for religious vision. It leads to a turning-away from self, a self-surrender, a self-submergence in God, and finally to that which the Hasidic mystic is wont to term bondage to God or *debequth*.[12] Solomon Maimon writes about it in his autobiography, after his journey to the Maggid of Meseritz: "As long as a man acts from himself, he is incapable of receiving the effect of the Holy Spirit. For this purpose he must comport himself like an instrument, only passively."[13] A

11. S. A. Horodezky, *Religiöse Strömungen im Judentum. Mit besonderer Berücksichtigung des Chassidismus* (Bern and Leipzig, 1920), p. 87.
12. Cf. especially G. Scholem, "Devekuth or Communion with God," *Review of Religion* (Columbia University Press, 1950).
13. Solomon Maimon, *Lebensgeschichte*, with Introduction and notes by Dr. Jakob Fromer (Munich, 1911), p. 200.

student of the Great Maggid who later became famous, R. Shneur Zalman of Ladi, says: "While our blessed Maggid spoke of the Torah, the Shekhinah spoke through his mouth, and the Spirit of God in him, but he was completely detached from the world." [14] Solomon of Lusk writes in a very similar vein: "The Maggid said to us: 'I will teach in what disposition one can best speak about the Torah. It is the state in which one no longer has any sense at all of one's own self, is all ear, so that it is not the speaker himself who speaks, but the world of speech in him." [15]

The use of the expression "self" could be misunderstood, but the whole context shows that the Great Maggid naturally did not understand "self" as that which we mean by it psychologically. On the contrary, he sets this "self" of his own over against the "world of speech" or his egoistic personal sphere against the suprapersonal. The relationship to this other world and to prophecy is for him the criterion by which to measure a man's penetration into the real unconscious, the *qidmat-ha-sekhel*.

When we now relate the Great Maggid's concepts of the unconscious to those of modern psychology, certain parallels can be established. To be sure, C. G. Carus already has stated: "The key to the understanding of the conscious life of the soul lies in the region of the unconscious," [16] and Eduard von Hartmann has spoken of that which is divine in us, which contains both conscious and unconscious.[17] But to both Carus and Hartmann the unconscious is metaphysical in nature and is hence a concept of philosophy. Freud, for whom the unconscious was mainly what has been repressed, and Adler, for whom it represents, more or less, a mere "artifice of the psyche," have attempted to explain the unconscious from the conscious standpoint and to find its source in consciousness.

14. Horodezky, *op. cit.*, p. 78.
15. *Maggid debarab le-Jaaqob*, Introduction.
16. C. G. Carus, *Psyche*, (Jena, 1926), p. 1.
17. Eduard von Hartmann, *Die moderne Psychologie* (Leipzig, 1901), p. 33.

With the Maggid of Meseritz the process is exactly reversed: consciousness derives from the unconscious because for him the unconscious is primary and pre-existent, a preconsciousness which precedes consciousness. It also contains man's creative powers, which manifest themselves in consciousness as sudden intuitive ideas. This brings us close to the view of C. G. Jung, for whom the unconscious is the origin of consciousness and the real source of man's creativity. Perhaps we may therefore call our author one of the forerunners of modern psychology.

In conclusion I should like to attempt to answer two further questions.

1. How can we explain the fact that in our texts the unconscious appears as masculine and the conscious as feminine? This question can be answered from the symbolic as well as the psyshological standpoint.

First it must be pointed out that one and the same symbol, depending on the particular situation, may emerge from the unconscious into consciousness in either a masculine or a feminine form. For this the symbolism of sun and moon offers numerous examples. This holds to an exceptional degree for Sefiroth symbolism. So—to give one example—the Sefirah *malkuth* contains *hesed* as well as *din*, that is, both the masculine and the feminine aspect. Whether *malkuth* appears masculine or feminine will depend upon which aspect predominates.

Looked at from the standpoint of masculine consciousness, one could say that the active consciousness would seem masculine, while the unconscious would be felt as something alien and feminine. But if the situation is reversed by the transference of the activity of masculine consciousness into the unconscious, then the active unconscious appears to the passive consciousness as something masculine, while consciousness feels itself to be feminine. This fact throws an interesting light on the psychological attitude of the Great Maggid. It appears that with him it is above all the unconscious that assumes the leadership, so that his feminine, passive, receptive consciousness encounters it as something masculine, active, and shape-giving.

2. At the outset of our study we brought up the question of what it was that could have moved the Great Maggid to speak in diverse vocabularies. We also wondered why he employed ancient images and symbols from Jewish mysticism, like Divine Wisdom, discriminating intelligence, Primordial Point and Palace, Father and Mother, the Mystery of Union, etc., to describe phenomena like consciousness and the unconscious. In this connection we asked ourselves, further, what led him, along with this Kabbalistic symbolic language, to coin what may well be called a modern scientific language of his own.

This problem is related to another question, which has been posed by Scholem. In the article that we have often cited, he asks himself in what sense—the theological (or, as he calls it, theosophical) or the psychological sense—the terms *sekhel* and *qadmut-ha-sekhel* are used, which aspect of these concepts is in the foreground. Scholem believes that with the Great Maggid the theological-mystical aspect of the concepts is unimportant and that psychological problems predominate throughout. "It is clear to every reader that the Maggid speaks in a theosophical language on questions and problems of human thought and its stages of development. Not the divine *binah*, but its reflection in the human soul, the human *binah* or thinking"[18] is the starting point for the author's speculations. Further, "every reader of the book *Maggid debarab le-Jaaqob* is convinced that the author has no interest in the explanation or exploration of the divine realm that was closed to him; on the contrary, he is always interested in explaining [problems] of man and his soul, while consistently employing a fixed Kabbalistic terminology."[19]

18. G. Scholem, *Ha-bilti moda we-mussag qadmut-ha-sekhel be sifruth ha-hassidith* ("The Unconscious and the Concept *qadmut-ha-sekhel* in Hasidic Literature") (Jerusalem, 1944), p. 4.
19. *Ibid.*

According to this conception, there exists no immediate connection between the divine realm of the Sefiroth and the image of the Sefiroth in the human soul, except insofar as human wisdom is a mirroring or reflection of divine wisdom. Such a conception is indeed supported by the Kabbalah, which teaches that "the Sefiroth are not restricted to the divine world" but also constitute "the essential structure of every single being." [20] There is much to be said for this conception. However, in my opinion it requires further elucidation from the psychological standpoint. For it is still an open question why the Great Maggid made use of the *"fixed Kabbalistic* terminology," when a *scientific* terminology lay at his disposal.

It seems to me that precisely this "dual" situation in the divine *and* human realms led the Great Maggid—consciously or unconsciously—to make use of two vocabularies: one theological-mystical and the other psychological-conceptual. This hypothesis is supported first of all by the fact that the personality of the Maggid discloses two sides, two ways of being, as is shown by the account of his transformation experience. On the one hand, he is a rational Talmudist whose consciousness is determined by his adherence to the world of Jewish tradition and law, but, at the same time, he has very deep ties to the world of Jewish mysticism. As rational thinker, he inclines to abstract intellectualization, but, as irrational mystic, Kabbalistic symbol and image are for him alive and present. Moreover, it is entirely possible that we also have here the indications of a general contemporary problem. The Great Maggid found himself in a kind of borderline situation, since in him was accomplished a transition from symbolic-pictorial to conceptual-discursive thought. I believe this hypothesis may throw some additional light on the problem of why the Maggid created his own conceptual language to use along with the fixed language of symbols.

The phenomenon of double or multiple vocabulary, or

20. *Ibid.*

whatever we want to call it, is always found whenever the attempt is made to represent a wholly or partly unconscious psychological process. A myth, for example, depicts an inner psychological event in narrative form and vivid pictorial language. Yet the same event—if recognized as a psychological phenomenon—can also be described in terms of psychological concepts. But in reality the language of myth and the language of concepts are interpreting the same unknown process, only by different methods. So the subject is one and the same, whether our author speaks of the "union of Father and Mother," "Primordial Point and Palace," etc., or of the "union of consciousness and the unconscious." At best, the psychological terminology expresses a recognition of the projection factor; not much more is said of the real nature of the process than is possible in the language of myth or religion. For we learn nothing further about the nature of the unconscious than we would by calling it Primordial Point, Father, spiritual *hylē*, or pre-intelligence.

Possibly the concepts coined by the Maggid are in many ways not very adequate for the interpretation of the nature of unconscious processes. But are not the scientific terms of modern psychology, like the "self" or the "unconscious," awkward substitutes also—mere transliterations or technical terms for things which only with great difficulty can be captured in words or rational concepts? It can surely be said that the Great Maggid, in his effort to point out such complex phenomena of the soul as consciousness and the unconscious, was not far from the mark with his concepts of *sekhel* and *qadmut-ha-sekhel*.

Ideas of the unconscious, similar to those of the Great Maggid and his student, the Maggid of Shitomir, can also be found in a younger pupil of the Maggid, Shneur Zalman of Ladi, who was the founder of the so-called Habad (= *hokhmah, binah, daath*)—the Lithuanian Hasidic movement. In our Introduction we referred to the concepts *qadmut-ha-sekhel* (the unconscious) and *sekhel-ha-neelam* (hidden consciousness)—or, as A. Marcus translated them, pre-intelli-

239 Psychological Aspects in Early Hasidism

gence and unconsciousness—cited by Marcus from Shneur Zalman's work *Likkute Torah*.[21] The same concepts, taken from the Maggid, appear in Shneur Zalman's *Tanya*, where again their double signficance, in the human and in the divine world, is clearly evident.[22]

Apart from these students of the Maggid, such concepts cannot, so far as I know, be found thereafter anywhere in Hasidic literature. They vanish as suddenly as they emerged, and with them all speculation regarding the unconscious and its symbolism.

This brings us to the end of our discussion. Our starting point was provided by certain concepts of the Great Maggid which coincide in many ways with our modern concepts of consciousness and the unconscious. Further, it was found that such concepts spring from an archetypal background and are to be explained on this basis. Archetypal motifs pervade the whole field of Jewish mysticism. The knowledge and understanding of these primal dominants or principles of psychic structure are an inner necessity for conscious modern man. The present work represents a tentative effort to come closer to the deeper archetypal levels of the Jewish soul. An adequate presentation and clarification of the relations between psychology and Kabbalah—though of pressing importance—remains for the time being a desideratum.

21. Shneur Zalman of Ladi, *Likkute Torah* ("Explications of the Torah") (Shitomir, 1848).
22. Shneur Zalman of Ladi, *Likkute amarim* ("Collection of Quotations") or *Tanya* (Vilna, 1930), pp. 212 ff.

INDEX

Subject Index

Abba, 183
Abstraction, unconscious source of, 179
Abyss, in Gnostic thought, 107
Acquired intellect, 188; and Islamic Aristotelians, 188n; and Maimonides, 188
Active imagination, 199
Active intellect, 232; and Aristotle, 187; and Maimonides, 187; outside the human soul, 188; and prophecy, 187
Adam ha-rishon, as first human being, 203
Adam qadmon, 111n; earthly correspondence to, 203; as totality of Sefiroth, 202
Aesthetics, 69. *See also* Beauty
Affects, 172
Africa, symbolic meaning of melon in, 99
Aggadah, 157, 219
Aion, 108
Air, 195, 216, 218
Albedo, 217
Alchemical opus, tree as symbol of, 111
Alchemists, 101 f., 109 f.
Alchemy: 109 ff., 118, 119n, 120, 163, 198, 200 f., 209, 225; axiom, 92; decad in, 224; and Descartes, 61, 120 f.; and Kabbalah, 208; lexicon of, 117; as *opus contra naturam*, 208. *See also* Kabbalah
Aleph, 192; as father symbol, 207; as masculine principle, 185, 192
Alexander, Legend of, 111
Alphabet. *See* Letters
Amr, mystical interpretation of, 207
Analytical geometry. *See* Geometry
Angel(s), 194n, 221. *See also* Baruch, Gabriel, Michael, Nuriel, Raphael
Anger, 172
Anima, 82, 102; acceptance of, 106; as concealed in a fruit, 103; Descartes's exclusion of, 87; melon as symbol of, 101 f., 115; problem of Descartes, 84n; symbol of, 101
Anima Catholica, 118
Anima mundi, 83, 84n, 224. *See also* Soul
Anima possibilis, 104
Animals. *See under* individual animals
Animus possession, 64
Anxiety, 38, 172
Apocalypse, 157, 221
Apocrypha, 225

INDEX

Apple, 100; as embryo of possibility of consciousness, 105; of Paradise, 104 f.; trees, 111
Aql, 174
Aqua: nostra, 101; *permanens*, as fiery water, 183; *vitae*, 102
Arbor philosophica, 111
Archetype(s), 106n, 198, 225; and collective unconscious, 225; constellation of, and synchronicity, 87; and ordering of thought processes, 71 f.; possession by, 90; *scintillae* as description of, 120; of Self, 93
Archetypal: contents, accompanied by thunder, 117; dream, 58; images, 59, 170n, 178; process in history, 81
Archons, 104, 108
Argentum vivum, 102
Arithmetic, 67
Asceticism, 158
Asmodeus, 193
Associations, 95, 95n
"Assumptio Mariae," 115. See also Church
Astronomy, 67
Astrum, 119
Athens, 140
Âtman, 9
Âtman Purûsha, 9
Atum, 9
Auditor, 114
Azkaroth, 193

Ba, 3, 9 ff., 18, 21 ff., 25, 28 f., 31, 33 f., 37 f., 40, 42, 44 ff.; aim of, 48; and attitude to the Beyond, 42; as autonomous power, 38; as bound in body, 13; compared to man's wife, 31; demands of, 34; faith in, 48; as faultless, 24; first parable of, 29 ff.; and funeral rites, 28; and heart, 20; and heirs, 28; his happiness in the Beyond, 26; hostility of, 38; as incarnation of a god, 18; and man, 48; power of, 50 f.; and redemption, 49; rejects idea of "free death," 27; relation of, to man, 51; resistant to conscious intentions of man, 20; second parable of, 32 ff.; and self-knowledge, 37; split from man, 37; and suicide, 48; true nature of, 22, 31, 46 ff.; universal, 9; as unmasker, 37; and wholeness, 23, 26, 48, 51; wisdom of, 29
Bahir, Book of, 162, 164, 167, 170, 170n; on *he*, 211 f.; on *malkuth*, 207 f.
"Barbelo" Gnostics, 108, 111. See also Gnosticism
Baruch (angel), 111
Beauty, in mathematics, 69
Berlin Hieratic Papyrus 3024, 5
Bereshith, 196n; and *beth*, 180; and Genesis, 180
Beth, 183n; and *binah*, 185; containing ten Sefiroth, 185; and *daleth* and *waw*, 185; as feminine, 185, 191 f.; and *hokhmah*, 185; as Palace of all letters, 180; as Primordial Point, 180
Beyond, the, 7, 18, 23; Ba's attitude toward, 42; Ba's happiness in, 26; concern for, 28; desire for, 47; extolled, 36; as home, 43; Ra's power in, 50; and redemption, 49. See also Heaven
Bible, 100, 167, 174, 185, 231; and Koran, 183n; numbers in, 74n
Binah, 170, 172, 177 f., 198 f., 200, 236; and *beth*, 185; as discriminating consciousness, 175; as discriminating between opposites, 171; and Gnostic *sophia*, 184n; and *he*, 185; as higher Shekhinah, 206; and *hokhmah*, 171, 181; as intellectual power, 171; and *malkuth*, 184, 206; as mother, 184n, 206; as Palace, 184; as upper mother, 184. See also Heart, *Hokhmah*
Bird dung, smell of, 34 f.

Index

Birth, of dormant treasure, 31
Black, 182, 216; fire, 217
Blood, 102, 172
Blood-soul, 172
Body, 233; Ba bound in, 13; and psyche, 127
Body and soul, 87, 121n; and pineal gland, 87. *See also* Opposites, Psyche and matter
Book, 77, 124. *See also* Dictionary
"Book of Creation," 167
"Book of the Dead," 9
"Book of the Dead of Ani," 20
Brahman, 194n
Brazier, 12, 44
Bread, 105n; of life, 110
Breasts, poetic similes for, 103n
"Brontologia," 116. *See also* Thunder
Brothers, 38 f.
"Brothers of the Free Spirit," 90
Burial, ritual of, 19

Cabala. *See* Kabbalah
Cabin, 96
Canticles III. 11, 207
Castration. *See* Complex
Catholic, Descartes as, 98
Catholics, 93n. *See also* Church
Caucasus, Rock of, 139
Causa finalis, 86n; in natural events, 83
Causality, 127; and God, 85 f.; principle of, 127
Center, infallible, 110; distillation of, 118
Chanukah, 218n
Chaos, 119; in Gnostic thought, 107
Chastity, 108; and Manichaeans, 104
Ch'ien, 100
Child: as life, 31; perishes, 29; stubborn, 35
China, 101 f.
Chinese imagery of melon, 100 f.
Chons, 12, 16

Christ, 104; in Gnostic creation myth, 107; number value of word, 181n; as serpent, 181n; and suffering, 104; symbol of, 114; as symbol of Self, 114. *See also* Messiah
Christianity, 157 f.
Christians, sacraments of, 114n
Church, 95, 123; and Descartes, 98, 114; as dream symbol, 93; as Mater Ecclesia, 82; paganism surviving in, 115; and Reformation, 114 f.; as symbol of Self, 114. *See also* Catholic
Circle, 92, 226
Circumambulation, 195
Citrinitas, 217
City: as analogy of man, 37; dangerous, 35
Coagulation, 197
Coffin texts, 9
Cognition, 191
Coitus, 123n
Collective: life, and Descartes's fear, 88; norm, 26, 29, 44; resistance to, 96; rules, 18
Collective unconscious, 82, 163, 170n; and archetypal images, 170n; and contamination, 93. *See also* Unconscious
Colors. *See under* individual colors
Compensation, 88, 92, 96, 113, 130; and intellectual attitude of Descartes, 114
Complex, castration, 88n
Confession, negative, 18
Conflict, emotional, 34
Coniunctio, 201, 205, 215, 224; archetypal background of symbolism, 208 f.; as central problem in Kabbalah, 198; in human soul, 228; *oppositorum*, 200; and problem of three and four, 215; and *sekhel-qadmut-ha-sekhel*, 228; suprapersonal background of, 226n; as symbol of wholeness, 208. *See also* Double *coniunctio*, Union

Conscious thought, and Descartes, 111
Consciousness, 164, 180, 229; achievement of, and melon, 106; apple as embryo of, 105; awakening of new, 92; as coagulation, 197; collectivity of, 31; dependent upon unconscious, 189; of Descartes, 112; and Descartes's dream, 57; development of, 225; and differentiation of God-image, 228; as feminine, 235; as hammer, 189; hubris of, 91; as human, 176; as immanent in instinctual nature, 119; latent in archetypes, 120; means of producing, 112; and mind, 80; and process of becoming, 92 f., 101; reflecting unconscious processes, 227; right side as symbol of, 88n; as symbolized by light, 120; and thinking, 80; and time, 197; unity of, 134. *See also Sekhel*, Unconscious
Conscious(ness) and the unconscious, 164 ff., 176, 234, 236; and chaos, 209; collision between, 209; forming psychic totality, 208; and *nigredo*, 209; opposite character of, 197; as phenomenon of soul, 238; separation of, in heart, 228
Consonants, as profane and mystical, 192
Copper, 217
Corpse, 23
Corpus: astrale, 110; *lucens*, 110
Correspondences, doctrine of, 83, 86n. *See also Correspondentia*
Correspondentia, 86, 86n, 129
Cosmos, seed of, 109; in Sethian thought, 106 f.; in soul of man, 73
Counter Reformation, 91, 93
Counting, various forms of, 223
Covenant, 155
Creation: through wisdom, 186 f.; of world in Gnostic thought, 107
Creation myth: of Basilides, 109; Ophitic, 107
Creation story, 222
Creativity, and reversal of direction, 195
Crippling of lower limbs, 88n
Crocodile-god, 29
Crocodiles, 29; smell of, 35
Crown, 229
Cucumbers, 99, 104, 104n; symbol of seeds of, 109

Daath, 170
Daimon, 96
Daleth, 185, 224
"Dark for spirit," 129
Dark forces, 101
Darkness: as feminine principle, 100 f.; in Gnostic thought, 106 f.
Dead: host of the—*see* Wotan; judges of the, 11, 18; judgment of, 19; man, 18; sacrifices for the, 28, 88; spirits of the, 124n; underworld and the, 11; weighing of hearts of the, 19
Death, 7 f., 12 f., 27 f., 139; as belonging to life, 20; day of, 13; drift toward, 17; as fate, 23; as "free death," 27; freedom to attain, 49; from grief, 47; heirless, 26, 28; longing for, 7, 47; and Manichaeans, 104; and melon, 101n; mystery of, 111; path of, 50; as ravisher, 24; as redemption, 41 f., 49; wish for, 38, 49
Debequth, 233
Decad: in creation, 222; and quaternion, 222; and Sefiroth, 222; and ten Sefiroth, 223; as totality, 224
"Declaratio Solemnis," 115
Demons, 193
Descartes: and "absolute knowledge," 72; and "absolute truth," 71; and alchemy, 61, 120 f.; and anima, 82, 87; and

anima problem, 84n, 93; and archetypal images, 74; and body and soul, 87, 121n; as a Catholic, 98 f., 116; and causality, 85 f.; and child, 63; and Church, 98; and consumption, 100; and cosmogonic theory, 58n, 92; on creation, 89n; death of, 64; and discoveries, 80; education of, 60, 97, 97n; and emotions, 126 f.; and evil, 127; and faith, 98; and father, 59; and fear of evil spirits, 116; and fear of exposure, 97, 97n; and fear of impotence, 88n; and fear of life, 88; and fear of love, 96; and fear of unconscious, 87, 122 f.; and feeling, 63, 121n; and feeling of inferiority, 135 f.; and feeling problem, 63f., 88n, 96, 126, 126n, 131 ff., 135 ff.; and feminine, 64, 82, 82n, 106; and feminine problem, 88, 93, 97; and freethinkers, 62; and Galileo, 61, 63; and Germany, 66; and God, 84, 85, 105n, 124, 128n; and good and evil, 105; and inflation, 90; introversion of, 88; intuition of, 70; life of, 59 ff.; and life, urge for, 88n; and life purpose, 65; and light, 130; and *Logos spermatikos*, 90n; on love, 89n; and *lumen naturale*, 113; and macrocosm, 110, 110n; and magic, 61, 61n; and materialism, 129; on matter, 84; and matter and psyche, 93; mechanistic views of, 83, 93; and melon, 105, 113; and mistress, 63; and morality, 115n, 131n; and mother, 59, 81 f., 135; and nature, 62, 80n, 83 f.; and numbers, 74; and Paris, 60; and *passiones*, 87; personality of, 115 f., 134; philosophy of, 124 f.; physical description of, 64; and pineal gland, 87, 127; and possession by archetypes, 90; and possession by Holy Ghost, 90n, 91n; and psychic reality, 95 f., 112; and reason, 121, 121n; and religion, 63, 97; and Rosicrucians, 61, 66, 74; and St. Augustine, 74n; and Scholasticism 98n; and science, 62, 67, 70 ff., 80n, 85, 90, 91n; and sex, 90n; and shadow, 96, 99, 112, 114; and sin, 116; as soldier, 60; and spirit, 89n; and synchronicity, 86, 86n; and thinking, 80, 85, 91, 91n, 93, 111, 113, 125, 130; and thinking function, 80 f., 132 f.; and time, 86, 86n, 89n; as tutor of philosophy, 64; and unconscious, 59, 66, 87, 125, 132, 136; and whirlwind, 63n; and *Zeitgeist*, 96 f.

Descartes's dream, 57, 102, 107; associations to, 130 f.; events preceding, 64; Freudian interpretation of, 88n; influence of, 91n; premonition of, 66, 96, 96n; publication of, 64; text of, 75 ff.

Descartes's works: *Cogitationes privatae*, 78n, 89n, 113n, 126n, 127, 127n; Letter to Elizabeth von der Pfalz, 121n; Letter to Mersenne, 63n, 80n; *Meditation* III, 125n; *Meditation* IV, 83n; *Meditation* V, 125n; *Meditation* VI, 84n; *Principia* II, 84n; *Principia phil.* I, 85n; "Recherche de la vérité par la lumière naturelle," 125n, 134n; *Regulae*, 124n, 126n

Despair, 18; over life, 17; and redemption, 50; and suicide, 20 and terror, 10

Deuteronomy 29:29, 176n

Devil, 88n

Dew of light, 107

Diaconi, 105n

Dictionary, 77 f., 124, 133

"Didactic Treatises of the Old Kingdom," 17
Din, 235
Discrimination, 236
Disorientation, 209
Distillation, 200; of the Center, 118
Double *coniunctio*, 206 f.; in Kabbalah, 209 f.
Dove, 103
Dream, Descartes's. *See* Descartes's dream
Dreams, 161, 230; archetypal, 58; big, 93; compensatory, 88; Freudian interpretation of, 97n; ghostly images in, 86; Maimonides on, 232; of modern people, 118; parapsychological events in, 86; prediction of, 66, 96, 96n; and prophecy, 231; as prophetic vision, 231; Talmud on, 231; as "teacher," 119; and unconscious, 117n; and visions, 232
Drunkenness, and death, 41
Dung, bird, 34 f.
Dying, 18
Dynasty, 12th, 49

Eagle, 218
Earth(ly), 93, 95, 97, 106n, 113, 113n, 195, 216, 218; forces, 101; and melons, 112; as mother, 113n; and water, 102
East, symbolic meaning of melon in, 99
Egg, 29, 109
Ego, 80 f., 81n, 137; and body, 233; -complex, 118; and self, 112; and thinking, 134
Egypt, 99, 169; meaning of melon in, 99
Electi, 103 f., 105n. *See also* Manichaeism
Electus, 114
Elohim, 204 f.; number value of, 181n
Emotion, 172; Descartes's attitude toward, 126 f.; as psychological event, 87; and synchronicity, 87
Emotional shock. *See* Shock, emotional
En Sof, 168 f., 173, 182, 223; containing opposites, 226; and *kether*, 170; outside space and time, 168
Enemy, 39
Episcopi, 105n
Ets hayim, 158
Europe, southern, symbolic meaning of melon in, 99
Eve, Gospel of, 108
Evil, 127, 129, 172; demon in Japanese fairy tale, 102 f.; and Descartes's exclusion of, 87; divine reality of, 105; as a *privatio boni*, 105, 130; problem of, 102 f., 136; problem of, and melon, 103 f.; and Sefiroth, 178; smells, 34 f.; and *Zohar*, 178. *See also* Good and evil
Evil spirit, 87, 116, 126, 129. *See also* Spirit
Exile, 202
Exodus, 99; dual meaning of, 169
Experience, inner, 120
Eye(s): as symbol of self, 120; spiritual, 119

Fairy tale(s), 102 f.; European, 103; "Princess Melon," 102; "The Three Melons," 103
Faith: and Ba, 48; and Descartes, 98
Fate, is death, 23
Father, 93, 198, 236; in Gnosticism, 107, 109; wind as image of, 90n
Fear, 172, 177; Descartes's, 88; of evil spirit, 116; of falling in Descartes's dream, 93; of feeling, 63 f.; of impotence, 88n; of love, 96; of unconscious, 122 f. *See also* Sin
Feeling, 80, 172; and creativity, 69; function, Descartes's, 63 f.; heart as organ of, 19; problem

Index

of Descartes, 88n; and rationalism, 137; sphere of body, 80n
Feminine, 93, 235; and Descartes, 106; the left as symbol of, 88; melon as, 106; splitting-off of, 202 f.; symbols of, in *Zohar*, 206 f. *See also* Symbol(s), Yin
Field, tilling of, 29
"Fiery sparks," 116, 118, 122
Filius philosophorum, 226
Fire, 12, 59, 110, 182 f., 195, 216 ff., 225; as metaphor for grief, 17. *See also* Sparks of fire
Fish, 26, 99, 218n; smell of, 34
Fishermen, 35
Five, 101, 105n, 210
Flames, 122n. *See also* Fire
Flood, smell of, 37
Food: for shadow, 114; vegetarian, 104. *See also* Ritual food
Four, 92 f., 108, 117, 128, 215 ff., 224; and decad, 224; elements, 217, 224; fishes, 218n; omitted, 218; stages in alchemy, 216 f.; and ten and seventy-two, 220
Fourth: as doubled, 218 f.; from triad plus one, 218 f.
French, and Germans, 66
Freud, and dreams, 58, 88n
Friends, 38
"Friends of God on the Rhine," 90. *See also* Holy Ghost movements
Fruit, 59, 110; and anima, 103; and consciousness, 101; and Descartes, 113, 113n
Funeral, 26, 28; rites, 25, 26, 29; texts of Old Kingdom, 19
Funerary inscriptions, 20
Future, trees that tell the, 111

Gabriel (angel), 216 f.
Galuth Shekhinah, 202
Garden of Eden, 178n; as *binah*, 206 f.; as *malkuth*, 206 f. *See also* Paradise
Garden of the Hesperides, 111
Garlic, 99

Gemarah, 155
Gematria, 181 f.
Genesis, 128, 167, 180, 203; *Zohar* exegesis of, 217; (passages) 1:1, 182; 2:4, 203, 220n; 2:7, 195n; 5:1, 203; 5:2, 204; 46:2, 232
Geometry, analytical, Descartes's theory of, 58n, 67
German mythology, 91, 91n. *See also* Mythology
Germany, 66, 91
Ghost, 75, 79, 81 f., 88 ff., 102n, 123; in dreams, 86; -figure, 91n; symbols, 75. *See also* Spirit
Glory, 178n
Gnosis: of Justinus, 111; and tree, 111
Gnosticism: Barbelo sect, 108; and Basilides, 108 f.; Christian, 163; cosmogony of, 182; and Manichaeism, 109; Ophitic sect, 107 f.; Sethian sect, 107
Gnostics, 222; and Manichaean thought, 108 f.
Goal: of life, 21 f.; of man, 48
God, 10, 76, 139, 168; cognitive experience of, 105; consciousness of, 126; and correspondence in man, 228; in Descartes's dream, 94; in Descartes's thought, 113; Descartes's understanding of, 124; Descartes's view of, 84; and evil, 177; in Gnostic thought, 108 f.; "Golden treasure of," 109; inner life of, 169; as *intelligentia pura*, 126 f.; and Kabbalah, 153; Kepler's view of, 84; and man, 51; melon as golden treasure of, 104, 104n; name of, and magic power, 193; names of, 204 f.; needs man, 202; presence of, in Beyond, 43; and principle of causality, 85 f.; proof of existence of, 85; separation from, 50; seventy-two letter name of, 221; spirit of, 118; as trickster, 84; unity and diversity in, 227;

vision of, 95; of wind and storm, 91n. *See also Elohim, Life, Tifereth,* YHWH
Godhead, and human soul, 171
Gods: endowed with magic power, 21; as judges, 20
God, 217; and melon, 101n
Golden treasure, melon as, 109
Golem, 194, 197; life and death of, 194 f.
Good: concern for, and goal of life, 21 f.; and evil, 76, 105, 106, 127, 178; as funeral rites, 25
Grapes, 105n
Grave, 28, 47
Greek mythology. *See* Mythology
Greeks, and melon, 100
Green, 182, 216, 222; fire, 217
Grief, 18; leading to death, 47

Habanah, 165, 171 f.
Halakhah, 156
Harpocrates (Horus), 88n
Harvest, 29, 31
Hashob, 175
Hasidism, 152, 167, 171; and Aggadah, 157; and alchemy, 158; archetypal foundation of, 224; and Baal Shem Tov, 158; history of, 153; and individual religious experience, 155; and Jewish mysticism, 163; and Kabbalah, 153, 202; Lithuanian, 238; and Orthodox Judaism, 155; and Rabbinical Judaism, 155; and Talmudic period, 163; and unconscious, 152; and unity of God and nature, 155. *See also* Baal Shem Tov (Index of Names), Talmud
Host, 114
He, 176n, 180 f., 184, 219; and *binah,* 211; creation of, 212; and *malkuth,* 211; and number value, 210; and soul, 210; upper and lower, 211

Heart, 23, 165, 172n; in Biblical literature, 172; and *binah,* 172; and brains and liver, 173; covetousness of, 38 f.; and evil, 172; and *habanah,* 172; hardness of, 32 ff., 37 f., 48; as king of organs, 172; language of, 19; number value of, 173; as organ of thoughts and feeling, 19; as seat of knowledge, 172; as seat of Sefiroth, 173; and soul, 172; and Talmud, 172; as unconscious, 19; weighing of dead man's, 19
Heat: as love, 8n; and passion, 17
Heaven, 106n; burning of, 34; forces of, 101; formation of, 225; seventh, 108; symbolized by melon, 100
Heirs, 23, 26, 28; and Ba, 28
Hell, 178n
Hephaestus, 88n
Heracleopolitan era, 9
Hesed, 177, 201, 212, 235
Hesperides, Garden of, 111
Hieros gamos, 200, 208
Hiphil, 171
Hippolytus, 139
History of psyche, vii ff.
Hod, 201; as testicles of primal man, 204
Hokhmah, 170, 176n, 177 f., 195, 198 f., 200 f., 204, 215; and *ayin,* 229; and *binah,* 200; as father, 184n, 206; and Gnostic *sophia,* 184n; as Golem, 194; as higher degree, 171; as *hylē,* 186; and *kether,* 229; as preconscious, 173; as *prima materia,* 194; as *qadmut-ha-sekhel,* 174; as skill, 190; and time, 196; and *yod,* 180, 211
Holy Ghost, 119; and Descartes, 90n, 91n; movements, 90
Holy Spirit, 233
Home: and the Beyond, 25 f., 43; and redemption, 49
Homunculus, 194

Horus. *See* Harpocrates
House, 26
Hubris, 91n, 116; of consciousness, 91
Human knowledge. *See* Knowledge
Humidum radicale, 110
Hunger, 110
Huntsman, 91. *See also* Wotan
Hylē, 174, 186, 194, 198
Hylic intellect, 188 f.; and Maimonides, 188

I Ching, 100, 143
"Ideal forms," 106n, 119
Identification, 80
Image. *See* Symbol
Imagination, 230, 232; Descartes's definition of, 127
Imma, 184
Impatience, Descartes's fear of, 88n
Incest, as archetypal, 208, 208n
Indians, American, 132n
Individual, relation of, to himself, and sin, 19
Individuation, process of, 129, 209
Inferior function. *See* Psychological function(s)
Inferiority complex, 135 f., 136n
"Infinite," 168, 183
Inflation, 80, 90
Inspiration, 69
Instincts, 89
Intellect, compensation for one-sided, 114. *See also* Acquired intellect, Active intellect, Hylic intellect, Passive intellect
Intellectus acquisitus, 188n
Intellectus agens, 187 f., 232
Intelligence, 165, 228; and creativity, 69
Introverted thinking. *See* Psychological functions
Introversion, 88, 233
Intuition, 91n, 125, 126n; and mathematical discovery, 67 ff.

Iron, 217
Irrational, 162
Isaiah (passages), 6:13, 182; 10:6, 197; 29:16, 197; 44:18, 174; 58:11, 204n
Isdes, 12
Isis, 88n
Israel, 176n, 202, 215; as chosen people, 155. *See also* Jews

Japanese fairy tale, 102 f.
Jeremiah 9:23, 174
Jerusalem, 205, 218; creation of, 212
Jesuit education of Descartes, 97, 97n
Jesuits, 134
Jews, 99 f.
Job 28:12, 195 f.
Judaism, 186; and Christianity, 157; mystical side of, 157; Rabbinical, 155
Judgment of the Dead, 19
Jung, Carl Gustav, iv, 72n, 73n, 79n, 80n, 81n, 82n, 83n, 89, 89n, 91n, 92n, 94n, 95n, 101n, 102n, 104n, 105n, 109n, 110n, 111, 111n, 112n, 114n, 117n, 118, 118n, 120n, 127, 127n, 129n, 134n, 143, 154, 174n, 179, 179n, 190n, 197n, 199n, 208n, 209n, 214n, 215, 215n, 217n, 224n, 225; on "active imagination," 199; on archetypal dreams, 58; on *coniunctio*, 200; on *coniunctio* symbolism, 208 f.; on dual *coniunctio*, 209; on ego and surrounding luminosity, 118; on Gnosis, 111; on light in man, 110; on mother-son relationship, 82; on opposites, 201n; on Primordial Point, 183n; on *quaternio*, 214 f.; on quaternity as two triads, 129; on the Self, 72 f., 112; on the Self and multiple luminosities, 120; on symbols of wholeness, 209 f.; on synchronicity, 86 f.;

on the Trinity, 129; and the unconscious, 235
Jung's works: *Aion,* 80n, 94n, 109n, 127, 183n, 209n; *The Archetypes and the Collective Unconscious,* 73n, 79n, 109n, 117n, 129n, 209n; "Brother Klaus," 95; *Mysterium Coniunctiones,* 201n, 214n; "On the Nature of the Psyche," 118n; *Paracelsus,* 82n, 109n, 110n, 119n, 134n; "The Phenomenology of the Spirit in Fairy Tales," 79n, 80n, 129n; *The Practice of Psychotherapy,* 134n, 209n, 224n; *Psychological Types,* 81n, 92n, 114n, 174n, 179n; *Psychology and Alchemy,* 73n, 92n, 101n, 102n, 104n, 109n, 208n, 215n, 217n, 224n; *Psychology and Religion,* 92n, 95n; "The Psychology of the Transference," 134n, 208n; "The Relations between the Ego and the Unconscious," 199n; *The Spirit Mercury,* 197n; *The Structure and Dynamics of the Psyche,* 89n; "A Study in the Process of Individuation," 117n; *Two Essays on Analytical Psychology,* 199n; "The Unconscious as Multiple Consciousness," 118n, 120n; "Wotan," 91n; (with Kerényi), *Introduction to a Science of Mythology,* 112n; (with Pauli), *The Interpretation and Nature of the Psyche,* 83n
Jupiter, 116, 139, 216
Justice, as Maat, 18

Ka, 9
Kabbalah, 152, 154, 157, 162, 165, 167, 170, 173, 178, 182n, 186, 198, 225; and alchemy, 158, 200, 228 f.; dominant concepts of, 153; and Gnostic systems, 168; and God-image, 168; historical development of, 166; and numbers, 233; and psychological interpretation, 153; symbols in modern dreams, 163; and tree of life, 111n; and the unconscious, 152. *See also* Hasidism
Kether, 170 f., 177, 211, 229; as "Ancient Holy One," 206
King(s), 182, 190, 201, 226; become gods, 28
Knowledge: Descartes's thoughts on, 122; dictionary as symbol of, 124. *See also* Wisdom
Koran, 183n

La Flèche, 77n, 93, 124
Lapis, 102
Law, respect for and identification with, 19
Laws of nature. *See* Nature
Leeks, 99
Left, 107; as chthonic, 88n; as feminine, 88; and inferior function, 88n; and right, 75 f.
"Legend of Alexander," 111
Lemons, 103, 103n
Letters: as conscious thought, 195; as creative instruments, 191 ff.; as masculine and feminine, 210; and numbers, 223; and unconscious, 195. *See also* individual letters; Words
Leviticus 17:14, 172n
Life: as child, 31; clinging to, 44, 47, 50; cruelty of, 30; as a cycle, 12; and death, 7, 36, 45; despair of, 17; dissatisfaction with, 139; enjoyment of, 27, 29, 31; goal of, 21; as harvest, 31; love of, 7; mystery of, 111; negation of, 7; philosophies of, 7 f.; remote from God, 43; tree as symbol of, 111; and union with God, 227; value of, 30; weariness with, 7, 21 f., 131; will for, 7, 49
Light, 89n, 120; in alchemy, 110; forces, 101; as garment, 210n;

Index

germs, 104, 106, 109; in Gnosticism, 106 f.; lightning as birth of, 117; natural, 119; sparks of, 107; as symbol of consciousness, 120. *See also* Lumen naturale, Seeds, Sparks
Lightning, 74, 117. *See also* Thunder
Lilith, 216; and name of God, 212
Lion, 218
Lithuania, 154
Logos, 198
Logos spermatikos, 90n
Loneliness of man, 40
Loretto, Madonna of, 115
Lotus, and death, 41
Love, 177, 205, 212; heat as, 89n; lack of, 38
Lucidum corpus, 110
Lumen naturale, 119, 121, 124; and archetypes, 120; in Descartes's thought, 113, 120
Luminosity. *See* Light, *Lumen naturale*
Lungs: Descartes's weakness of, 100; melons as cure for inflammation of, 100
Lurianic Kabbalah, 162, 201, 206
Lysis, 136

Maaseh: bereshith, 167; *merkabah*, 167
Maat, 12, 18 ff., 43; as religious law, 50; Scribe of, 16
Madonna of Loretto, 115, 135
Maggid debarah le-Jaaqob, quoted, 165 f., 175, 176, 180
Maggid of Meseritz: and Baal Shem, 159; and *Bahir*, 162; and *coniunctio*, 198; language of, 165; and Luria, 162; as mystic, 237; and opposites, 188; and psychological concepts, 162; scientific terminology of, explained, 237; and symbols, 162; as Talmudist, 237; works of, listed, 160; and *Zohar*, 162

Magic, 91n, 124, 124n; and mysticism, 193; power of gods, 21; and power of words, 192
"Magic trickery," 59
Mahashabah, 174 f.
Malkuth, 177, 201, 204, 211, 215, 235; as daughter, 207 f.; as feminine, 206; as lower mother, 184; as lower Shekinah, 206; as mother, 207 f.; as sister, 207 f. *See also* Binah, He
Man: in alchemical thought, 110 f.; and Ba, 48, 51; city as analogy of, 37; in Descartes's dream, 76, 98, 100; exchange of roles with soul, 8; as fourth, 218; in Gnostic thought, 107; and God, 51; and nature, 80; problem of modern, 136; relation of, to mind, 80; relation of, to wife, 33 f.; tree born of, 111; and union of male and female, 204. *See also* Primal man, Primitive man
Mandala(s), 72 f., 109, 120, 208; and Descartes, 73; magical powers of, 73
Manichaeism, 103 f., 105n, 115, 163; connection of, with Gnosticism, 108 f.; and meaning of the melon, 105 f., 109, 123
Manna, 99
Marriage, 225n; *quaternio*, 209
Mars, 139, 216
Masculine, 93, 235
Mask, 97, 97n
Massoretes, 191n
Material world. *See* Physical world, Matter
Materialism, Epicurean, 130
Mathematical creativity: and beauty, 69; and feelings, 69; and intelligence, 69
Mathematical discovery of Descartes, 61, 67, 70; and intuition, 67, 70; and preconscious, 68; psychology of, 67 ff.

Mathematical proofs, 67 f.; and intuition, 67 f.
Mathematical schools: "formalistic," 69; intuitive, 69
Mathematics, 67; and Descartes, 60; and the mystery of the transcendent, 71
Matter, 186; in Descartes's laws of nature, 84
Matter and psyche, 17, 83, 83n, 93. *See also* Synchronicity
Mechanics, 67n
Mechanistic: thought, 83; view of nature, 113
Mediterranean, symbolic meaning of melon in, 99
Melo, 100
Melon(s), 97 ff., 136; as anima symbol, 101 f., 103, 115; called *spermatias*, 100; and closeness to earth, 112; and connection to sparks, 123; in Descartes's dream, 114 f.; and Descartes's knowledge of Manichaean symbol of, 105; and evil, 103 f.; and the feminine, 100 f., 106, 115; as golden treasure of God, 104, 104n, 109; and Greeks, 100, 109; green, 105n; in *I Ching*, 100 f.; as latent conscious order, 101; as light-containing fruit, 104 f.; as mandala symbol, 109; and Manichaeans, 104, 104n, 123; as microcosmos, 110; as moon-shaped, 103n; as poetic simile for woman's breasts, 103n; Princess, 103; as remedy for phthisis, 100; as ritual food of *electi*, 103 f.; as something strange, 112; in Spanish culture, 101n; spirit, 103; spoilability of, 100; as symbol of achievement of consciousness, 106; as symbol of Self, 109, 115; as symbol of Yin, 101; as uniting symbol, 115; water, 100; as watery fruit, 101 ff.; yellow, 105n. *See also* Fruit, "Princess Melon"

Men, as mother symbol, 207
Mercurius, 117, 132n
Mercurius vivus, 102
Mercury, 216
Merkabah, 167
Messiah, 117, 178n. *See also* Christ
Metternich Stele, 16
Michael (angel), 216 f.
Midrash, 172, 196, 221, 225, 231
Mind: and man, 80; of man and God, 84; and mandala symbol, 73; in primordial form, 81
Mind and body. *See* Body and psyche
Mishnah, 155
Mitnagdin, 155
Model: of human mind, 73; of universe, 73
Monas, 134
Moon, 102, 105n, 201, 235; and melon, 103n; and sun-trees, 110
Moorish woman, 103
Moriah, 218
Mother, 82, 88n, 93, 97, 97n, 236; Descartes's image of, 81 f.; early death of, 82; earth, 113n; of God, 90n; and son, 82
Mound, man cast on, 26
Mount Sinai, 155
Mummy, belongs to the Ba, 25
Mustard seed, 109
Mysterium coniunctionis, 200
Mystery: of death, 111; of life, 111; of rebirth, 111
Mysticism, 117n, 225; Jewish, 163, 165; Jewish and archetypal motifs, 239; Jewish and non-Jewish, 227; and Maimonides, 168; and power of words, 192; and Saadia, 168; *Yetsirah*, 195. *See also* Magic
Mythology: Germanic, 116; Greek, 116; Roman, 116
Myths, creation, 92. *See also* Creation myth

Name: as essence, 37; magical power of, 193; man's, 36

Index

Natural light, 119, 121. *See also* Lumen naturale
Nature, 117, 157; laws of, 84 f., 113; and man, 80; order in, 83. *See also* Opposites
Neighbor, 39
Neoplatonism, 163, 169, 186 f.
Netsah, 201; as testicles of primal man, 204
New Kingdom, funeral texts of, 19
New Testament, 51
Night, as origin of water, 102
Nigredo, 209, 216
North, 88n, 94
Nothing(ness), 168, 177, 196
Number mysticism, 223
Numbers, 121, 121n, 223; as archetypes, 74; in Bible, 74n; Descartes's theory of, 67; of Gnostics, 181n; and letters of alphabet, 181; primal, 167; and Sefiroth, 167. *See also* individual numbers
Numbers 12:6, 231n
Nuriel (angel), 216 f.

Objective psychic factor, 83, 83n
Objectivity, 83n
Odin. *See* Wotan
Oedipus, 88n
Old Kingdom, 31; judgment of dead in, 19
Old Testament, 221, 225
One, 181, 223
Onions, 99
Ophites, 107, 181n. *See also* Gnosticism
Opposites, 46, 140, 157n, 170 f.; evolution of pairs, 182 f.; in God, 105; and Great Maggid, 188; and Kabbalah, 200. *See also* Pairs of opposites
Optics, 67n
Or ha-emeth, text passages quoted, 189 f., 197 ff., 229
Oranges, 103, 103n
Order, 202; of Cosmos, 73; as union of opposites, 209

Original sin. *See* Sin
Osiris, 25
Ox, 218

Pagan religion, 116; surviving in Church, 115; unconscious, 99
Pairs of opposites: above-below, 200; day-night, 200; good-evil, 200; heaven-earth, 201; *hokhmah-binah*, 201, 206; king-queen, 201; light-darkness, 200; male-female, 200; *malkuth-tifereth*, 201; right-left, 200; spirit-nature, 157; sun-moon, 201; *tifereth-malkuth*, 206; white-red, 200. *See also* individual pairs, e.g., Matter and psyche
Palace, 180 f., 236; as mother, 184; as new form, 183
Parables, of Ba, 44
Paradise: apple of, 105; fruits and powers of, 114n
Parapsychology, and events in dreams, 86
Partsufim, theory of, 206
Passiones, 87; *animae*, 126
Passive intellect, 187
Pearl, of great price, 49
Pears, 103n
Penance, 178n
Penitence, 158
Perfume, of Pneuma, 106 f.
Persia, and quince, 103n
Persona. *See* Mask
Personality, 133 f.; and Descartes, 95 f.; inner ripening of, 116; split, 96
Phantoms. *See* Ghost
Pharaoh, as God, 50
Pharisees, 155
Philoctetes, 88n
Philosopher's stone, 226
Philosophy: Hermetic, 169; Jewish, 168
Phylacteries, and three and four, 219n

Physical, 93. *See also* Matter
Physical world, projections onto, 83 f.
Physics: and Descartes, 60, 86n, 129 f., 130n; of Newton, 86n
Pineal gland, 87, 127
Plants, 104, 110 f.
Plērōma, 184n
Plum tree, 102
Pneuma, 90; in Gnostic thought, 106 f., 109
Point. *See* Primordial Point
Poland, 154
Polarities, of the world, 9
Polytheism, 99
Possession, animus, 64
Power, and transformation, 49
Preconscious, 68, 72, 151 ff.; and mathematical discovery, 70
Prediction, and Descartes's dream, 96, 96n
Pride, sin of, 37
Prima materia, 194, 196; and opposites, 200
Primal Man, 107
Primitive man, and ghosts, 79
Primordial Point, 180 ff.; in alchemy, 183n; as father, 183 f.; in Islamic literature, 183n; as new form, 183; and *Zohar,* 180 f., 182
"Princess Melon," 102 f.
Privatio boni, 105, 127, 130
Projections, 66, 92, 127; by Descartes on Socrates, 96; of Trinity on material world, 83 f.; of unconscious content, 226
Prometheus, 139
Prophecy, 186 f., 234; combining imagination and intellect, 232
Proverbs (passages), 1:8, 215; 4:23, 172; 5:4, 216; 15:14, 172n
Psalms (passages), 104:2, 210n; 133:3, 205
Psyche: in history, vii ff.; and matter, 74; water as symbol of, 101, 103

Psychic totality, 110. *See also* Self
Psychological, and mythological, 238
Psychological function(s): of Descartes, 80n, 81n; feeling, 80n; feeling as fourth, 133; feeling as inferior, 88n, 96; inferior, 92 f.; introverted thinking, 96; thinking, 80 f., 81, 95 f., 125, 132 f.
Psychological type(s), of Descartes, 95 f., 121n
Psychology, 152; and Kabbalah, 239; of mathematical discoveries, 67 ff.
Punic wars, 139
Pyramid: builders of, 26; texts, 9
Pythagoreans, 140, 220; and number ten, 221

Qadma, 174. *See also Qadmut*
Qadmut, 173 f.; and time, 174 f.
Qadmut-ha-sekhel, 151 f., 165, 175 f., 176n, 180, 186, 189 f., 197 ff., 228 ff., 233 f.; and divine realm, 198; double aspect of, 197 f.; and Dov Baer, 152; and Kabbalah, 166; in *Maggid debarab le-Jaaqob,* 165 f., 175 f., 180; in *Or ha-emeth,* 189 f., 196 ff., 229 f.; as pre-intelligence, 152; as psychological concept, 166; and Shneur Zalman, 152; and *sekhel,* 181; summary of, 198; and unconscious, 161, 175; union with *qadmut,* 200. *See also* Sekhel, Unconscious
Qidma, 174. *See also Qadmut*
Quaternio, 209; of Sefiroth, 214
Quaternity, 129, 224; examples of, 216. *See also* Tetrad
Queen, 201, 226
Quince: -apple, 100; in Persia, 103; as poetic simile for breast, 103n. *See also* Apple, Fruit, Melon

Index

Ra, 12, 16, 41; and the Beyond, 50; as divine Judge, 43 f.; as father of Pharaoh, 50; the Sun-god, 49
Rabbinism, and Halakhah, 157
Raphael (angel), 216 f.
Ratio, 174
Rationalism, 136 f.
Rays, 118, 118n. *See also* Fiery sparks, Sparks
Reality, 233
Reason, human, as symbolized by *lumen naturale*, 121
Rebirth, mystery of, 111
Red, 102, 182, 216; fire, 217
Redemption, 107; and Ba, 49; for Barbelo Gnostics, 108; and despair, 50; of God, 203; longing for, 49; and world order, 202
Reed bank, 35
Reflection, 88n, 228, 236
Reformation, the, 91; and the Church, 114 f. *See also* Counter Reformation
Religion, and Descartes, 63. *See also* Church
Religious: tradition, 7; worship, as collective rite, 31
Renaissance, 90
Repression, 234
Resh: as son, 207; as *tifereth*, 207
Reshith, 185
Resistance, to collective, 96
Revelation of Justinus, 111
Ripening: of melon, 113; of self, 110; symbolism, 101
Rites, formal, 34
Ritual food of the *electi*, 103 f.
River bank, 26, 28, 35
Roman mythology. *See* Mythology
Romania, 154
Romans, Epistle to the, 51
Rope, 12
Rosicrucians, 74; and Descartes, 61, 61n, 66
Rotundum, 110
Rubedo, 217

Russia, 154

Sabaoth, 108
Sabbatianism, 167
Sacraments, of Christians, 114n
Sacrifice(s), 43, 50; for the dead, 28; of heir, 23; tables of, 26, 28
Safed movement, 167
Saguntum, 140
Salvation of germs of light in Manichaeism, 109
Satan, spirit of, 94; three-headed, 129n
Saturn, 118, 139, 216
Savior. *See* Christ
Scent. *See* Perfume
Scholasticism, 128
Science: Descartes's belief in, 90n, 91n; materialistic, 129 f.; as mother, 82; as woman, 82n
Scientific: method, and Descartes, 72; thinking, Descartes and development of, 90n, 91
Scintillae, 118 ff., 118n; as description of archetypes, 120. *See also* Fiery sparks
Scriptures, 178n; and creation of world, 178
Seed, 108 f., 113, 113n; in fruit, 109; imagery of Descartes, 113, 113n; of light, 119 f.
Sefiroth, 167, 169, 173, 180, 198, 206, 237; arrangement of, 170, 206; as aspects of Godhead, 171; and divine names, 193; each containing others, 199; and letters of alphabet, 181; and manifest God, 193; and *partsufim*, 206; and Plotinus, 169; as potencies, 173; and Proclus, 169; as psychic reality, 173; as structural elements of psyche, 228; symbolism of, 235; union of, 211; upper and lower, 177; and Valentinus, 169
Sekhel, 165; as consciousness, 174 f.; etymology of, 174 f.; and *mahashabah*, 175; as spirit, 174

256 INDEX

Sekhel ha-neelam, 152
Sekhel ha-nibdal, 188
Sekhel ha-poel, as active intelligence, 188
Self, 93, 109 f., 114, 134, 137; as appearing remote, 112, 115; awakening and development of, 118; eye as symbol of, 120; and horoscope, 73; knowledge of, as life goal, 48; and magic circle, 72 f.; and mandala form, 73; melon as symbol of, 109, 115; realization and transformation, 44; redemptive aspect of, 114; as "regulating factor," 73; in relation to ego, 112; star as symbol of, 120
Semen, 108
Sensation, 172
Sensus naturae, 119n
Separation, producing consciousness, 112
Serpent, number value of word, 181n
Sethians, 106; three principles of, 106
Seven, 108, 195; days, 177; and eight, 207; thoughts and Sefiroth, 177
Seventy, 181n
Seventy-two, 220
Sex(ual): act, 90n; mysteries of, in Kabbalah, 227 f.; symbolism pronounced in spiritual realm, 228
Shaareh orah, 164, 167
Shadow: of Descartes, 112, 114; in Descartes's dream, 96, 99; Germany as, 66; of Jews, 99 f.; as un-Christian figure, 99
Shekhinah, 184, 202 f., 234; exile of, 202, 212 f.; as feminine part of Primal Man, 202
Shemoth, 193
Shin, and three and four, 219
Ship, 29
Shock, emotional, 118
Shulhan arukh, 157
Silver, 217; and melon, 101n

Simulacrum Dei, 110
Sin(s): of Descartes, 116; fear of, 20 ff., 29, 34; lamented over, 37; original, 114; relation of individual to, 19; and suicide, 50
Sinai, 221
Sine umbra peccati, 114
Six, 210 f.; directions, 210n
Smell(s): of crocodile, 35; evil, 34 f.; of fish, 34; of flood, 37
Snake, 94
Sol invisibilis, 120
Solomon's temple, 218
Son, 190
Song of Solomon, 225, 227
Sonship, in Gnostic light, 109
Sophia, 184n
Soul, 83, 83n, 159, 163, 168, 172, 210, 232, 236; attitude of, toward suicide, 7; Ba as aspect of, 9 f.; and Christ's suffering, 104; concentrating of, 73; containing five parts, 210; containing four elements, 224; containing three parts, 210; and Descartes, 80, 80n; and emotional life, 3; exchange of roles with man, 8; Jewish, 239; and Kabbalah, 153; and life, 7; and Maggid, 164; and man in mandalas, 73; needs of, 50; and psychology, 164; responsibility to, 44; universal, 118, 118n; viewpoints of, 7. *See also* Body and soul, Heart
South, 88n
Space, 121
Spain, 167; and melon, 101n
Sparks: of fire, 59, 78, 118, 118n, 122n, 123, 134; in flint, 131
Spiral, 92
Spirit, 89, 93, 157, 186, 193; and Descartes, 66; divine, 90; evil, 76, 94 f.; eyes, 119; of God, 118; primordial form of, 79; as wind, 89n. *See also* Opposites.
Spiritus: familiaris, 129; *vegetativus*, 111
Square root, 223

Index

Star(s), 182; of David, 226; in man, 110; as symbol of Self, 120
Stone, alchemical, 102. *See also* Philosopher's stone
Storm, 90 f., 90n, 95, 97, 107, 113, 124n, 131. *See also* Wind
Succus lunariae, 102
Suffering, 104
Suicide: and Ba, 48; contemplation of, 10; and despair, 20; incidence of, 50; and soul's attitude toward, 7; as sin, 50
Summa theologica, 157n
Sun, 26, 105n, 109, 118, 178n, 201, 235; Descartes's image of, 122; Kepler's view of, 122n; light of, 28; and moon-trees, 110 f.; setting of, 29
Sunbark, 12, 16, 41
Supernal point, 182
Stoics, 122n
Swamp, 35
Sweden, 100
Symbol(s): alchemical, 118; as archetypal images, 59; dark forces of, 101; of God, 76; of numbers, 74; of psyche, 101; of unconscious contents, 123
Synchronicity, 86, 86n, 87, 135

Tabula rasa, 187
Talmid hakham, 155
Talmud, 155, 167, 230; on creation through alphabet, 192; and Hasidism, 154, 156; and heat, 172; and Rabbinism, 156; and rationalism, 154; and religious experience, 154; and Torah, 155
Talmudic period, 163
Tao, 101
Targum, 185
Temenos, 97, 194
Temple, 178n
Ten, 181, 210, 220; and four, 223 f.; and tetrad, 224; as unity, 221 f. *See also* Decad
Ten Commandments, 221

Tereus, 139
Terror and despair, 10
"Tertiaries," 90. *See also* Holy Ghost movements
Testicles, 88n
Tetractys, 220
Tetrad: and decads, 221; and divine name, 214. *See also* Quaternity
Tetragram, 176n, 216; identity and difference in, 213 f.; and Kabbalah, 211 f.; and Pythagorean tetractys, 220; and Sefiroth, 210 f.; in *Zohar*, 210 f.
Thesaurus, 109, 109n
Thinking, 80, 232, 236; autonomous nature of, 81; and consciousness, 80; and Descartes, 80 f., 80n. *See also* Intellect
Thirty-two, 222
Thor, 116
Thoth, 12, 16, 20; as moon-god, 19
Thought: heart as organ of, 19; inner process of, 113; as qualities, 177; and unconscious, 190
Three, 92 f., 105n, 106, 109, 128, 129n, 215, 231; and four, 215, 219. *See also* Shin
"Three Lemons, The," 103
Three Principles of Sethian thought, 106
Throne, 178n
Thunder, 76, 108, 116 ff.; in mythology, 116
Tifereth, 201, 204, 210n, 215; as nuptial sexual act, 226n; as son, 207; as YHWH, 205. *See also* Waw
Tikkun ha-olam. See Order
Time, 89n, 121, 121n, 196 f.; Descartes's view of, 86, 86n; and physics, 86n
Titans, 116
Tohu-wa-bohu, 221 f.
Tongue, 11
Torah, 155, 192, 234
Torah she-bikhtav, 155

258 INDEX

Tragedy, human, 10
Transformation: of man, 48 f.; the unconscious as substance of, 118
Treasure: dormant in womb, 31; melon as, in Manichaean thought, 109
Tree, 12, 102 ff., 110 f.; apple, 111; in Barbelite thought, 111; future-discerning, 111; lemon, 103; of life, 111n, 218; as metamorphic form of man, 111; the philosophical, 110; plum, 102; of Sefiroth, 215; sun and moon, 110 f.; as symbol of alchemical opus, 111; as symbol of Gnosis, 111; as symbol of life process, 111; as symbol of wisdom, 111. See also *Arbor philosophica*
Triad, of fishes, 218n
"Trickster," 132; and God, 84
Trinity, 83 f., 128 f.; of *netsah, hod,* and *yesod,* 205. See also Triad
Truth, individual, 19 f.
Twenty-two, 222
Two, 181, 223
Types. See Psychological types

Unconscious, 111, 152, 163, 166, 175 ff., 198, 229; and abstraction, 179; and Adler, 234; and bonds of senses, 230; and compensation, 110; and consciousness, viii, 180, 190; and Descartes, 59, 87, 111, 125; as divine, 176; and dreams, 86; entering consciousness, 206; as father of son, 190; fear of, 122 f.; and Freud, 199, 234; and Hartmann, 151; and Hasidism, 153; having own law, 189; and heart, 19; as hidden, 176; as higher god, 180; higher than consciousness, 190; as *hokhmah,* 180, 190; as *hylē,* 238; image-creating activity of, 79; inspiration in Lullus, 72; intuitive side of, 91n; and Jung, 235; and Kabbalah, 153; and Kant, 153; known through effect on consciousness, 191; left side as symbol of, 85n, 89; and Leibniz, 151, 153; and Maggid, 235 f.; and Maggid of Shitomir, 238; Maggid's concept of, and modern psychology, 234; and Marcus, 151; as masculine, 235; and mathematical discovery, 68; as metaphysical concept, 234; pagan, 99; part of Descartes's personality, 98 f.; possibilities in, 31; as *prima materia,* 197; as Primordial Father, 238; projection of, 66; ripening process, 101; and Schelling, 151, 153; as source of thought, 190, 196 f.; and space, 197; and time, 197; as transformative substance, 118; and values, 164. See also Collective unconscious, Conscious and unconscious, Consciousness, *Qadmut-ha-sekhel, Sekhel-ha-neelam*
Underworld, 11, 23
Union, 204 f.; of Christ and Ecclesia, 227; of Christ and the soul, 227; of conscious and unconscious, 198 f., 225, 238; in divine sphere, 227; of fire and water, 225 f.; of God and Israel, 225, 227; of *hokhmah* and *binah,* 198 f., 225; of King and Queen, 227; of masculine and feminine in first man, 203; as mystery, 200, 236; of Sol and Luna, 226; of son with mother-daughter-sister, 208; in unconscious, 227; of *waw* and *he,* 212; of *yod* and *he,* 212. See also *Coniunctio*
Union of opposites, 200, 225; in Kabbalah, 203; in Jewish mysticism, 224
Uniting function, 114n

Values: erupting into consciousness, 147; new, 29
Vegetarianism, 104
Via purgativa, 66n
Vinum ardens, 102
Viriditas, 217
Vishnu, 194n
"Visio Arislei," 110
Vision: and ego detachment, 233; of Ignatius of Loyola, 94 f.; intuitive, 69; of Niklaus von der Flüe, 95; prophetic, 230

Water(s), 23, 29, 110, 182 f., 195, 216, 218, 225; alchemical names for, 101 f.; earthiness of, 102; nocturnal origin of, 102; primal, 107; as symbol of psyche, 101, 103
Waterfowl, 35
Watermelon, 100
Waw, 185; creation of, 212; as masculine, 191; as middle line, 211; as mystery of union, 211; number value of, 210 f.; and *tifereth*, 211
West, the, 12, 23, 29, 44
Wheat, 105n
Whirlwind, Descartes's theory of, 63n. *See also* Wind
White, 182, 216; fire, 217
Wholeness, 129; and Ba, 23, 26, 48, 51; human, 47; and life, 96; symbols of, and individuation, 209 f.; as union of opposites, 209 f.
Wickedness of the world, 7
Wife, 29, 32 ff.
Will, free, 19
Wind, 90, 96, 98, 107, 115; as father image, 90n; symbols of, 75 f.; as whirlwind, 75 f.
Wisdom, 119, 130 f., 196, 198, 207, 228, 237; like sparks in flint, 131; tree as symbol of, 111
Wise man, 40
Woman: first, and Gnosticism, 107; ill-reputed, 35

Words: as animating dead matter, 194; as creative force, 192
World: and Kabbalah, 153; mechanistic conception of, 83; as water, fire, and air, 218
"World-soul." *See Anima mundi*
Wotan, 91, 91n, 124n

Y, 220
Yaldabaoth, 104, 108
Yehi, 184
Yesod, 198; as aspect of unconscious, 199; as bridge between conscious and unconscious, 206; as mediator for union, 200; as phallus, 204; as procreation, 204; as uniter, 204
Yetsirah, 167, 173, 222
YH, 219 f.
YHW, 220
YHWH, 175, 176n, 184, 204 f.; magic power of, 193; and Sefiroth, 180; symbols of, 219 f.; used to form delta, 220
YHY, 219
Yin, 100 f.
Yod, 176n, 181, 212, 219; and *he*, 184; and *hokhmah*, 180, 211; as light, 186; as masculine, 191; as matter, 186; number value of, 181, 210; as Primordial Point, 180; as *qadmut-ha-sekhel*, 186; as source of all things, 181. *See also* Unconscious
Yorde merkabah, 167
YWHY, four variants of, 220

Zaddik, 176; personality of, 156
Zechariah 14:9, 202
Zeus, 116
Zion, 205
Zodiac, 72
Zohar, 157n, 162 f., 167, 178, 183, 186, 201, 203, 203n, 205 f., 215; commentary on Genesis, 232; on correspondence, 191; on death of Rabbi Simon ben

Yochai, 204 f.; feminine symbols in, 206 f.; and secret of Torah, 192
Zohar references: Zohar I, 15a, 184n; 15b, 185n; 28a, 207n, 212n; 30a, 185n; 48a, 203n; 133b, 219n; 141a, 204n; 149b, 232n; 247b, 206n, 207n; Zohar II, 55a, 203n; 85a, 215n; 100b, 207n; 164b, 210n, 225n; Zohar III, 29a, 201n; 62a, 204n; 70a, 169; 93a, 202n; 227b, 216n, 220n; 288a, 215n; 290a, 184n; 296a, 203n, 205n

Index of Names

Aaron ben Jacob ha-Cohen (Rabbi), 219n
Abraham ben David, 167
Abraham ben ha-Yarchi (Rabbi), 219n
Abraham ibn David, 188
Abraham ibn Ezra, 221n
Abraham, Magen, 219
Abulafia, Abraham, 167
Adam, Charles, 57, 59n, 61n, 62n, 63n, 64n, 67n, 80n, 97n, 142
Adler, Alfred, 234
Aescoli-Weintraub, A. Z., 159n
Agrippa of Nettesheim, 61, 119, 223
Akiba (Rabbi), 166 f., 220n
Albertus Magnus, 224 f.
Alexander of Aphrodisias, 188
Amora (Rabbi), 210n, 211n
Andison, M. L., 57n
Apuleius, 88n
Aquinas, Thomas, St., 97n, 157
Aristotle, 97n, 186
Augustine, St., 74n, 104, 104n, 105, 128
Ausonius, 77, 131, 132
Azriel of Gerona, 167, 169n, 181, 210n

Baal Shem Tov (Rabbi), 158, 159n, 160
Bachofen, J. J., 88n, 142
Baer, Dov (Rabbi), 152, 158, 160
Baillet, Abbé Adrien, 64, 75, 75n, 79n, 136n
Baptista, Joannes, 61

Barth, Heinrich, 71n, 72n, 80n, 85, 85n, 122n, 142
Basilides, 168
Baur, Ferd. Chr., 104n, 142
Baynes, Cary F., 100n, 143
Beeckmann, Isaak, 60, 66, 130
Beeson, C., 104n, 142
Bennet, E. A., 58n, 87n
Bergman, Hugo, 151
Bergson, Henri, 82n, 142
Bernhard de Clairvaux, St., 227
Beyme, F., 58n
Bischoff, E., 216n, 226n
Bloch, Philipp, 232n
Blüher, 226n
Boehme, Jakob, 117, 168n, 223
Bolte, J., 103n, 142
Bombach, S. J., 179n
Bonaventura, St., 157
Breasted, James H., 5, 52
Brochard, Jeanne, 59
Brockdorff, Cay von, 62n, 63n, 87n, 113n, 126n, 142
Bousset-Gressmann, 186n
Bruno, Giordano, 73
Brunschvicg, Léon, 67n, 129, 129n, 142, 221n
Buber, M., 153n, 158n, 159n
Buber, S., 193n

Carus, C. G., 153, 234, 234n
Cassirer, E., 122n, 142
Celsius, 99
Chandoux, 62
Cohen, G., 66, 142

Index

Cordovera, Moses, 157, 191, 223, 223n

David (King), 220
David abu Simra (Rabbi), 185, 185n
De Berulle, Cardinal, 62
de Buck, A., 6, 9n, 47, 52
Dee, John, 183n
Descartes, René. *See* Subject Index
Diederichs, E., 102n, 143
Dorn, 183n
Dorneus, Gerhardus, 110, 119, 120
Dornseiff, Franz, 183n, 193n
Dubnow, S., 158n, 160n

Eckhart, Meister, 168n, 186
Eleazar (Rabbi), 215
Elijah (Gaon), 157n
Elimelech, 161, 161n
Epiphanius, 108, 108n
Erman, Adolph, 5, 10 f., 13 f., 16 f., 21, 40, 42 f., 52
Ezekiel, 167, 218

Faulhaber, Johannes, 74
Feibush, Meshullam (Rabbi), 160
Felsch, Carl, 83n, 85, 85n, 127, 127n, 142
Fichte, 152
Ficino, Marsilio, 73
Figulus, Benedictus, 111
Finke, Heinrich, 53
Fischer, A., 103n, 143
Fleckenstein, J. O., 63n, 86n, 92, 92n, 143
Franck, A., 166n
Franz, Marie-Louise von, ix, 14, 99n, 143
Freud, S., 58, 199, 199n, 226n, 234
Friedländer, M., 222n
Fromer, Jakob, 233n
Funk, Philipp, 94n, 143

Gagnebin, S., 58n, 63n, 113n, 115n, 130n, 143
Galileo, 61 f., 83

Gardiner, Alan H., 5, 10, 13 f., 18, 27, 32 f., 39 ff., 43, 45 f., 52
Gehrhardt, G. L., 125n
Gesenius-Buhl, 174n
Geulincx, Arnold, 87
Gibieuf, P., 143
Gikatilla, Joseph, 164, 167
Gilson, Etienne, 60n, 122n, 123n, 126n, 143
Goethe, 126n
Goldschmidt, L., 191n
Golenischeff, Waldemar, 16
Gonseth, F., 71, 71n, 81n, 143
Gordon, H. L., 157n
Gorion, Misha ben, 178n
Gouhier, H., 143
Grapow, Hermann, 52
Grasowsky, J., 171n, 174n
Graziano, Abraham, 173n
Grouhier, J. H., 135n
Grünwald, M., 194n
Gulkowitsch, Lazar, 196n
Gunn, Battiscombe, 5, 10, 13 f., 27
Gutmann, J., 188n

Hadamard, Jacques, 70, 143
Hammer, J. von, 174n
Hartmann, Eduard von, 151 ff., 153n, 234, 234n
Hayim ben Atar, 152
Hermann, Alfred, 8, 10, 17, 30 f., 45, 52
Herrera, Rabbi, 213n, 214
Hieronymus, 223, 223n
Hippolytus, St., 106n
Horodezky, S. A., 154n, 155n, 224n, 233n, 234n
Hovorka, O. von, 100n, 143
Hull, R. F. C., 144n
Hurwitz, Siegmund, ix, 111n, 157n

Ignatius of Loyola, St., 94, 94n
Irenaeus, St., 107n, 111, 222, 222n
Isaac, 218
Isaac the Blind, 167, 173
Isaiah (Rabbi), 160
Israel (Rabbi), 208n

262 INDEX

Jacob ben Asher (Rabbi), 157
Jacobsohn, Helmuth, viii f., 52
Jefferson, Geoffrey, 87n, 143
Ježower, I., 57, 75n, 77n, 143
Joel, D. H., 166
Johanan (Rabbi), 231
John, St., 110
Joseph ben Shalom ha-Ashkenazi (Rabbi), 195n
Jung, Carl Gustav. See Subject Index
Junker, Hermann, 5, 7 f., 27, 43, 53
Justinus, 111
Justus-Lipius, 122n

Kant, 85, 153, 153n
Karo, Joseph (Rabbi), 157, 157n
Kepler, 83, 83n, 122n, 129
Kerényi, C., 112
Khunrath, Heinrich, 118, 118n, 120, 183n
Kircher, Athanasius, 61
Kluger, Rivkah, 225n
Kronfeld, A., 100, 143

Lanczkowski, Günter, 6n, 53
Laporte, J., 71n, 113n, 125n, 128n, 145
Laser, S. M., 174n
le Coq, A. von, 105n, 145
Leibniz, 86n, 125n, 151, 153
Leisegang, Hans, 106n, 107n, 108, 108n, 145, 222n
Lepsius, Richard, 5, 53
Leroy, Maxim, 57, 57n, 145
Levy, Isaac (Rabbi), 160
Loew (Rabbi), 195
Löwith, Karl, 125n, 145
Lullus, Raimundus, 61, 72 f.
Luria, Isaac, 158, 167, 171

Macrobius, 88n
Maggid of Meseritz. See Subject Index.
Maimon, Solomon, 233, 233n
Maimonides, 156, 167 f., 179, 186, 188n, 231n, 232n
Mani, 105n

Marcus, Ahron, 151, 151n, 152, 174, 238
Margulies, Reuben, 162n
Maria Prophetissa, 92 f.
Maritain, Jacques, 57n, 63n, 66n, 70n, 81n, 90, 90n, 117n, 128, 128n, 145
Markion, 168
Matthiessen, Wilhelm, 119n
Maximilian of Bavaria, 93
Mendel (Rabbi), 160
Mersenne, Marin, 63n
Metrodorus of Skepsis, 72
Michel (Rabbi), 160
Migne, Jacques Paul, 94n, 104n, 128, 145
Milhaud, G., 67, 74n, 79n, 145
Misha Joseph ben Gorion, 178n, 195n
Mogk, E., 91n, 145
Molitor, J., 223n
Morienus, 118n
Moses, 99, 193, 222
Moses de León, 217n
Müller, Ernst, 220n, 221n

Nachmanides, 167, 181n
Nahum of Chernobyl, 161, 161n
Neumann, Erich, 208n
Newton, Isaac, 86n
Nietzsche, Friedrich, 90n, 145
Niklaus von der Flüe, 95
Ninck, Martin, 91n, 145

Otto, Eberhard, 9

Paracelsus, 82n, 110, 114n, 117, 119, 119n, 121
Paul, St., 51
Pauli, W., 83, 83n, 87n, 122n, 129, 145
Pauly, August Friedrich von, 146
Pauly-Wissowa, 100n
Pfalz, Elizabeth von der, 121n
Philo, 186n
Phineas ben Yair, 193
Pico della Mirandola, G., 73
Platzeck, E.-W., 146

Index

Pliny, 100n
Plotinus, 169
Plutarch, 88n
Poincaré, Henri, 67 ff., 67n, 146
Polivka, G., 103n, 142
Proclus, 169
Pseudo-Democritus, 62
Puech, H. C., 104n, 146
Pythagoras, 79

Quiring, Heinrich, 57n, 146

Rabinowitsch, W., 154n
Rashi, 231n
Regardie, I., 226n
Reuchlin, Johannes, 216, 220, 223
Rittmeister, J., 58, 88n, 90n, 137, 146
Röd, Wolfgang, 59n, 85, 85n, 146
Rosenroth, Knorr von, 204n, 207n, 216n
Rossi, Paolo, 73, 73n, 135n, 146
Rulandus, 117

Saadia, 167
Sainte Fare Garnot, J., 6, 53
Sardanapalus, 140
Satornilos, 168
Scharff, Alexander, 5 ff., 23 f., 27 ff., 32, 34 ff., 38 ff., 44 f., 53
Schelling, 151 ff.
Schnürer, Gustav, 53
Schönenberger, Stephen, 120, 120n, 121n, 123n, 146
Scholem, Gershom, 151 ff., 151n, 159n, 160 f., 160n, 161 f., 166, 168n, 169n, 173n, 181n, 182n, 192n, 194n, 195n, 202n, 210n, 211n, 217 f., 217n, 218n, 227, 227n, 233n, 236, 236n
Sebba, G., 59n, 146
Sethe, Kurt, 5, 8, 10, 13 f., 16 f., 30, 35 f., 41 f., 53
Silz, Priscilla, 83n
Simon, Maurice, 162n
Simon ben Yochai (Rabbi), 204
Sirven, J., 61n, 65, 66n, 70, 70n, 74n, 75n, 81n, 82n, 83n, 96, 96n, 97n, 105n, 117n, 127, 128n, 146
Socrates, 96
Solomon ibn Gabirol, 186

Solomon of Lusk, 160, 234
Sperling, Harry, 162n
Spiegel, Joachim, 5, 6n, 18 ff., 40, 43, 53
Spinoza, 85
Steindorff, G., 35
Stock, Hyman, 84n, 123n, 124n, 126n, 130n, 146
Stöckel, A., 186n
Storch, A., 58, 146
Strachey, James, 57n
Sudhoff, Karl, 119n, 147
Suys, E., 5, 28, 53

Tannery, P., 57, 142
Thausing, Gertrud, 8n, 9n, 13, 53
Tishby, I., 154, 162n, 169n, 186n, 196n
Torczyner, H., 174n

Valentinian, 168
Vanini, Lucilio, 62
Vital, Hayim, 158
Vitellio, 83n
Vogelsang, F., 30, 54

Waerden, B.-L. van der, 70n, 147
Waite, Arthur E., 226n
Walter, Balthasar, 182n
Weill, Raymond, 6, 8, 10, 13 f., 17, 24, 27 f., 32, 36, 45 f., 54
Wendland, P., 106n
Werblowsky, R. J. Z., 188n
Whitehead, A. N., 71n, 147
Wilhelm, Richard, 100, 143
Wischnitzer-Bernstein, Rahel, 218n
Wisdom, J. O., 88n, 90n, 91n, 113n, 126n, 133n, 147
Witelo. *See* Vitellio
Wolf, Zeev, 161, 161n, 229, 229n
Wünsche, August, 208n, 220n, 225, 226n

Yates, Frances, 73n, 147
Yehudah ben Ileai (Rabbi), 215, 219n
Yitzchak (Rabbi), 215

Zalman, Shneur, of Ladi, 151n, 152, 160, 234, 238, 239n